D1806280

THIS BOOK SHOULD BE RETURNED ON OR BEFORE THE LATEST
DATE SHOWN TO ANY LANCASHIRE COUNTY LIBRARY

SYS. HOLD
FROM ZB
TO

14 OCT 2004

SUBJECT TO RECALL

28 JUN 2006

2736067
QL/P-3

RS

- SUBJECT
TO RECALL

2 1 MAR 2007

PLA76140.
QL/P-3

06 APR 2017

25 MAY 2017
18 JLY 2017

AUTHOR   BENDER, R.J.

CLASS
741.683

TITLE   Postcards of Hitler's Germany

Lancashire County Library

30118095828046

Lancashire
County Council

LANCASHIRE
COUNTY LIBRARY
Bowran Street
PRESTON PR1 2UX
LL1   Recycled

POSTCARDS

Postal Stationery/Printed to Private Order/Propaganda

of HITLER'S GERMANY

VOLUME 1

1923 TO 1936

BY R. JAMES BENDER

LANCASHIRE COUNTY LIBRARY	
09582804	
H J	03/09/2004
	£39.46

1st Edition

Copyright 1995 by Roger James Bender

Published by R. James Bender Publishing,
 P.O. Box 23456, San Jose, California 95153

Printed in the United States of America

All rights reserved. This book or parts thereof,
 may not be reproduced in any form without
 permission of the author.

ISBN No. 0-912138-60-2

Foreword

This ten-year study was produced because of an early fascination with the colorful and historical propaganda postcards of the Third Reich era. Studying them and the events they portrayed created a hunger for more knowledge about the German postal system and its function. I soon learned there was much more to this hobby than just propaganda cards. Cards flooded the postal system carrying their blatant, and sometimes subtle, messages alongside equally interesting "official issue" postcards (Amtliche Ausgaben) and the "printed to private order" postcards. It is these three categories of Third Reich postcards that I have addressed in this work.

The "official issues" were available at all post offices or at special counters at exhibitions. Their issuance was ordered by the postal authorities. They are the most common of the postcards encountered because of their numerous distribution outlets. Postage stamps are imprinted.

The "printed to private order" postcards were produced to commemorate special events, from local postal exhibitions to city and district commemorations. Some are common because of their profuse useage over a long period of time (sometimes months), and some are very rare as they may have been produced in limited numbers for a week-end event. On this wide range of subject cards, the postage stamps are also imprinted.

The third category covered in this study is that of "propaganda" postcards. These are the most colorful of the three and are generally political in nature. They required a postage stamp.

As I observed the thousands of cards available to me I noted that all three catagories, in their own way, depicted a mini-history of Germany during the Third Reich period. When I put the three groupings of cards together in a chronological order, I not only saw most every event that was important to the German populace portrayed, but also the complex latticework of German culture and society. Not only did they portray the frustrations with the Versailles Treaty, but at the other end of the spectrum, the status of females in the "new order" to the love of nature. It was with this enlightenment that the format you are about to view was developed.

For a purely philatelic approach to the subject of "official issues" and "printed to private order" postcards there are no better references than Michel's "Ganzsachen-Katalog Deutschland," "Privatpostkarten-Katalog Deutschland: Deutsches Reich 1873-1945," "Bildpostkarten-Katalog Deutschland," and Borek's "Ganzsachen-Spezial-Katalog Deutschland ab 1933." Although they are in German, they go into much greater detail on not only postcards but also special cancels. They were my bibles when cross-referencing or confirming details I had gathered from the numerous international collections I was permitted to study and photograph.

What has developed from my years of research are three volumes on the above subject. They are as follows:

Vol. 1: 1923-1936. Only Party struggle cards from 1923 to 1933, and from 1934 to 1936, any dated card in a chronological order.

Vol. 2: 1937-1939. Any dated card in a chronological order.

Vol. 3: 1940-1945. Any dated card in a chronological order plus the postal stationery of annexed and occupied territories (presently in development).

It should be noted that as extensive as my search was for appropriate cards for this series, I know that I have only scratched the surface and welcome contact from fellow collectors who hold hidden "gems" in their collections which are unknown to me. With their assistance I would like photos of such postcards, special cancels, and publishers' details, which can make up an expanded series in the future.

Roger James Bender

Acknowledgments

This is probably the most difficult part of doing this series...how to thank the dozens of individuals who gave so freely of their knowledge, advice, guidance and the use of their prized collections. This series would have been pamphlet-size without them. In the many years of researching various subjects I have never worked with a more generous group of individuals. Near the top of this list is John Ziegelhofer. We had never met but he trusted me enough to send six massive albums of his personal postcard collection to photograph. Over the years he was always there with his valued input plus new cards as they were discovered. When it came to "printed to private order" cards, Robert Dunn taught and guided me through the complex maze. He provided numerous cards for photography and kept me updated as new ones came on the market. The detailed coverage of these volumes would be non-existent without him. And by his side, his friend and fellow collector, James Franz, filled in the photographic gaps giving you, the reader, a more complete and illustrated study. Franco Mesturini, a leading Italian card collector, photographed several thousand cards and sent them to me for examination and inclusion. John Webb of England also sent major portions of his collection across the Atlantic for me to photograph. He continued his support with corrections and additional cards as they became available. I believe this series is linguistically near perfect because of Egon Gogolinski. He not only added guidance and cards, on numerous occasions he went through each word of text to make sure the translations were accurate, based on 1930s useage. Joan Panettiere also corrected numerous versions of the manuscript for grammatical errors, and was one of the driving forces to continue bettering what I already felt was the best I could do. Tom Capparelli jolted me with phone calls every few months to find out what I needed and always supplied what he had. Francis Catella, who had produced his own wonderful series on the subject, never hesitated to help where he could and never asked anything in return. When we discuss rally cards, Mike Passmore was always ready to aid me and also corrected different versions of the manuscript.

Besides the above contributors there were individuals who immediately stepped forward and offered their cards, inspiration and knowledge. Without them all I would not have the pride in this series that I currently do. I offer my sincerest thanks to the following friends and colleagues:

J.R. Angolia	Bob Lyons
Philip Baker	Larry Noder
Terry Bart	G. Notarpole
Cherokee	John Pechy
G.V. Comer	John Rawlings
George Crabb	N. David Ripley
Alfred Ex	Erik Rundquist
David Geary	Larry Smith
Richard Geliebter	Charles Snyder
Derek Gloster	Otto Spronk
John D. Griffin	E. Talacko
Friedrich Herbst	J.B. Terry
Bob Jackson	Randy Treadway
H.J. Kaiser	M.C. Voit
Doug Kay	

Table of Contents

───────────Type Styles Referred to:───────────

Fraktur - "Gothic" is considered a sub-style of this old face of type.

𝕻𝖔𝖋𝖙𝖐𝖆𝖗𝖙𝖊

𝕻𝖔𝖋𝖙𝖐𝖆𝖗𝖙𝖊

Antiqua - Originating from Roman capital letters with "serifs" (the small hooks at the ends of the letters). Comes in various type styles.

POSTKARTE

POSTKARTE

POSTKARTE

Grotesk - A more modern sans-serif (without serifs) type face which is also called a block-letter style.

Postkarte

P O S T K A R T E

POSTKARTE

Postkarte

Format Examples

This volume on Third Reich-era postcards illustrates any card that can be dated or tied to a particular event, which in reality, presents a mini-chronological history of Hitler's Germany. Postcards without a double border or separate stamp (indicating imprinted) is a privately published card. These cards are in the greatest numbers of variations and are classified as "Propaganda Cards." Most often these cards are of a political nature and always require a postage stamp.

Cards with a double border and separate stamp indicates "Official Postal Stationery" with imprinted stamp. These official issues (Amtliche Ausgaben) are quite common as they were available at all post offices or at special counters at exhibitions and events.

Cards without the double border, but with a separately illustrated stamp, indicate "Printed to Private Order" postcards with imprinted stamps. These issues were printed to commemorate special events.

Official Postal Stationery

☐ 1941, 1 Aug.-May 1945—6 Pf. (grey-green), with printed "Postkarte."

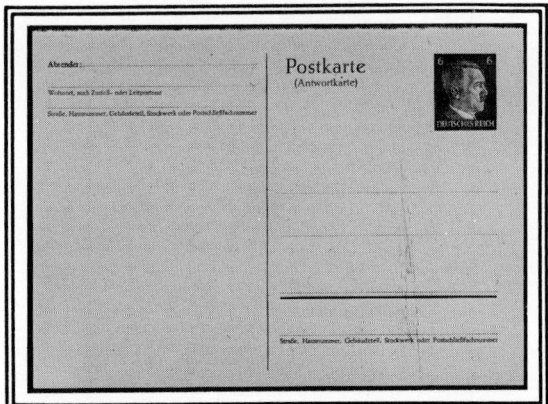

Printed to Private Order

☐ 1938, 9 Jan.—Dessau, 2nd Postage Stamp Show of the "Merkur" collectors' association. 5 Pf. Luftpost (green).

1923

□ 1923—Early propaganda card dedicated to the leader of the German freedom movement— Adolf Hitler. Publ.: Verlag der Nationalen Propaganda in München.

John D. Griffin

8

☐ 1923—Early National Socialist letter stationery with words and music for the song, "Deutschland, erwache!" on the inside. Distributed only in the Munich area.

☐ 1923—Austria. "National Socialism . . . the future of the German People."

1924

☐ 1924, June—Landsberg am Lech, commercially produced postcard commemorating Hitler's imprisonment at Landsberg Prison. His portrait and a 11 May 1924 statement is imprinted on the obverse. The card, send on 16 June 1924, tells of the sender's visit with the Führer. Publ.: A. Samweber (J. Kistler), Landsberg am Lech.

M.C. Voit

☐ 1924—Early portrait of Hitler, Publ.: J.F. Lehmanns Verlag, München. Illustration by Prof. von Kursell.

Mesturini

☐ 1924—Bruchsal, commemorating German Day, as well as the foundation of the NSDAP.

☐ 1924, 15-17 Aug.—Weimar, commemorating the first meeting of the National Socialist Workers movement.

1925

☐ 1925—Commemorating the propaganda voyage of four National Socialists in a home-made sailboat in 1925.

PROPAGANDAFAHRT
von 4 National-Sozialisten im selbstgebauten Segelboot

1926

Ziegelhofer

Adolf Hitler
Führer der Nationalsozialistischen Deutschen Arbeiterpartei

☐ 1926—Illustration made from a photo on the occasion of Hitler's speech in Eutin/Holstein on May 9, 1926. Publ: Fridericus-Verlag, München.

1927

☐ 1927, 19-21 Aug.—Commemorating the 1927 Reichsparteitage in Nuremberg. Publ.: Photo-Hoffmann, München.

☐ 1927, 19-21 Aug.—Commemorating the 1927 Reichsparteitage. Publ.: Photo-Bericht, Hoffmann, München.

Reichsparteitag
d. N.S.D.A.P.1927 in Nürnberg

☐ 1927, 19-21 Aug.—Reichsparteitage Nuremberg, "Zur Freiheit!" (To Freedom). Designed by Mjölnir to advertise for subscriptions to "Völkischer Beobachter," which was the Party's newspaper edited by Alfred Rosenberg.

□ 1927, 24 Aug.—"The future is ours." Propaganda card promoting a subscription to "Illustrierte Beobachter," the illustrated newspaper of Hitler's movement . . . "In the struggle for justice and truth, Hitler's press provides clarity." Publ.: Verlag F. Eher, München. Illustrated by Mjölnir.

□ 1927—"Marxism shall die so that Socialism may live!" Designed by Mjölnir and published by "Kampfverlag" which was owned by Gregor and Otto Strasser (the Party's internal opposition to Hitler). Note the swastika on the belt buckle. Mjölnir purposly copied the style and coloring of Communist and Spartakist propaganda cards. There are six cards in this series of which only two are illustrated at right.

□ 1928—Six card fund-raising and propaganda series. The artist is Mjolnir. Publ.: NSDAP Gau Berlin. (Illustrated on facing page.)

Gogolinski

☐ "Freedom is not
   yet lost."

☐ "The banner
   is up!"

Gogolinski

Gogolinski

☐ "And yet!"

Gogolinski

Gogolinski

☐ "Over graves, forward!"

☐ "Over graves,
   forward!"

☐ "Freedom on
   its way."

Gogolinski

1929

☐ 1929—Fund-raising card for National Socialist prisoners and wounded. Painting by Felix Albrecht. "Your will is demanding victory," a statement by Ernst Röhm.

Ziegelhofer

☐ 1929, 1-4 Aug.—Nürnberg, commemorating the 1929 Reichsparteitage. "Join the SA."

☐ 1929, 1-4 Aug.—Official Party Day card Nr. 1 commemorating the 1929 Reichsparteitage. Publ.:
Kunst-Verlag Peter Triem, München.

☐ 1929, 1-4 Aug.—Official Party Day card Nr. 2.

☐ 1929, 1-4 Aug.—Commemorating the triumphant march of the SA to Nürnberg for the 1929
Reichsparteitage.

Capparelli

☐ 1929—"Germany Awaken!"

1930

☐ 1930—Horst Wessel's SA comrades commemorate his death with this card.

Ziegelhofer

☐ 1930, May—Bayreuth, commemorating Gau Parteitag in Oberfranken. Houston Stewart Chamberlein (1855-1927) is featured. Hailed by the Germans as a Nordic prophet, he exposed the thesis that they were the master race and the creators and sustainers of civilization.

☐ 1930—Commemorating Hitler Day in Braunschweig. Publ.: Dr. jur. J. Schröder Verlag, München.

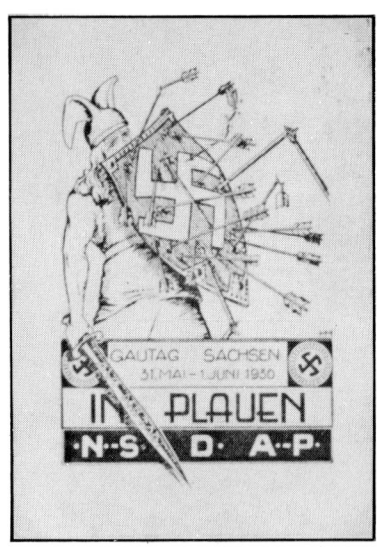

☐ 1930, 31 May-1 June—Plauen, commemorating
Gau Day in Saxony with illustration showing attacks against the NSDAP.

Kaiser

☐ 1930, 30 June—Commemorating the final Allied
evacuation of the Rhineland. "The Rhine
is free!" Pub.: Eduart Theile, Ludwigshafen am Rhein. Illustration by A. Zobel.

☐ 1930, 30 June—Commemorating the final Allied
evacuation of the Rhineland. Publ.:
Verlag Webeko, Mainz. Illustration by
Theo Matejko.

Ziegelhofer

☐ 1930, 2-3 Aug.—Falkenau, commemorating People's
Day.

1931

☐ 1931, 1 Jan.—A patriotic card calling for victory in 1931. Publ.: Grossdeutscher Lehrspiel-Verlag, Dresden.

Ziegelhofer

Mesturini

☐ 1931, 28 Jan.—Early Hitler portrait by Kursell. Publ.: Verlag Hoffmann, München.

☐ 1931—"Happy Easter." Alexander Schaaff Verlag. Dresden.

☐ 1931, May 30-31—Breslau, commemorating the 12th Stahlhelmtag (Steel Helmet (Veterans) Day).

☐ 1931, 11-12 July—Teplitz-Schönau, commemorating People's Day.

☐ 1931, 18 Oct.—Commemorating the consecration of the standards at Braunschweig.

Ziegelhofer

☐ 1931, 18 Oct.—Braunschweig, commemorating the SA unit deployment in that city.

Ziegelhofer

☐ 1931, 18 Oct.—Braunschweig, commemorating SA Day.

Ziegelhofer

☐ 1931, 29 Oct.—Berlin, fund-raising card for the political struggle of the NSDAP, produced by Gau Berlin. Painting by Felix Albrecht. "No one shall run short of breath," by Dr. Goebbels.

☐ 1931, November—Hesse, commemorating Hitler days in that state as well as the November elections.

☐ 1931—"Kampf Heil!" Publ.: Alexander Schaaff Verlag, Dresden. Note that this card is identical to the 1 Jan. 1931 card, but without the "1931" date.

□ 1931—"Heil Hitler." This card indicates the time has come for the National Socialists. Publ.: Alexander Schaaff Verlag, Dresden.

□ 1931—Adolf Hitler. Publ.: Alexander Schaaff Verlag, Dresden.

□ 1931—Anti-semetic card with an SA man showing Jews "the way home." Publ.: Alexander Schaaff Verlag, Dresden.

☐ 1931—"The Young Plan—the day is coming!" This plan was put forward in 1929 specifying a fixed amount of war reparations to be paid by Germany ($9 billion) and a fixed date this burden of guilt would end (1988). Hitler saw it as another inequity of the Versailles Treaty. Publ.: Alexander Schaaff Verlag, Dresden.

☐ 1931—An SS man. Publ.: Alexander Schaaff Verlag, Dresden.

☐ 1931—Depicting a sleeping press as the National Socialist movement marches forward. Publ.: Alexander Schaaff Verlag, Dresden.

☐ 1931—"Freedom and Bread" The brown platen rolling over enemies of the people. Publ.: Alexander Schaaff Verlag, Dresden.

☐ 1931—"Heil Hitler!" The SA symbol is shown piercing a snake's head. Publ.: Alexander Schaaff Verlag, Dresden.

☐ 1931—"The way into the Third Reich" This anti-semetic card depicts a board game showing the Jewish obstacles in the way of a National Socialist Third Reich. Publ.: Alexander Schaaff Verlag, Dresden.

□ 1931—Commemorating the SA martyr, Horst Wessel.

□ 1931—Commemorating the SA martyr, Horst Wessel, who was killed on 23 February 1930, and his song. "Die Fahne hoch."

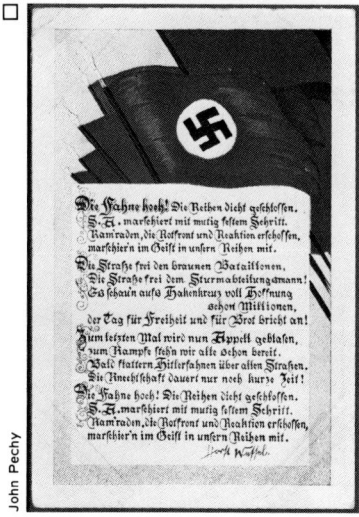

John Pechy

Webb

Webb

Publ.: NSDAP Ortsgruppe
Nordfront, Magdeburg.

Ziegelhofer

Ziegelhofer

Ziegelhofer

Publ.: Labi, Dresden.

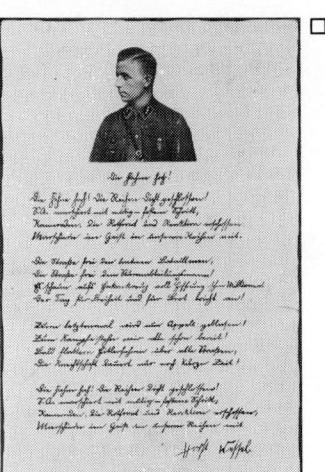

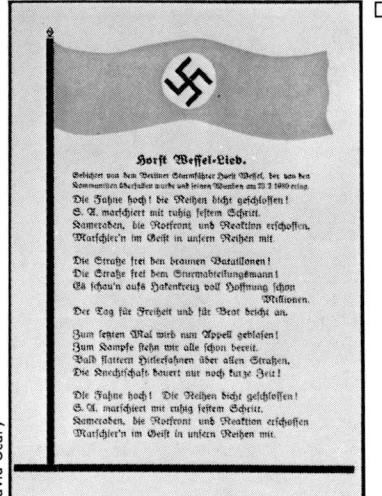

David Geary

David Geary

Horst Weſſel
Sturmführer 5, Gauſturm Berlin
† 23. Februar 1930

Die Fahne hoch!

Die Fahnen hoch, die Reihen feſt geſchloſſen, SA. marſchiert
mit ruhig feſtem Schritt; Kam'raden, die Rotfront und Reaktion
erſchoſſen, marſchier'n im Geiſt in unſern Reihen mit.

Die Straße frei den braunen Bataillonen! Die Straße frei dem
Sturmabteilungsmann! Es ſchau'n aufs Hakenkreuz voll Hoffnung
ſchon Millionen, der Kampf für Freiheit und für Brot bricht an.

Zum letztenmal wird Sturm-Alarm geblaſen, zum Kampfe
ſteh'n wir alle ſchon bereit; bald flattern Hitlerfahnen über alle
Straßen, die Knechtſchaft dauert nur noch kurze Zeit.

Die Fahnen hoch, die Reihen feſt geſchloſſen, SA. marſchiert
mit ruhig feſtem Schritt; Kam'raden, die Rotfront und Reaktion
erſchoſſen, marſchier'n im Geiſt in unſern Reihen mit.

Publ.: M. Blüdow,
Berlin.

Wessel's first verse of "Die
Fahne Hoch" is featured on
this card.

☐ 1931—"Germany Awaken! The victory is ours!"

Capparelli

☐ 1931—"Deutschland Erwache."
    (Germany Awaken).

David Geary

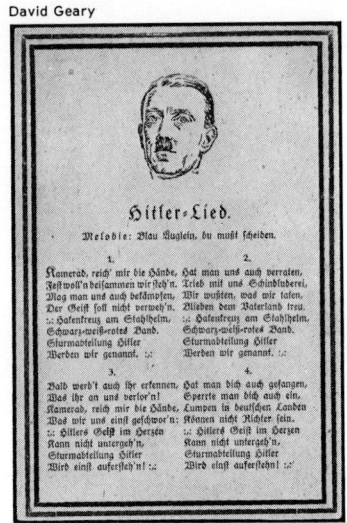

☐ 1931—Commemorating the "Hitler-Lied," to be
    sung to the melody of "Blue Eyes, you
    must depart."

Capparelli

☐ 1931— "Don't leave us in the lurch," depicting
    the period when SA men were arrested
    for wearing their uniforms.

1932

☐ 1932, 2 Feb.—Adolf Hitler.

Ziegelhofer

☐ 1932, 14 March—"Germany awaken!" The swastika sun is shown rising over Scheidegg (Allgäu).

Mesturini

☐ 1932, 18 April—Commemorating the Hitler rally in Görlitz on 18 April 1932. The Oberlausitzer Hitlerhaus is illustrated.

Mesturini

☐ 1932, April—2 Mark fund-raising card for the presidential election.

Ziegelhofer

☐ 1932, April—Commemorating the presidential elections of 1932. Frederick the Great is shown chasing out communists and corruption from the government. Publ.: Der Stahlhelm, B.D.F.—Bundesamt.

□ 1932, April—Set of four SS publicity cards distributed by the Berlin SS office. Publ.: Plakatkunstdruck Eckert, Berlin-Schönberg. Painting by Felix Albrecht, Berlin.

□ Nr. 1

□ Nr. 2

□ Nr. 3

□ Nr. 4

☐ 1932, April—"Create Work! Buy German products." National Socialist propaganda card for the upcoming elections. Publ.: Richard Kaufmann, Darmstadt.

☐ 1932, April—"The ploughman of the future." Publ.: Verlag für nationale Bildkunst, Rudolf Bischoff, München.

Ziegelhofer

☐ 1932, 1 May—Commemorating the Day of National Labor (May Day).   Publ.: Richard Kaufmann, Darmstadt.

☐ 1932, 29 July—Issued in memory of Hitler's visit to Radolfzell a. Bodensee on 29 July 1932. Publ.: Kunstverlag Franz Walter, München.

Deutschlands Rettung: Adolf Hitler

☐ 1932, 13 Aug.—"Don't yield! Remain firm!" from a speech by Hitler on this date. Publ.: Verlag Nationalsozialistisches Volksliederbuch, Berlin-Schöneberg.

☐ 1932, 14 Aug.—Commemorating the Rhine-Pfalz flight during the National Socialist Flying Sport Day.

□ 1932, 1 Oct.-30 June 1934—Set of six scenic cards in Esperanto (an artificial language based on the most common words in the important European languages and intended for international use). 5 Pf. Hindenburg (green), 5 Pf Schiller (green), 6 Pf. Ebert (olive), and 8 Pf Beethoven (dark green).

1. Berlin, Krögel

□ Hindenburg
□ Schiller
□ Ebert
□ Beethoven

Berlin, Krögel

La germana lefarbo havas boladtinde nor malmulte de vidindajoj, kiuj povas esti rigardataj kiel veraj antikvajoj. Sed tamen oni trovas en la malnovaj urbkvartaloj konstruajojn, kiuj rememorigas pri la jarcento antaŭ 200—250 jaroj. Ekde kaj vidindaj estas ekz. la kortoj de la malnovaj familiaj domoj, kiuj parte estas hodiaŭ konservataj. La tiel nomata "Krögel" sur la bildo estas unu el tiuj pentrindaj anguloj, kiujn la urba administracio nun gardas.

Dunn

2. Eisenach, Die Wartburg

□ Hindenburg
□ Schiller
□ Ebert
□ Beethoven

Eisenach, die Wartburg

"Ludwig der Springer" (la saltanto) metis, laŭ la legendo, la unuan fundament-ŝtonon por la konstruado de la kastelo jam en la jaro 1073, sed efektivo finkonstruis ĝin "Ludwig der Heilige" (la sanktulo) en la jaro 1223. La "Wartburg" estas la plej bona ekzemplo de primaj palac-loĝejoj el la deksesa jarcento kaj la barokteriaj partoj estas ankoraŭ hodiaŭ bone konservitaj. Sur la bildo estas videbla la antaŭkastela parto, kie Martin Luther restadis dum la jaroj 1521—22 kiel "Junker Jörg".

Dunn

3. Hildesheim, Knochenhauer-Amtshaus

□ Hindenburg
□ Schiller
□ Ebert
□ Beethoven

Hildesheim, Knochenhauer-Amtshaus

Hildesheim, la bela germana urbo, ekzistas jam depost pli ol 1000 jaroj. Unu el plej plej imponaj kaj kulturhistorie interesaj konstruajoj estas la "Oficejo de la enhakistoj", konstruita en la jaro 1529. La domo estas la plej granda konstruajo, kiun mezepoka gildo (la handstoj buliajoj) konstruis, kaj ĝi fariĝis kiel plej granda kaj belokonstruita dumĉarpentaĵo la insigno de Hildesheim.

Dunn

4. Innsbruck (Tirol), Goldenes Dachl

□ Hindenburg
□ Schiller
□ Ebert
□ Beethoven

Innsbruck (Tirol), Goldnes Dachl

Innsbruck, ronde ĉirkaŭita de altega rok-montaro, estas kvazaŭ Salzburg la plej bela loĝita urbo en la alstrivaj Alpoj. Krom multaj aliaj memorajoj el la dekdua jarcento poludas la mezgranda urba interesan kaj malofatan insignon, la "Oran tegmenton" (germane: Goldnes Dachl). La unuataj tegoloj faŭrmas antkonsial hodiaŭ tiel mirinda kiel antaŭ jarcentoj kaj rememorigas pri Maximilian I., kiu konstruis la belegan balkonajojn kaj tegmenton en la jaro 1500 je la memoro de sia edziĝo kun Maria Blanca Sforza.

Dunn

5. Kufstein (Tirol), Strateto

☐ Hindenburg
☐ Schiller
☐ Ebert
☐ Beethoven

Kufstein (Tirol), Strateto

Kufstein, alt-tirola lim-urbo, kun antikva fortikaĵo "Geroldeck", estas ĉirkaŭŝirata de altaj rokmuroj de la "Kaiser"-montaro kaj "Pendling". La malgranda urbo, kiu jin indiĝenis belegan monumenton de la Tirol-a liberec-batalinto Andreas Hofer, havas prizorĝe mirigan ĉirkaŭaĵon kaj estas mondkonata somera restadejo. Sur la bildo pentrinda strateto, en kiu troviĝas la malnovaj ĉentrinkejoj tirol-aj, la tiel konataj "Auracher Liedl" kaj "Batzenhäus'l".

6. Mittenwald (Germ.), Cefstrato kun pregejo

☐ Hindenburg
☐ Schiller
☐ Ebert
☐ Beethoven

Mittenwald (Germ.), Ĉefstrato kun preĝejo

Mittenwald, la malgranda germana Alp-urbo, konata pro la fabrikado de violonoj, gitaroj kaj citroj, estas lokita en vasta valfundo kaj ĉirkaŭita de potencaj rokoj de la "Karwendel"-montaro. La ĉirkaŭaĵo estas unika bela kaj multaj vojaĝantoj vizitas ĉi–are-kaj en la somero kaj en la vintro-la gasteman urbeton. Ankaŭ Goethe restis ĉi-tie kelkajn tagojn dum sia vojaĝo al Italio.

☐ 1932—"Germany is awakening!" This artist card illustrated by A. Müller, Nürnberg. Publ.: R. Sporer, Nürnberg.

Deutschland erwacht!

☐ 1932—"Friedrich the Great—Adolf Hitler, two men with the same determined will and the same objectives. Publ.: Deutscher Kunstverlag Franz Walter, München.

□ 1932—SA. A band member of Sturmbann 111/110 is depicted. "The horn will call just one more time."

Ziegelhofer

□ 1932—"The living front." Publ.: Verlag für nationale Bildkunst, R. Bischoff, München. Nr. 2.

Ziegelhofer

□ 1932—The SA marches.

Ziegelhofer

Ziegelhofer

□ 1932—Breaking the chains of the Versailles Treaty. Official postcard of Gau München-Oberbayern.

□ 1932—Propaganda postcard with Hitler saying. Publ.: Karl Kropp, Berlin-Schöneberg. "One Germany must be forged by those who do not want to be just citizens nor proletarians, but only Germans!"

Ein Deutſchland
muß geſchmiedet werden
von denen, die nicht
Bürger noch Proletarier
ſein wollen, ſondern
nur Deutſche!

Ziegelhofer

□ 1932—Fund-raising card for the Party's struggle to power. A 50 Pf. donation was requested. Illustration by Felix Albrecht. Publ.: F. Lück, Berlin-Spandau.

Ziegelhofer

John D. Griffin

„Wir brechen die Ketten, wir machen uns frei"!

Kampfschatzspende:
N. S. D. A. P. Gau Hessen-Nassau-Nord

20 Pfennig

□ 1932—Fund-raising card produced by NSDAP
Gau Hessen-Nassau-Nord. "We break the
chains—we will be free!"

Was Ihr ererbt von Euren Vätern habt,
erwerbt es um es zu besitzen !

Ziegelhofer

□ 1932—"What you inherit from your fathers, you must
earn to call your own!"

Deutschlands Erwachen.

□ 1932—Germany Awaken! Publ.: M. Lochner,
Berchesgaden.

1932......!

Mesturini

□ 1932—1932 will be the year of the National Socialists
in Germany.

☐ 1932—NSDAP fund-raising card, Gau Brandenburg. "Free the soil! Free the land!"

☐ 1932—Contribution card for the memorial fund of SA man, Hans Hobelsberger, killed by communists on 10 November 1931. Publ.: Josef Kinzer.

☐ 1932,—Fund-raising card produced for the NSDAP of Gau Greater Berlin. Publ.: Felix Albrecht, Berlin-Spandau.

42

☐ 1932—Fund-raising card for the SA in Lichtenstein-Callnberg.

☐ 1932—Awakening of the nation, from an original painting by Joh. Heinrich Pfaff.

Ziegelhofer

☐ 1932—Braunschweig, commemorating National Socialist Flight Day.

43

☐ 1932—"Alpenland, German and Free."

Capparelli

☐ 1932— "Work, Freedom, Bread."

☐ 1932—Patriotic slogan by Adolf Hitler. "We may do injustice, but in saving Germany we will eliminate the world's greatest injustice!"

☐ 1932—Berlin, commemorating National Front Soldiers' Day. "The new Germany is marching!"

☐ 1932—"All of Germany it should be!"

☐ 1932—Vote the people's block in the upcoming 1932 elections.

☐ 1932—"Towards Freedom. Vote for list 1 on November 6."

☐ 1932—"Hands off the Main River line! Vote the National Socialist list Nr. 2.

☐ 1932—Sent by Germans living overseas (here, Spain) urging a vote for Hitler in the 1932 elections. "We Germans in foreign countries ask: Give Hitler the power—vote National Socialist!"

☐ 1932—SS advertising card No. 1, "My Honor is Loyalty." Publ.: Wilh. F. Mayr, Miesbach. Illustration by F. Albrecht.

☐ 1932—SS advertising card No. 4, depicting grave sites of SS men who died during the early days of the struggle. Possibly part of the above series.

1933

In contrast with the chronological order in which dated postal stationery and propaganda cards have been listed, it is necessary to group the following cards with imprinted stamps by stamp denomination. Their introductory date has not been determined and are, therefore, listed by the stamp's issuance, in this case, 1933/1934. Outlined boxes plus descriptive text indicate that the card is known to exist, but a photograph is not available.

☐ 1933-1945—Blank card with no address lines and 1 Pf. (black) imprinted stamp.

Cards without illustrations or additional text.

143 x 106mm cream-colored stock.

☐   —München 8, Karl Rieger. 1 Pf. (black).

Card with five address lines and imprinted sender's name and address.

☐ —"Germany, your colonies!" Without inscription on lower left of card. 1 Pf.

☐ 1933-1945—Blank card with no address lines and 3 Pf. (brown) imprinted. Produced on white, off-white and cream-colored stock.

☐ White
☐ Off-white
☐ Cream

☐ —Blank card with one 72mm long address line. 3 Pf. (brown).

☐ —Card with "Achtung!/Briefmarken-/Sammler:/Ganzsache!" on left side, no vertical line, and three 36mm address lines. 3 Pf. (brown).

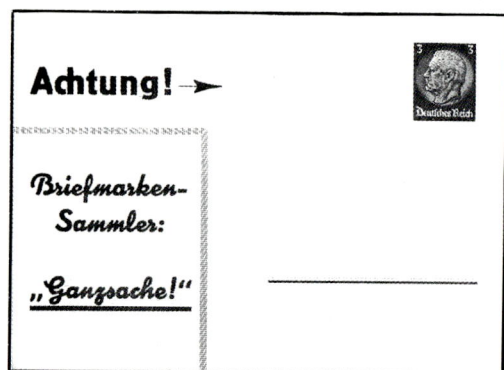

☐ 1933, April—3 Pf. (brown) with border and "Sonderpostkarte" (Special Postcard) imprinted. Two broken lines and one solid line.

☐ Also available with three broken lines and one solid line.

Blank cards with imprinted names/adresses of various collectors.

☐ —Aschersleben, Zahnarzt Wichmann. 3 Pf. (brown).

Cards for firms or associations.

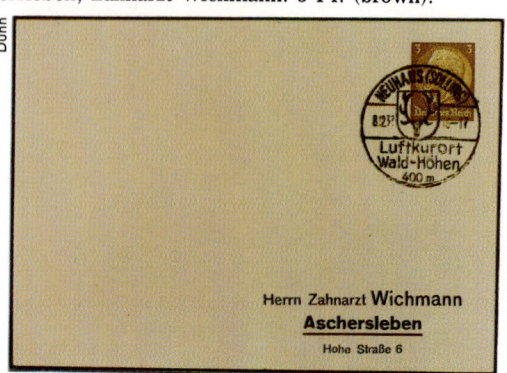

50

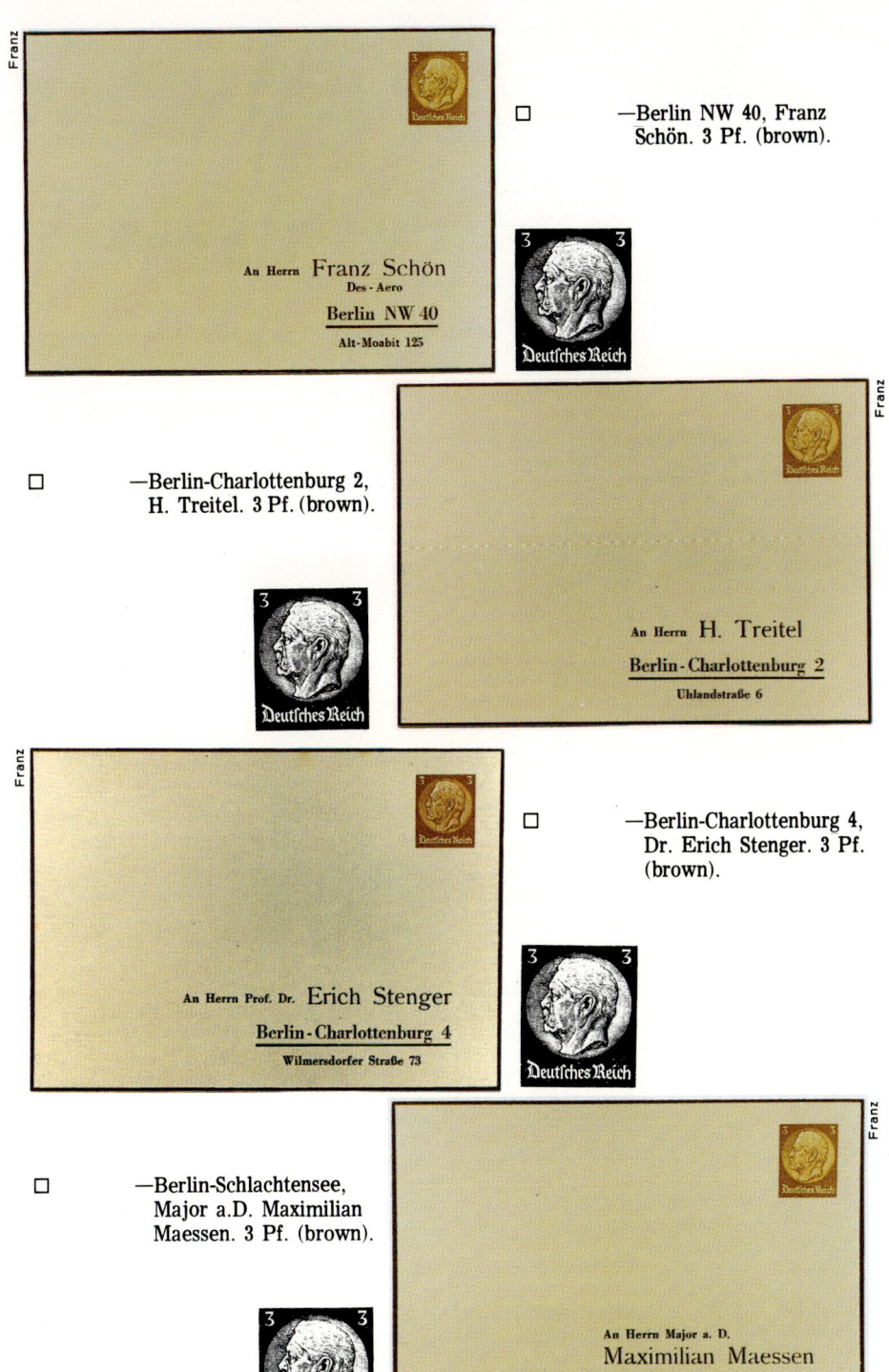

—Berlin NW 40, Franz
Schön. 3 Pf. (brown).

An Herrn Franz Schön
Des - Aero
Berlin NW 40
Alt-Moabit 125

Deutsches Reich

—Berlin-Charlottenburg 2,
H. Treitel. 3 Pf. (brown).

Deutsches Reich

An Herrn H. Treitel
Berlin - Charlottenburg 2
Uhlandstraße 6

—Berlin-Charlottenburg 4,
Dr. Erich Stenger. 3 Pf.
(brown).

An Herrn Prof. Dr. Erich Stenger
Berlin - Charlottenburg 4
Wilmersdorfer Straße 73

Deutsches Reich

—Berlin-Schlachtensee,
Major a.D. Maximilian
Maessen. 3 Pf. (brown).

An Herrn Major a. D.
Maximilian Maessen
Berlin - Schlachtensee
Heimstättenstr. 13

Deutsches Reich

An Herrn Georg Neumann

Berlin-Schöneberg

Hohenfriedbergstr. 20

Deutfches Reich

☐ —Berlin-Schöneberg, Georg Neumann. 3 Pf. (brown).

Dunn

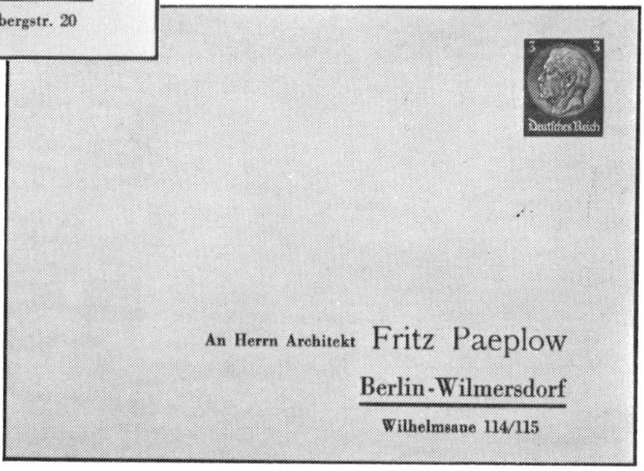

☐ —Berlin-Wilmersdorf, Fritz Paeplow. 3 Pf. (brown).

Deutfches Reich

An Herrn Architekt Fritz Paeplow

Berlin-Wilmersdorf

Wilhelmsaue 114/115

Cards with imprinted names/addresses of various collectors, plus "Drucksache."

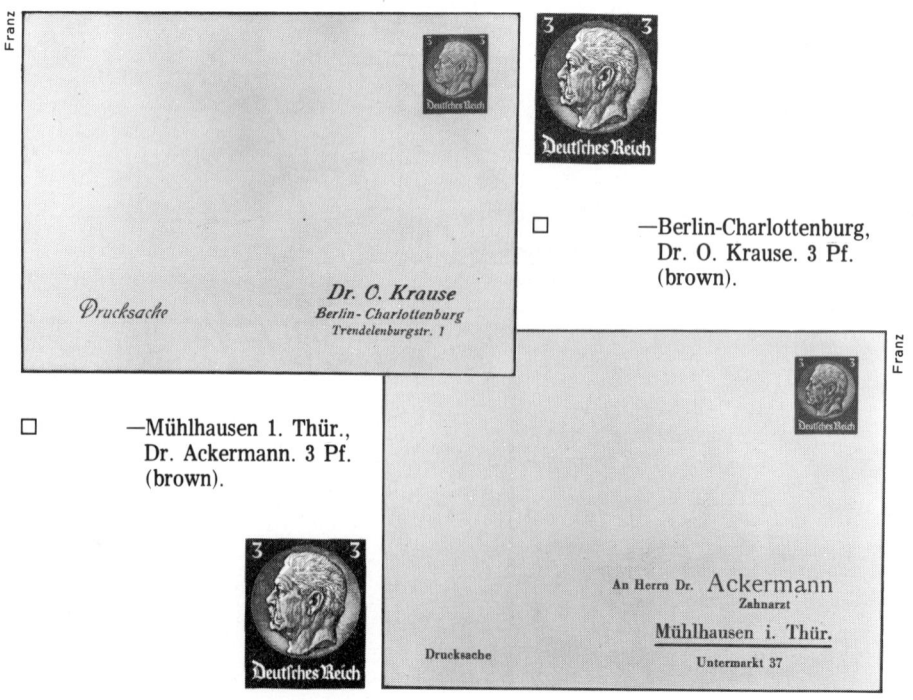

Franz

Drucksache

Dr. O. Krause
Berlin-Charlottenburg
Trendelenburgstr. 1

Deutfches Reich

☐ —Berlin-Charlottenburg, Dr. O. Krause. 3 Pf. (brown).

☐ —Mühlhausen 1. Thür., Dr. Ackermann. 3 Pf. (brown).

Franz

Deutfches Reich

An Herrn Dr. Ackermann
Zahnarzt

Mühlhausen i. Thür.

Untermarkt 37

Drucksache

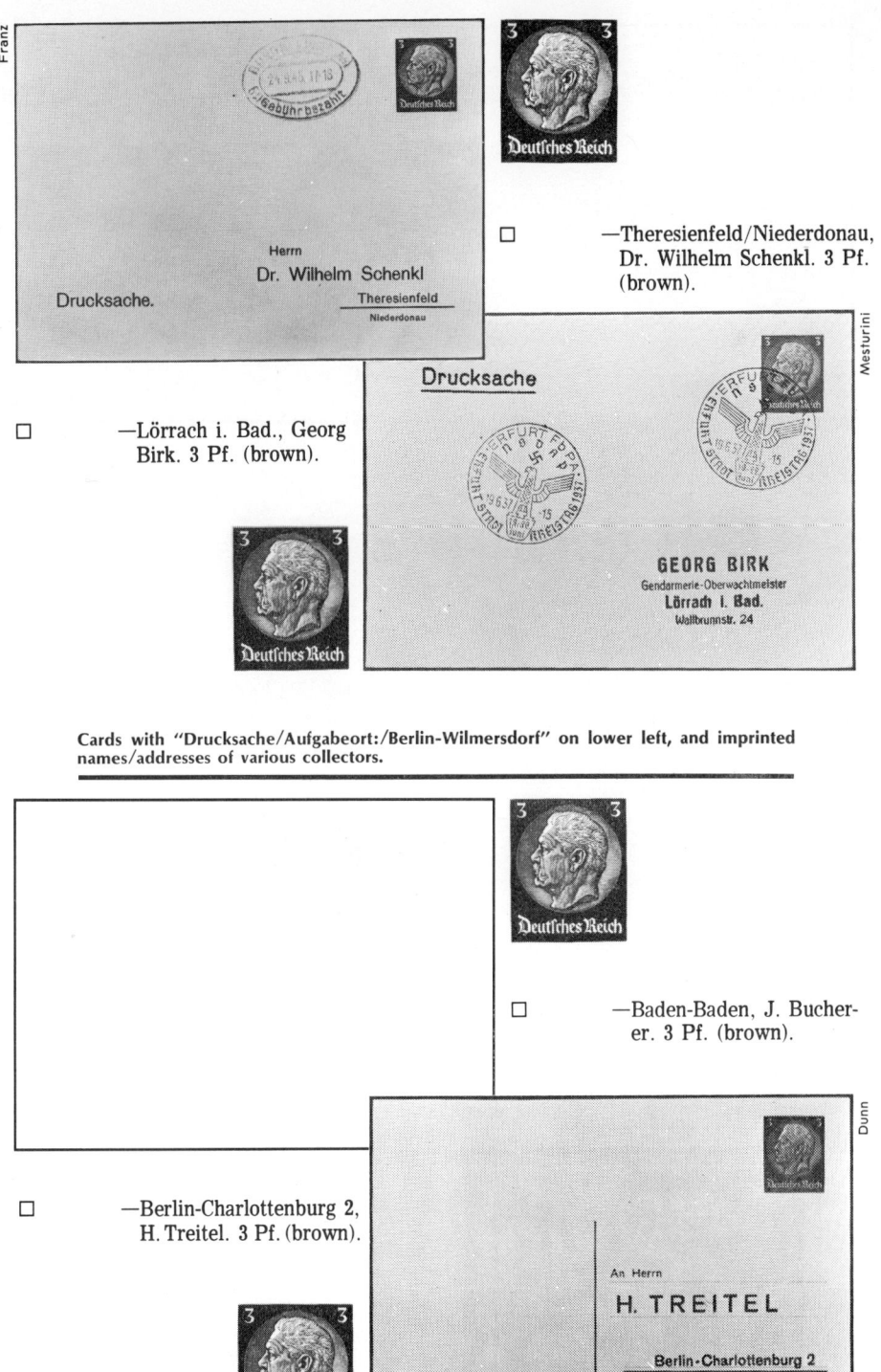

Franz

Herrn
Dr. Wilhelm Schenkl
Theresienfeld
Niederdonau

Drucksache.

□ —Theresienfeld/Niederdonau,
Dr. Wilhelm Schenkl. 3 Pf.
(brown).

Mesturini

Drucksache

GEORG BIRK
Gendarmerie-Oberwachtmeister
Lörrach i. Bad.
Wallbrunnstr. 24

□ —Lörrach i. Bad., Georg
Birk. 3 Pf. (brown).

Cards with "Drucksache/Aufgabeort:/Berlin-Wilmersdorf" on lower left, and imprinted
names/addresses of various collectors.

□ —Baden-Baden, J. Bucherer. 3 Pf. (brown).

Dunn

An Herrn

H. TREITEL

Berlin-Charlottenburg 2

Uhlandstraße 6

Drucksache
Aufgabeort:
Berlin Wilmersdorf

□ —Berlin-Charlottenburg 2,
H. Treitel. 3 Pf. (brown).

☐ —Berlin, Wilmersdorf,
  Paeplow. 3 Pf. (brown).

☐ —Cottbus, Richard Daniel.
  3 Pf. (brown).

☐ —Halle (Saale), T. Zirkenbach. 3 Pf. (brown).

☐ —Nürnberg N., Ernst
  Lebrecht. 3 Pf. (brown).

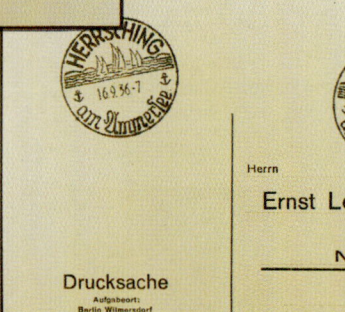

Cards with "Drucksache/Abs. Fritz Paeplow/Berlin-Wilmersdorf/Wilhelmsaue 114/15" on lower left, and imprinted names/addresses of various collectors.

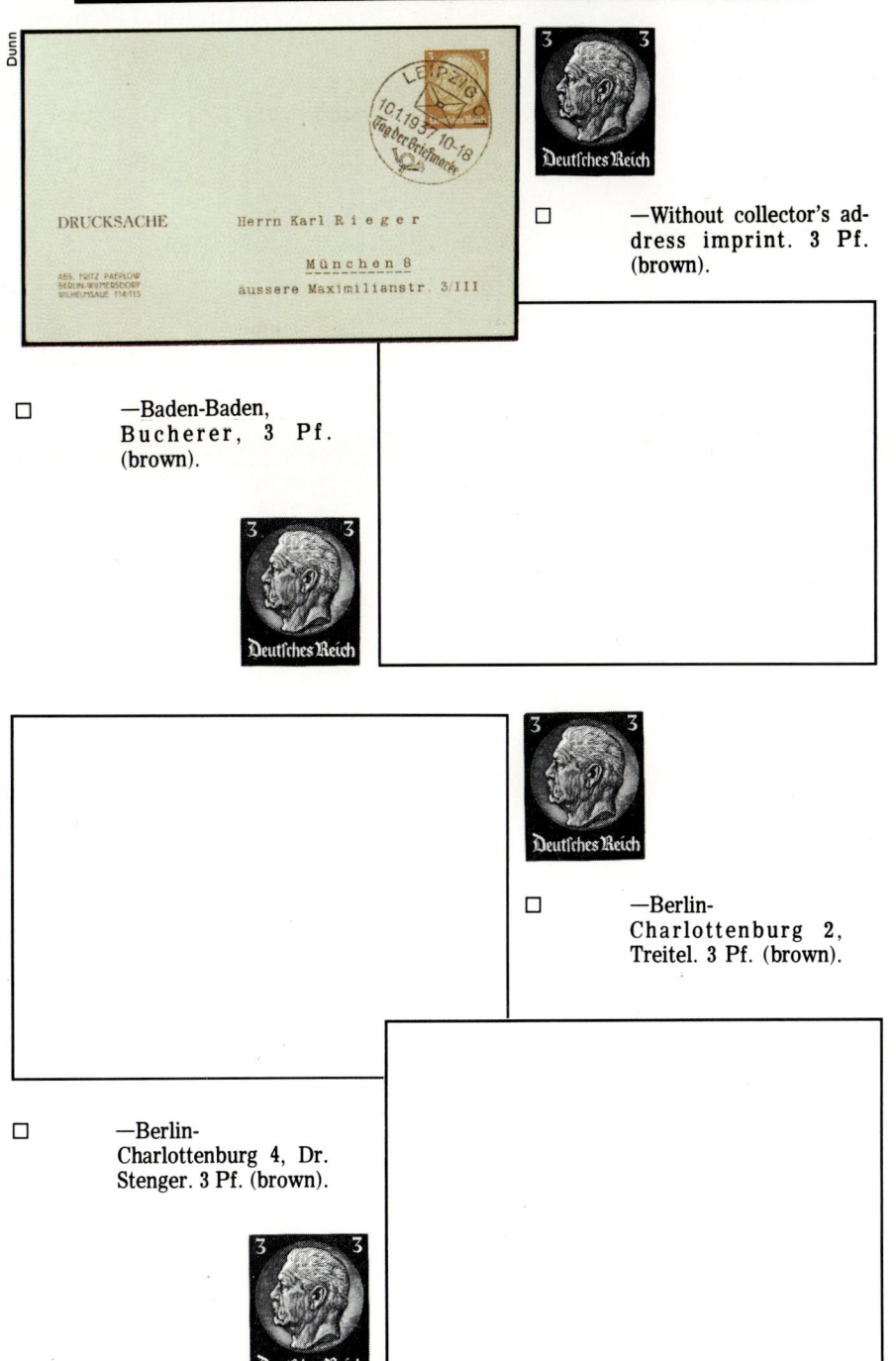

Dunn

DRUCKSACHE

ABS. FRITZ PAEPLOW
BERLIN-WILMERSDORF
WILHELMSAUE 114/115

Herrn Karl R i e g e r

M ü n c h e n 8
äussere Maximilianstr. 3/III

☐ —Without collector's address imprint. 3 Pf. (brown).

☐ —Baden-Baden, Bucherer, 3 Pf. (brown).

☐ —Berlin-Charlottenburg 2, Treitel. 3 Pf. (brown).

☐ —Berlin-Charlottenburg 4, Dr. Stenger. 3 Pf. (brown).

Franz

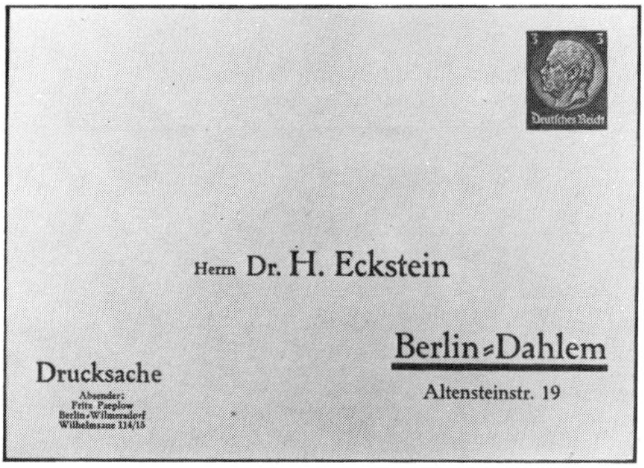

Herrn Dr. H. Eckstein

Berlin=Dahlem
Altensteinstr. 19

Drucksache
Absender:
Fritz Paeplow
Berlin-Wilmersdorf
Wilhelmaue 114/15

☐ —Berlin-Dahlem, Dr. H. Eckstein. 3 Pf. (brown).

☐ —Berlin-Wilmersdorf, Fritz Paeplow. 3 Pf. (brown).

☐ —Braunschweig, G. Dangers. 3 Pf. (brown).

☐ —Dresden A20, Oberlandesgerichtsrat Dietze. 3 Pf. (brown).

□ —Halle (Saale), Kurt
Zirkenbach. 3 Pf. (brown).

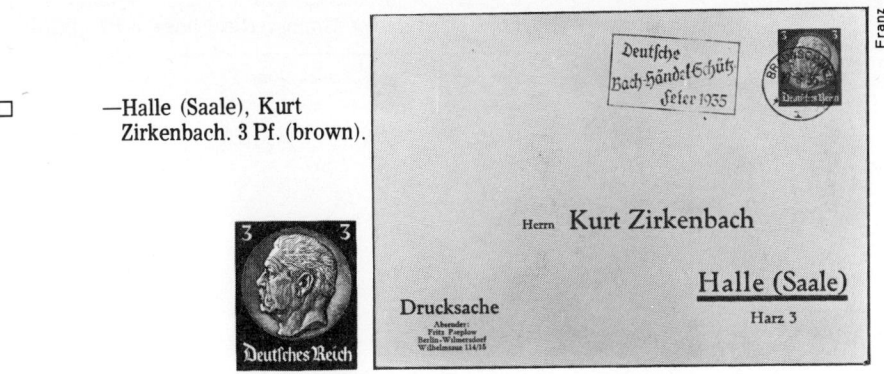

□ —Blank card with one line of text . . . "An." 3 Pf. (brown).

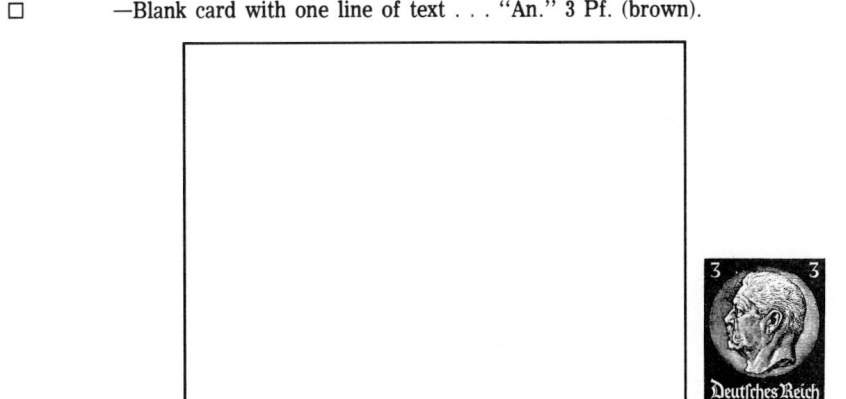

□ Blank card with five address lines (four broken, one solid) 38mm long. The vertical
division line is 61.5mm long. 3 Pf. (brown).

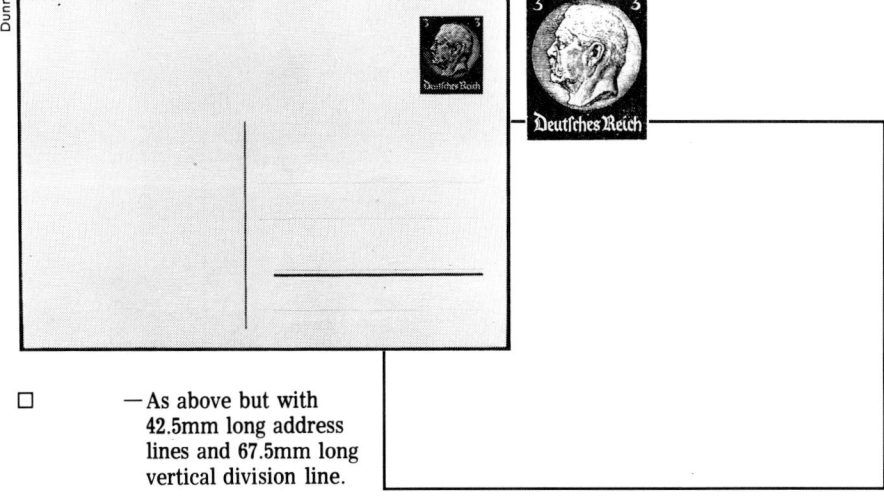

□ —As above but with
42.5mm long address
lines and 67.5mm long
vertical division line.

57

☐ —Blank card with "Drucksache" over two 23mm vertical lines. 3 Pf. (brown).

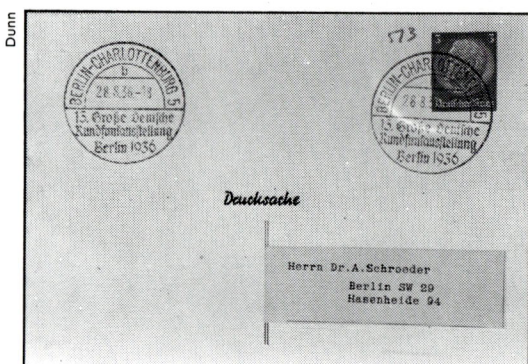

☐ —Blank card with "Postkarte" in Gothic type over 81mm vertical line. 3 Pf. (brown). Coated stock.

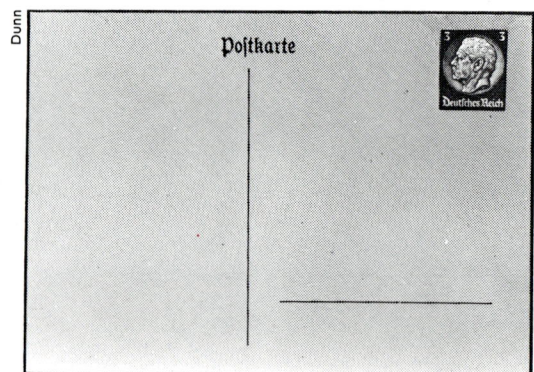

☐ —Blank card with "Drucksache," five address lines (four broken, one solid) 41.5mm long. The vertical division line is 90mm long. 3 Pf. (brown).

□ —Blank card without "Drucksache," five address lines (note different lengths). The vertical division line is 64mm long. 3 Pf. (brown).

□ — Aschersleben, Paul Koch, the producer and publisher of the "KA-BE" stamp albums. An album is illustrated on the reverse side. 3 Pf. (brown).

□ —Bad Weisser Hirsch, Kurt Horn. "May the tobacco business flurish." 3 Pf. (brown).

□ —Berlin W62, Walter Goecks. 3 Pf. (brown). At least seven variations exist, i.e., card color, length of name or location of name. Sender's notice at lower left of card.

□ Name 18mm long.
□ Name 22mm long.

□ —Berlin W62, Walter Goecks. Name in middle is 19mm long. 3 Pf. (brown).

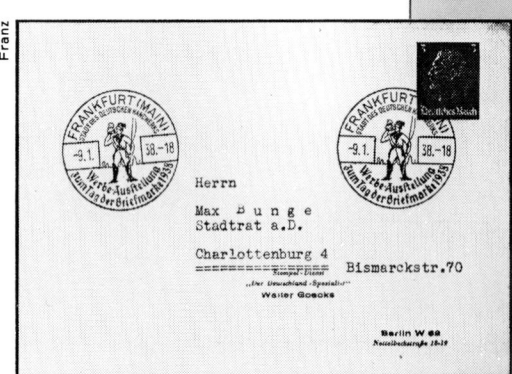

□ —As above, but with 22mm long name. 3 Pf. (brown).

□ —Berlin W62, Walter Goecks. Name is 28mm long. Cream-colored stock. 3 Pf. (brown).

☐ —Berlin W62, Walter Goecks.
Name is 28mm long. White
board stock. 3 Pf. (brown).

☐ — As above, but
name is 31mm long. 3
Pf. (brown).

☐ —Name in middle, with
additional address imprint
on lower right of card,
"Berlin W62/Nettelbeck-Stras-
se 18-19." 3 Pf. (brown).

☐ — Berlin W62,
Walter Goecks. Card
with "An" on obverse
and "Die neuen
Protektorats-Marken"
on reverse.

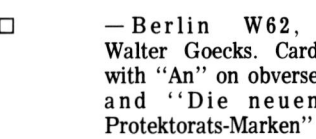

☐ —Berlin N31, Carl Kühne Wine Vinegar Company. 3 Pf. (brown).

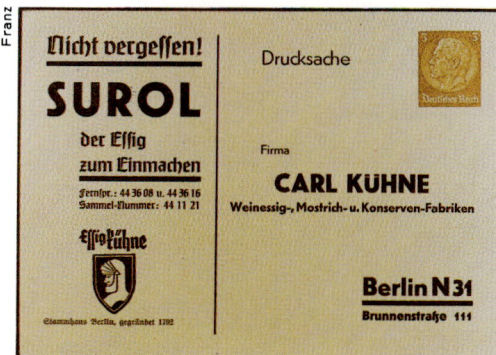

☐ —Berlin W35, Medizinischer Versand (Medical Supplies Shipper), on reverse is an order form for Haemasal. 3 Pf. (brown).

☐ —Berlin SW 61, Alfred Metzner Publishing Company. 3 Pf. (brown).

Heavy bar below Berlin is made of two lines:
☐ 20mm and 14mm   ☐ 14mm and 20mm

☐ —Berlin W15, Werner
Schüler. 3 Pf. (brown).

☐ —Berlin-Charlottenburg, Dr. O.
Krause Rundsendungsleiter, over
the sender's particu-
lars. 3 Pf. (brown).

☐ —Berlin-Charlottenburg 9, Major a.D. Th Junker—sender. 3 Pf. (brown).

☐ —Berlin-Lichterfelde-West, Max v. Bahrfeldt, on reverse is a receipt for an annual subscription to the BGSV society. 3 Pf. (brown).

☐   —Berlin-Wilmersdorf, Fritz Paeplow. 3 Pf. (brown).

FRITZ PAEPLOW
ARCHITEKT DWB
BERLIN-WILMERSDORF
WILHELMSAUE 114/15
POSTSCHECK BERLIN 16515
FERNRUF H7 WILMERSDORF 0660

☐   —BerlinWilmersdorf 2, fifteen different privately-printed promotional postcards for the firm of Albert Klickow Markenhaus (1933-1940). 3 Pf. (brown).

☐ Nr. 1

On left of card is store front with "Abstempelunge/Marken und Ganzachen..." Text in green below.

Ziegelhofer

Drucksache

☐ Nr. 2

Webb

☐ Nr. 3

Dunn

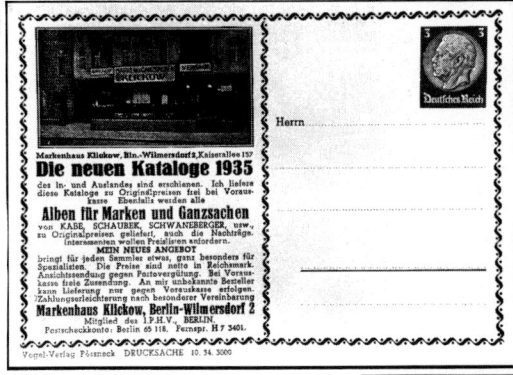

☐ Nr. 4

☐ Nr. 5

65

On left of card in brown, "25 Jahre Markenhandlung . . ."

□ Nr. 6

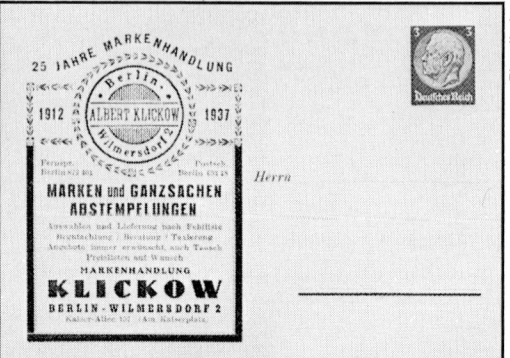

Ziegelhofer

□ Nr. 7

Dunn

□ Nr. 8

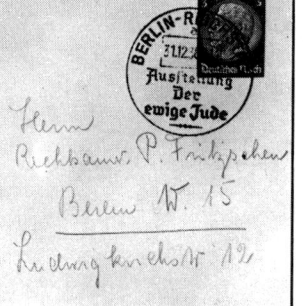

Dunn

□ Nr. 9

Dunn

Die deutschen

Wohlfahrtsmarken:

Sonderangebot

gebrauchter Stücke zu soliden Preisen. Jede Marke ist einzeln käuflich und können von einigen Wertes bis zu 10 Stück geliefert werden, solange mein Vorrat reicht. Ich ausgabe nachträge Bestellung auf Kasse. Nachnahmen kosten 1 RM. mehr. Für Anfänger:

36 verschiedene Wohlfahrtsmarken RM. 1.—
Auch liefere ich Zusammenstellungen für .... RM. 25.—
Nur verschiedene Wohlfahrtsmarken in guter Durchschnittsbeschaffung.
Vorauskasse oder Nachnahme.

MARKENHANDLUNG

Klickow

Berlin-Wilmersdorf 2

Kaiser-Allee 157 (Am Kaiserplatz)
Fernsprecher: 87 34 01

☐ Nr. 10

Dunn

✠✠✠ **1912-1937** ✠✠✠

25 Jahre
Markenhandlung
KLICKOW

Berlin-Wilmersdorf 2

Kaiser-Allee 157 (am Kaiserplatz)
Fernsprecher, 87 34 01
Postscheckkonto Berlin 65118

Auswahlen

und Lieferung nach Preisliste
Begutachtung Beratung Taxierung
Angebote immer erwünscht,
auch Tausch
Preislisten auf Wunsch

☐ Nr. 11

Dunn

FROHE OSTERN!

Ein Osterei für Sie!

☐ Nr. 12

☐ Nr. 13

Franz

Sonder-Angebot
zum
**Geburtstag der Briefmarke
am 6. Mai 1939**

Auswahlen

und Ansichtssendungen auf Wunsch.
Kassenaufträge werden bevorzugt und erbitte ich Zahlungen auf mein
Postscheckkonto Berlin 65118
Portospesen stets besonders. Die Preise sind netto in Reichsmark, die Angebote immer freibleibend. Erfüllungsort Berlin. Angebote — auch Tausch — immer erwünscht.

Herrn

Markenhandlung **Klickow**
BERLIN-WILMERSDORF 2
Kaiser-Allee 157 (am Kaiserplatz)
Fernspr. 87 34 01. — Geschäftsgründung 1912.

Reverse of Nr. 13.

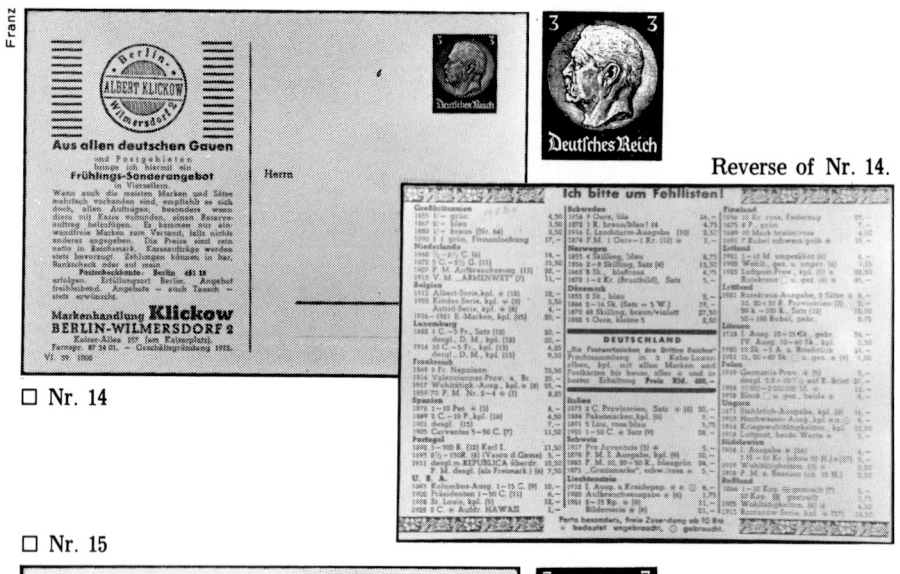

Reverse of Nr. 14.

☐ Nr. 14

☐ Nr. 15

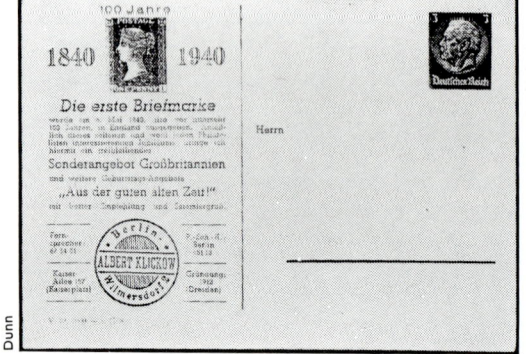

Folded double-card with title in green, "100 Jahre/1840 1940/die erste Briefmarke . . ."

☐ —Berlin, Berliner Ganzsachen-Sammler-Verein. 3 Pf. (brown). At least six different cards exist in this series. some with variant reverses.

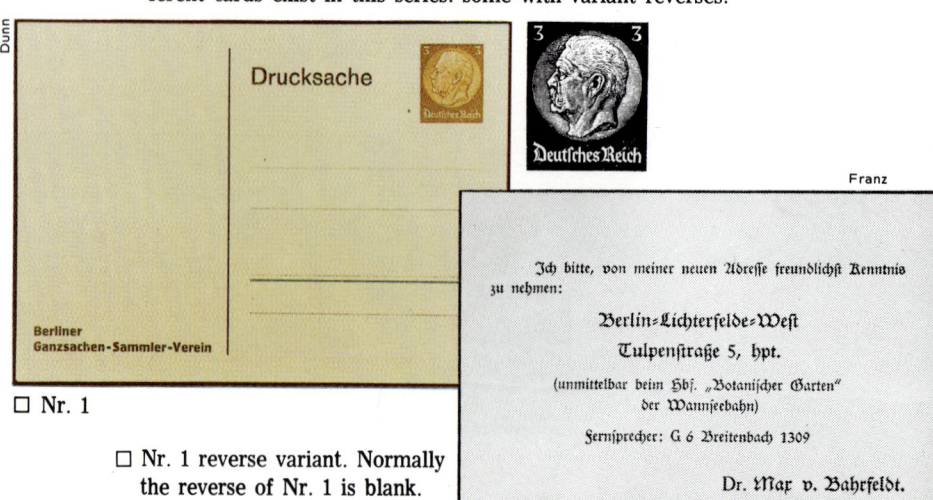

☐ Nr. 1

☐ Nr. 1 reverse variant. Normally the reverse of Nr. 1 is blank.

Deutsches Reich
3 3

Deutsches Reich

Drucksache

Berliner
Ganzsachen-Sammler-Verein
Rundsendungsleiter

☐ Nr. 2

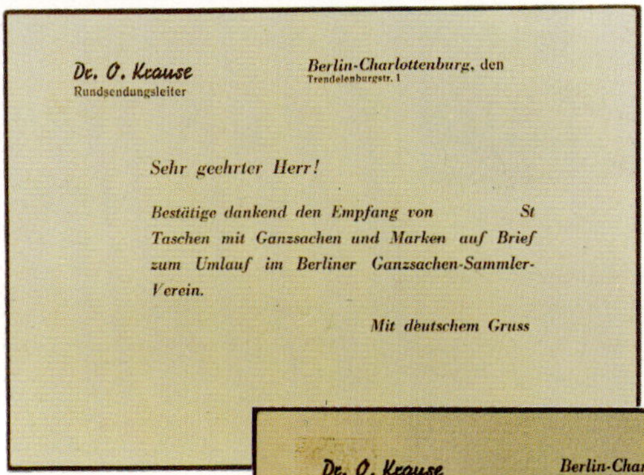

Dr. O. Krause
Rundsendungsleiter

Berlin-Charlottenburg, den
Trendelenburgstr. 1

Sehr geehrter Herr!

Bestätige dankend den Empfang von   St
Taschen mit Ganzsachen und Marken auf Brief
zum Umlauf im Berliner Ganzsachen-Sammler-
Verein.

Mit deutschem Gruss

☐ Reverse of
above.

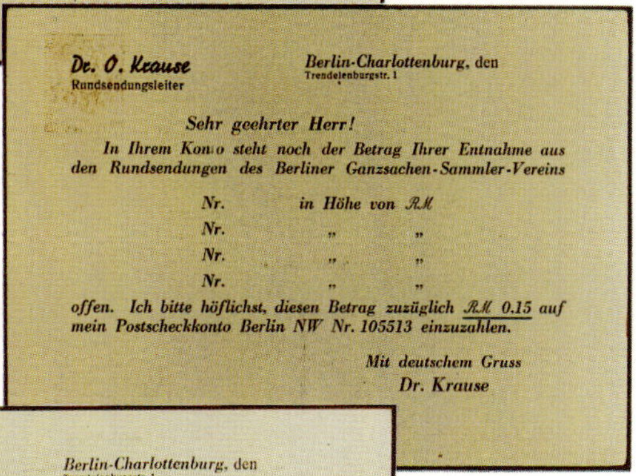

Dr. O. Krause
Rundsendungsleiter

Berlin-Charlottenburg, den
Trendelenburgstr. 1

Sehr geehrter Herr!
In Ihrem Konto steht noch der Betrag Ihrer Entnahme aus
den Rundsendungen des Berliner Ganzsachen-Sammler-Vereins

Nr.   in Höhe von ℛℳ
Nr.   „   „
Nr.   „   ,   „
Nr.   „   „   „

offen. Ich bitte höflichst, diesen Betrag zuzüglich ℛℳ 0.15 auf
mein Postscheckkonto Berlin NW Nr. 105513 einzuzahlen.

Mit deutschem Gruss
Dr. Krause

☐

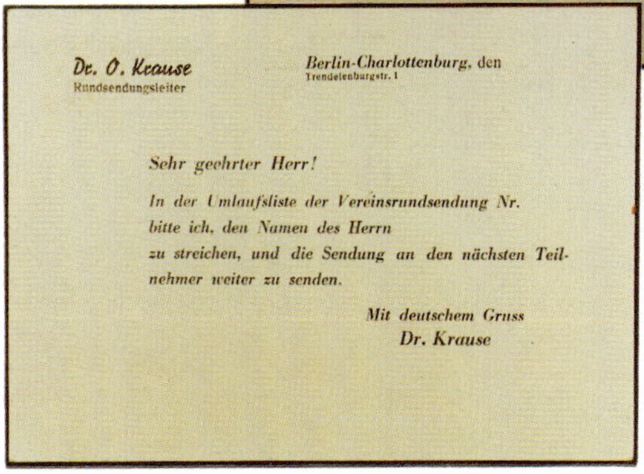

Dr. O. Krause
Rundsendungsleiter

Berlin-Charlottenburg, den
Trendelenburgstr. 1

Sehr geehrter Herr!

In der Umlaufsliste der Vereinsrundsendung Nr.
bitte ich, den Namen des Herrn
zu streichen, und die Sendung an den nächsten Teil-
nehmer weiter zu senden.

Mit deutschem Gruss
Dr. Krause

☐

Three different reverses for above, from Dr. O. Krause.

☐ Obverse as above but no reverse text.

□ Nr. 3
Berliner Ganzsachen-Sammler-Verein,
Major a.D. Th. Junker. 3 Pf. (brown).

□ Nr. 4
Berliner Ganzsachen-Sammler-Verein,
Fritz Paeplow. 3 Pf. (brown).
□ Reverse without text.
□ Reverse with statement of
account text.

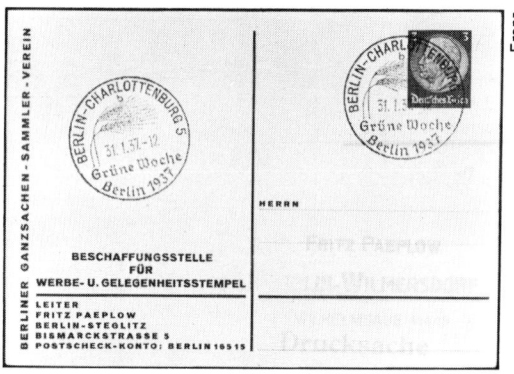

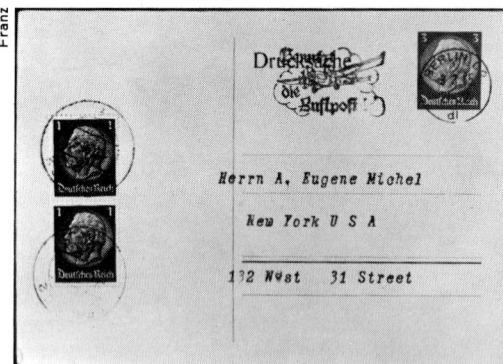

□ Nr. 5
Berliner Ganzsachen-Sammler-Verein,
with text on reverse announcing the 11
March 1935 Founders' Day. 3 Pf. (brown).

Berlin, den 27. Februar 1935

Sehr geehrter Herr!

Das diesjährige **Stiftungsfest** des Berliner Ganzsachen-Sammler-Vereins
findet am **Montag, den 11. März, 20⁰⁰**, in Form eines einfachen Essens (Gedeck
M 2.50, kein Trinkzwang) im Vereinslokal Landwehr-Kasino, Berlin-Charlottenburg,
Jebensstraße, am Bahnhof Zoologischer Garten, statt. Wir bitten, an dem Stiftungsfest
teilzunehmen und freundliche Zusage bis spätestens 8. März an Herrn Dr. Voelkel,
Berlin-Lichterfelde, Roonstraße 19, Fernsprecher F 6 Breitenbach 9415, zu richten.

Ein neues **Mitgliederverzeichnis** soll herausgegeben und allen Mitgliedern
zugesandt werden. Wir bitten, alle die eigene Person betreffenden Angaben nach-
zuprüfen und Fehler oder Veränderungen (Anschrift, Fernsprecher, Postscheckkonto) Herrn Dr. von Bahrfeldt, Berlin-Lichterfelde, Tulpenstraße 5, bis zum
10. März mitzuteilen.

Beabsichtigt ist, bei jedem Mitglied seine **Sammelgebiete** anzugeben, um
eine Belebung der persönlichen Beziehungen zu erreichen; wir bitten um Angabe
etwa wie folgt: Altdeutschland oder Uebersee gebraucht, einschl. Marken auf Brief
oder Karten und Kartenbriefe oder Privatganzsachen unter Hinzufügung von Kauf
oder Tausch.

Mit deutschem Gruß
Berliner Ganzsachen-Sammler-Verein.

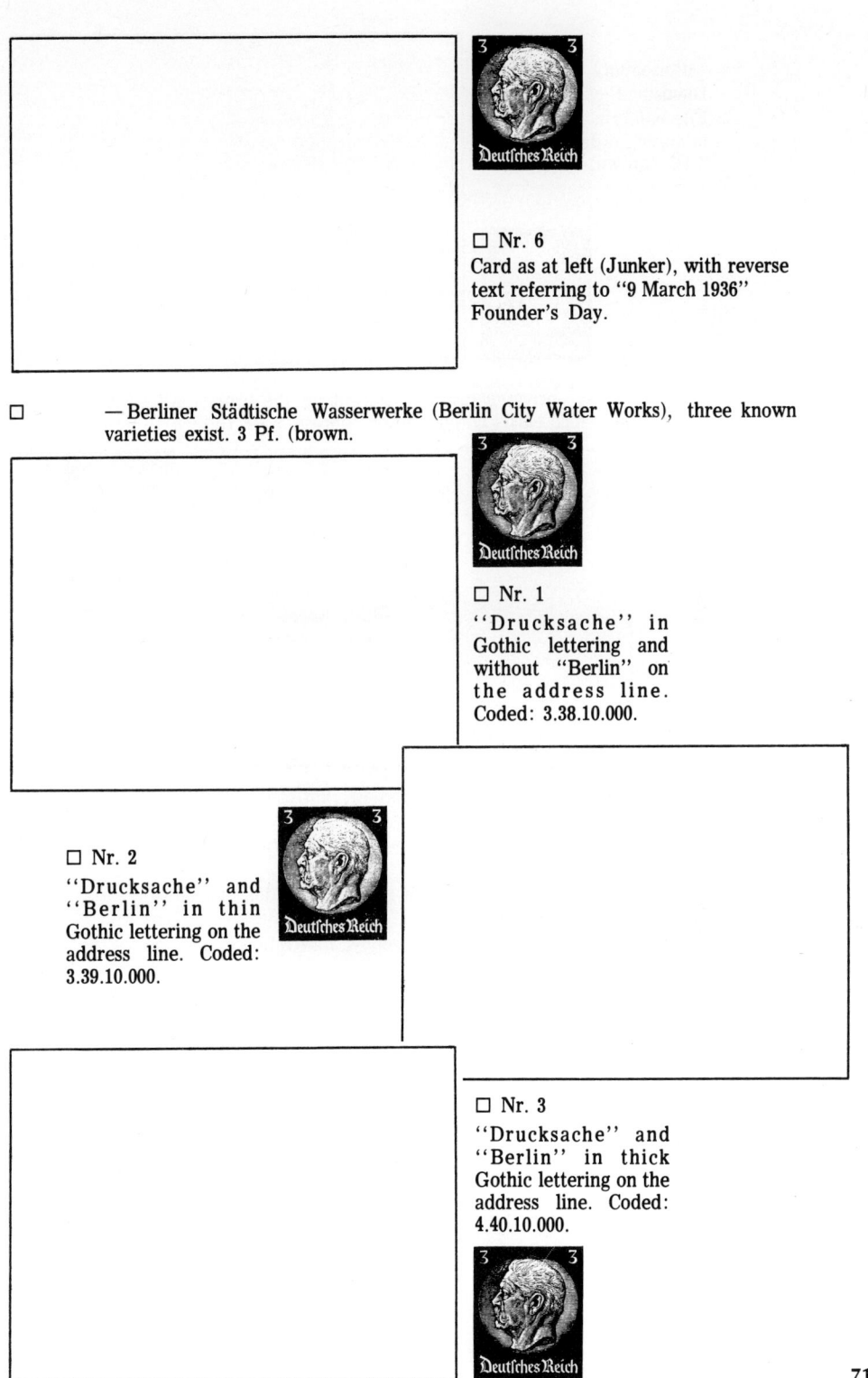

☐ Nr. 6
Card as at left (Junker), with reverse text referring to "9 March 1936" Founder's Day.

☐ —Berliner Städtische Wasserwerke (Berlin City Water Works), three known varieties exist. 3 Pf. (brown.

☐ Nr. 1
"Drucksache" in Gothic lettering and without "Berlin" on the address line. Coded: 3.38.10.000.

☐ Nr. 2
"Drucksache" and "Berlin" in thin Gothic lettering on the address line. Coded: 3.39.10.000.

☐ Nr. 3
"Drucksache" and "Berlin" in thick Gothic lettering on the address line. Coded: 4.40.10.000.

□ —Boizenburg (Elbe),
Duensing-Bicheroux-Werke
Fliesenfabrik (tile manu-
facturer), order inquiry.
3 Pf. (brown).

□ —Colditz I. Sa., privately-printed postcard for the firm of Alfred Kurth Brief-
markenhaus. Also exists without 4-line address. 3 Pf. (brown).

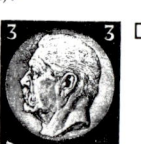

□ Frame around illustration in yellow, illustration in blue, address in grey.
□ Frame around illustration in yellow, illustration in blue, address in black.
□ Frame around illustration in green, illustration in reddish-
brown, address in black.
□ Frame around illustration in yellow, illustration in blue, no
4-line address imprint.

□ —Dresden A 16, Addressen-Müller, reverse has an order form for address labels.
3 Pf. (brown).

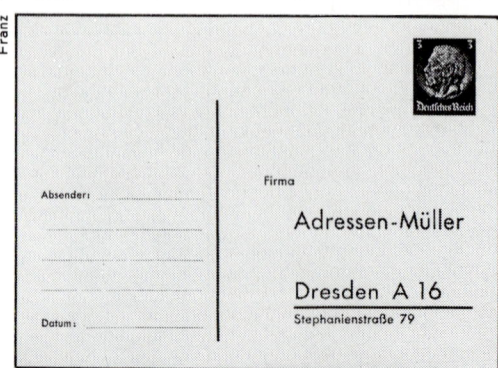

□ As above, but
with "Dresden
N 15" address.

—Füsilier-Bund 73, a monthly magazine, Major a.D. Th. Junker—editor. 3 Pf. (brown).

—Füsilier-Regiment Nr. 73, announcing a regimental evening. 3 Pf. (brown).

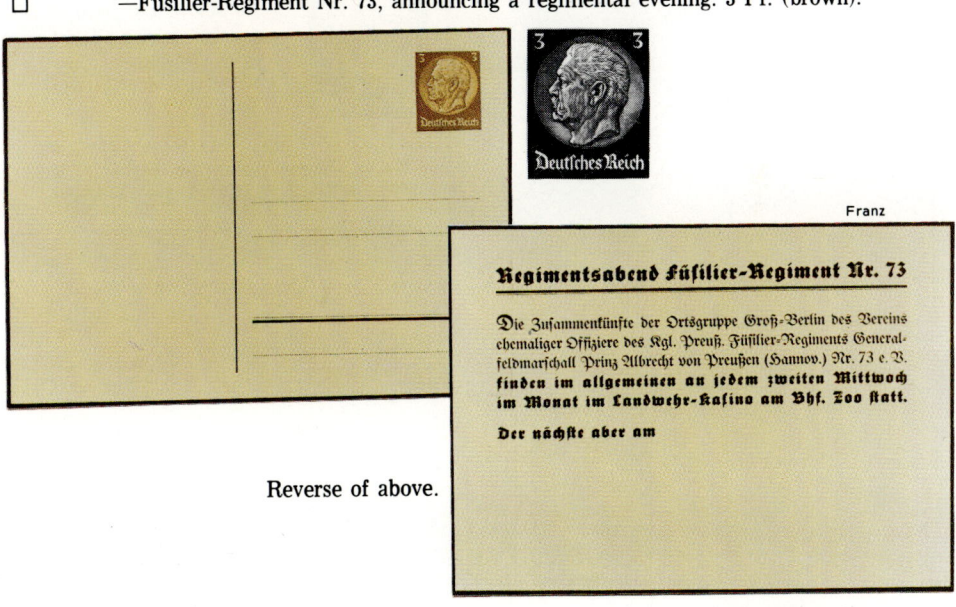

Reverse of above.

—Hamburg 8, Wilkening & Co. Schellack-Import-Gesellschaft, reverse has a price list. 3 Pf. (brown).

73

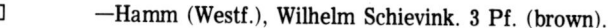
□ —Hamm (Westf.), Wilhelm Schievink. 3 Pf. (brown).

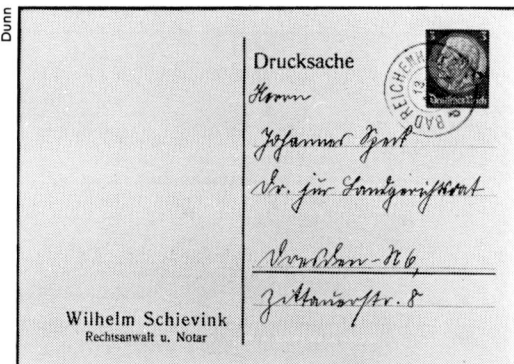

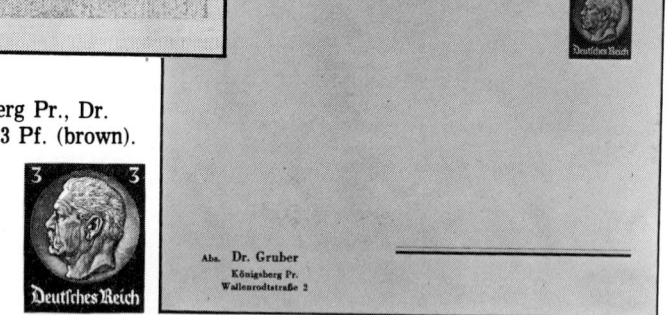

□ As below, but with "Dresden 16" stick-on label over Köln address.

□ —Köln, Addressen-Müller, reverse has order form for address labels. 3 Pf. (brown).

□ —Königsberg Pr., Dr. Gruber. 3 Pf. (brown).

□ —Landshut, Landwirtschaftliche Berufsgenossenschaft Niederbayern. Delivery information. 3 Pf. (brown).

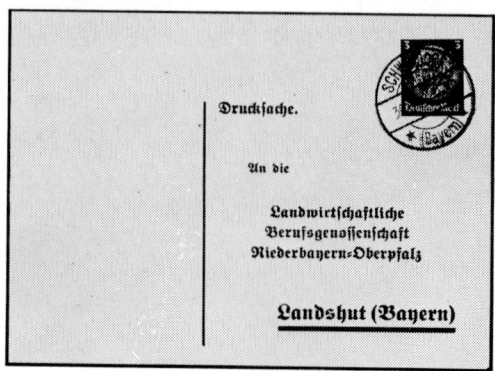

—Leipzig C1, Executive Committee of the Evangelical Society of the Gustav Adolf Institution. 3 Pf. (brown).

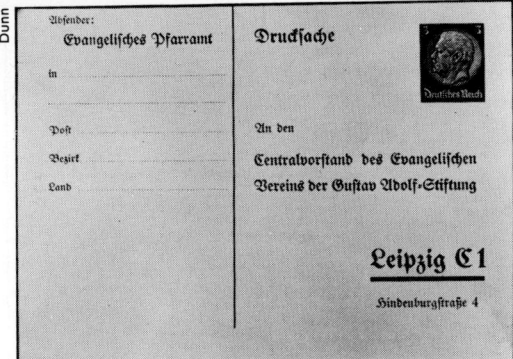

—München 8, Adam Ballinger (Sauerkraut manufacturer). 3 Pf. (brown).

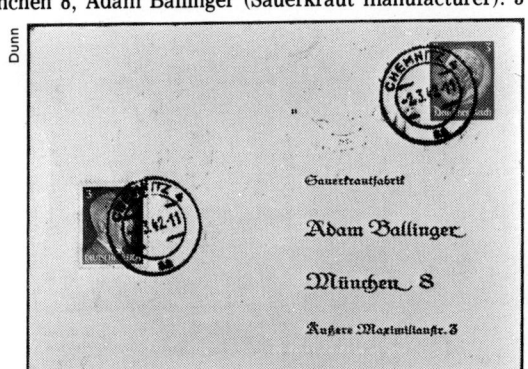

—München 8, Karl Rieger. 3 Pf. (brown).

As illustrated but with "Drucksache" above address lines.

—As above but with imprint on reverse. **3 Pf. (brown).**

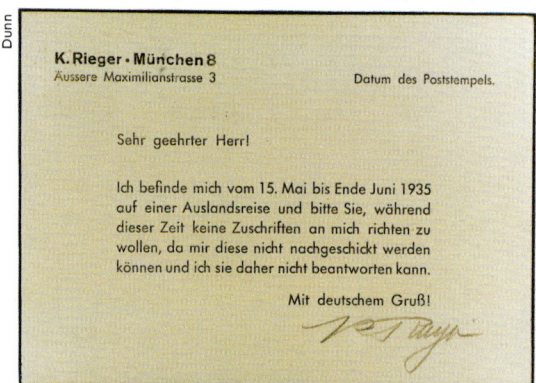

—München, promoting the Munich Postal Collectors' Society. **3 Pf. (brown), 6 Pf. (green) and 5 Pf. Luftpost (green).**

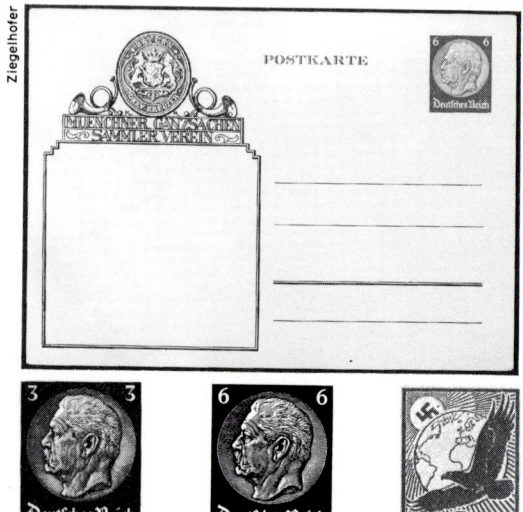

—As above but without "Postkarte." **3 Pf. (brown).**

□ —As above but with black border around card commemorating the death of Paul von Hindenburg. 6 Pf. (green).

Paul von Hindenburg

□ —Nürnberg-N, Ernst Lebrecht. 3 Pf. (brown).

□ —Rabenstein, Oskar Erich Peters; cream-colored, course card stock, in format 120:78mm with address imprint. 3 Pf. (brown).

□ —Düsseldorf, State Lottery Receipt (Franceson). 3 Pf. (brown). Also from "Groll" and "Schwarz."

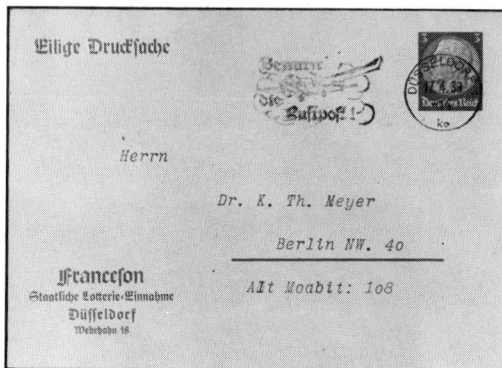

□ Franceson
□ Groll
□ Schwarz

□ —Tübingen (Württ.), Dr. Weissburger. Four known varities exist. 3 Pf. (brown).

□ Cream-colored stock, black printing.

□ Cream-colored stock, brown printing.

☐ Light-green stock, brown printing.

☐ Light-green stock, green printing. Reverse has order form.

☐ —Indanthren-Haus, five card advertising series for fade-resistant cloth. 3 Pf. (brown).

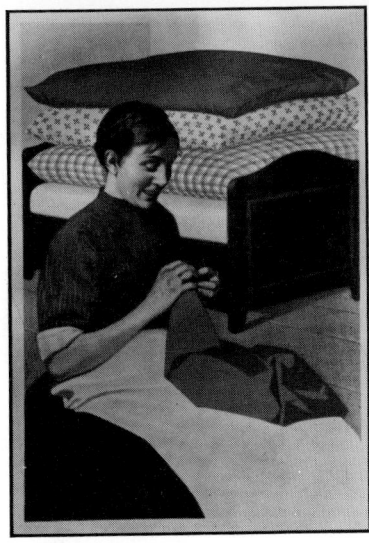

☐ Nr. 1

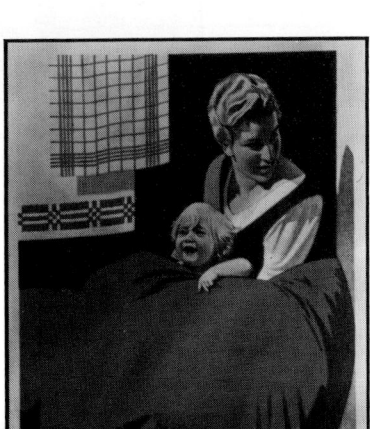

☐ Nr. 2

☐ Nr. 3

☐ Nr. 4

☐ Nr. 5

☐ —Kölnischwasser-Vernebler. 3 Pf. (brown).

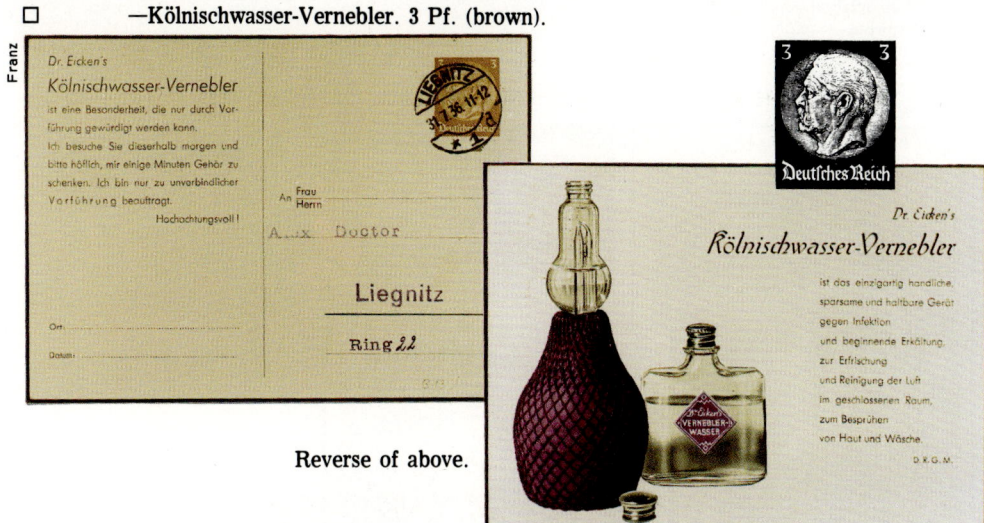

Reverse of above.

☐ —Schaubek Briefmarken-Album, seller of stamp albums world-wide. Reverse has a map of the world. 3 Pf. (brown).

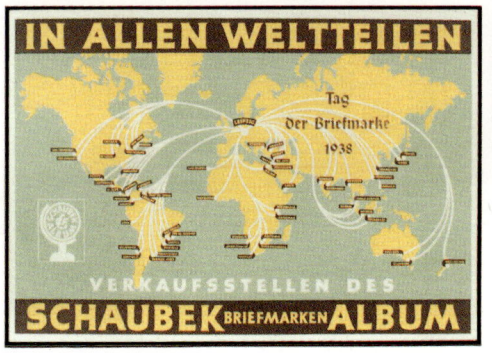

Event cards (also
firm and association
events) without
specific dates.

☐   —Heidelberg, three card set commemorating the National Festival. 3 Pf. (brown).

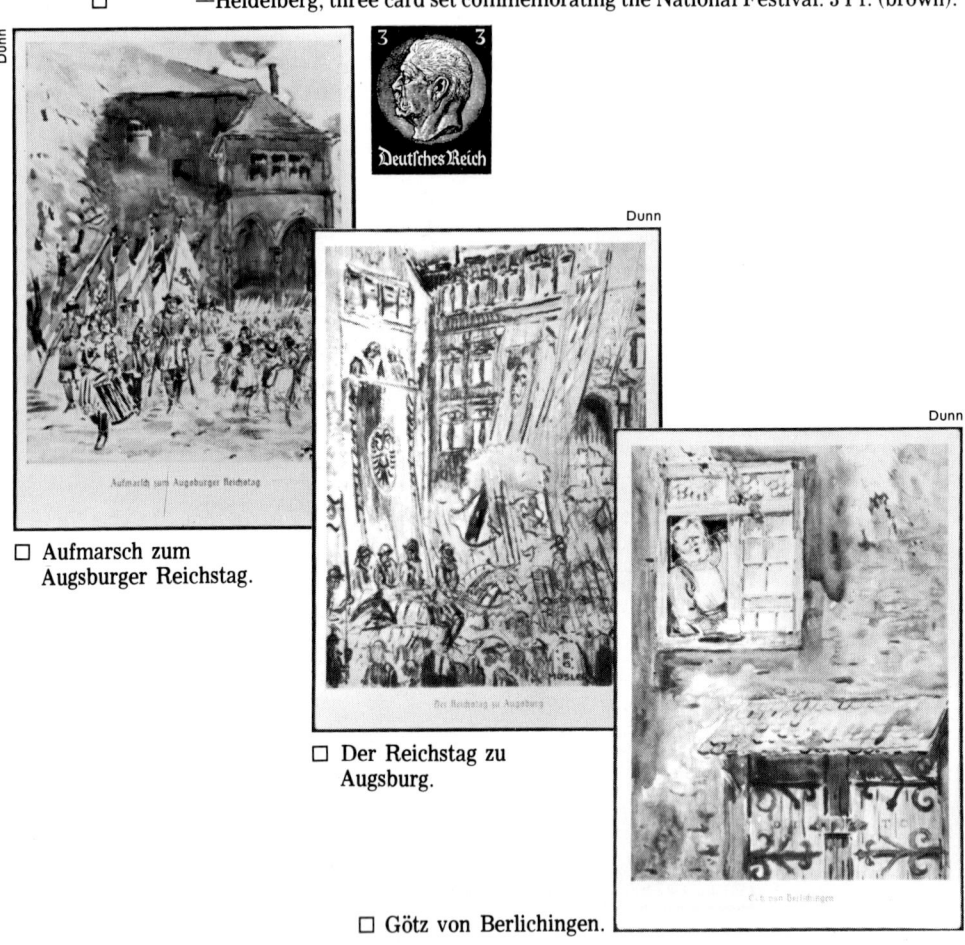

Dunn

Dunn

Dunn

☐ Aufmarsch zum
   Augsburger Reichstag.

☐ Der Reichstag zu
   Augsburg.

☐ Götz von Berlichingen.

☐ —Commemorating the Day of German Family Music. 3 Pf. (brown).

☐ —As above but with "Raum für Einladungstext" overprinted in black. 3 Pf. (brown).

☐ —Cherish home music. 3 Pf. (brown).

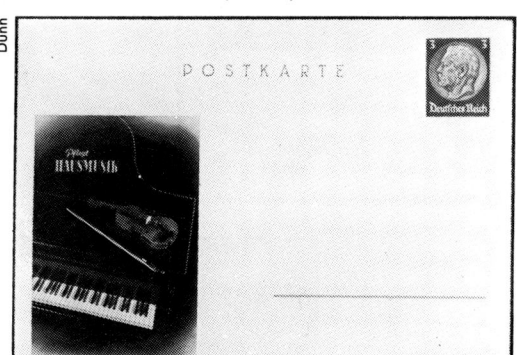

☐   —Marcophil postcard series consisting of sixteen cards depicting old German postilions and postmen. No imprinted stamp or 3 Pf. (brown). It is estimated that only 60 complete sets were produced with an imprinted stamp.

☐ Nr. 1 Grossherzogl. Baden'scher Postillon.
☐ Nr. 2 Königl. Württembergscher Postillon.
☐ Nr. 3 Kurhessische Postbeamte.
☐ Nr. 4 K.K. Oesterreichische Postillons.
☐ Nr. 5 Königl. Hannoverscher Post-Beamter.
☐ Nr. 6 Königl. Preuss. Postbeamter.
☐ Nr. 7 Fürstl. Turn u. Taxis'scher Postillon.
☐ Nr. 8 Grossherzogl. M. Schwerinsche Postbeamte.
☐ Nr. 9 Coburg Gotha'scher Postillon.
☐ Nr. 10 Koenigl. Bayerische Postillons.
☐ Nr. 11 Königl. Sächsische Post-Beamte.
☐ Nr. 12 Königl. Bayerischer Postbeamter.
☐ Nr. 13 Grossherzogl. Badischer Postbeamter.
☐ Nr. 14 Königl. Preuss. Postillon.
☐ Nr. 15 Königl. Sächs. Postillon.
☐ Nr. 16 Königl. Hannoverscher Postillon.

Grossherzogl. Baden'scher Postillon.

Nr. 1

Kurhessische Postbeamte.

Nr. 3

K.K. Oesterreichische Postillons.

Nr. 4

Fürstl. Turn u. Taxis'scher Postillon.

Nr. 7

84

Webb

Nr. 9

Dunn

Nr. 13

☐ —"Beautiful Germany," fund-raising series for the 1934/35 WHW lottery. 3 Pf. (brown).

☐ 1 Sylt/Strand (Nr. 7)
☐ 2 Paderborn (Nr. 15)
☐ 3 München, Frauenkirche (Nr. 21)
☐ 4 Schloss Linderhof (Nr. 28)
☐ 5 Magdeburg, Domhauptportal (Nr. 45)
☐ 6 Beilstein, Zehnthaus (Nr. 59)
☐ 7 Wolfachtal (Nr. 65)
☐ 8 Schloss Egg bei Metten (Ndby.) (Nr. 66)
☐ 9 Sächs. Schweiz, Basteibrücke (Nr. 75)

☐ 10 Burg Eltz (Nr. 76)
☐ 11 Bad Ems (Nr. 109)
☐ 12 Ostseebad Warnemünde, Hafen (Nr. 110)
☐ 13 Engen im Hegau m. Hohenhöwen (Nr. 111)
☐ 14 Potsdam, Marmorpalais am heiligen See (Nr. 112)
☐ 15 Bolkenhain mit Bolkeburg (Ndsch) (Nr. 113)
☐ 16 Poppelsdorfer Schloss (Nr. 114)
☐ 17 Dinkelsbühl (Nr. 115)

85

☐ —Berlin NW 87, Dr. Rudolf Reiss. Double-card with 3 Pf. (brown) on message card and on reply card. Four varieties exist.

☐
Separated/
used question
portion.

Nr. 2

☐ 1. Message portion blank on front and back, 17mm wide attachment affixed on bottom; reply portion (name of town in "Grotesque") has illustration on front moved to the left, and on back is a four-line order form.

☐ 2. As No. 1 above, but without attachment and line under Berlin on reply portion is 38mm long (Berlin in "Antique").

☐ 3. As No. 2, but line under Berlin is 45mm long.

☐ 4. Reply portion is blank on front, on back is a photo of a Rheumasan tube and bottle; reply portion has a space for address on front (in Grotesque), on left is a ten-line advertising, on back is an order form to request samples and information.

Nr. 3

☐ Attached.
☐ Separated message portion.
☐ Separated reply portion.

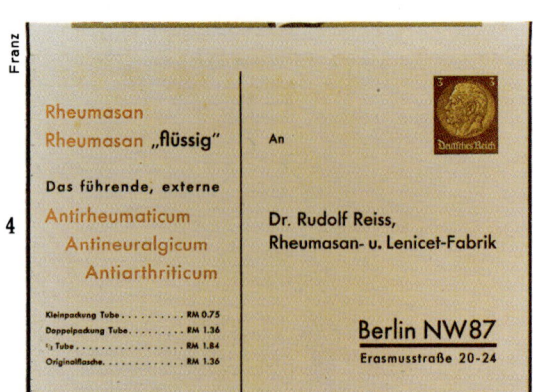

Nr. 4

☐ Attached.
☐ Separated message portion.
☐ Separated reply portion.

Reverse of message portion is blank.

☐   —Hamburg 26, Chemische Fabrik Promonta G.M.B.H. Two-part card with 3 Pf. & 3 Pf. (brown).

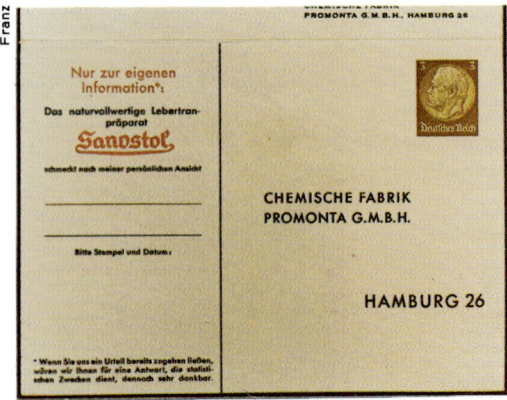

88   ☐ Attached.   ☐ Separated message portion.   ☐ Separated reply portion.

☐   —"Beautiful Germany," fund-raising series for the 1934/35 WHW lottery. These cards were two-part, printed in brown, and had 3 Pf. and 3 Pf. (brown) imprinted stamps.

☐ 1 Sylt (Nr. 7) & Schloss Linderhof (Nr. 128)
☐ 2 Paderborn (Nr. 15) & München (Nr. 21)
☐ 3 Magdeburg (Nr. 45 & Beilstein (Nr. 59)
☐ 4 Wolfachtal (Nr. 65) & Schloss Egg (Nr. 66)
☐ 5 Basteibrücke (Nr. 75) & Burg Eltz (Nr. 76)
☐ 6 Bad Ems (Nr. 109) & Trier (Nr. 124)
☐ 7 Warnemünde (Nr. 110) & Bolkenhain (Nr. 113)
☐ 8 Engen (Nr. 11) & Monreal (Nr. 118)
☐ 9 Potsdam (Nr. 112) & Burg Runkel (Nr. 117)
☐ 10 Poppelsdorfer Schloss (Nr. 114) & Schloss Hellenstein (Nr. 126)
☐ 11 Dinkelsbühl (Nr. 115) & Berneck (Nr. 116)
☐ 12 Saarburg (Nr. 119 & Kreuzeck (Nr. 122)
☐   Harburg (Nr. 120) & Trifels-Burgengruppe (Nr. 121)
☐ 14 Stralsund (Nr. 123) & Klosterruine Limburg (Nr. 125)
☐ 15 Palmnicken (Nr. 127) & Rothenburg o.T. (Nr. 128)
☐ 16 Balingen (Nr. 129) & München (Nr. 131)
☐ 17 Aachen (Nr. 130) & Kynsburg (Nr. 136)
☐ 18 Landsberg (Nr. 132) & Insel Reichenau (Nr. 133)
☐ 19 Abend im Spreewald (Nr. 134) & Ruine Trifels (Nr. 135)
☐ 20 Schneekoppe (Nr. 137) & Tübingen (Nr. 138)
☐ 21 Lindau (Nr. 139 & Brandenburger Tor (Nr. 149)
☐ 22 Rhein bei Speyer (Nr. 140) & Goslar (Nr. 150)
☐ 23 Hambacher Schloss (Nr. 141) & Hitzakker (Nr. 151)
☐ 24 Neu-Leiningen (Nr. 142) & Zugspitze (Nr. 160)
☐ 25 Leuchtenburg (Nr. 143) & Schloss Ettersburg (Nr. 153)
☐ 26 Wernigerode (Nr. 144 & Quedlinburg (Nr. 152)
☐ 27 Zeitz (Nr. 145) & Friedrichsh. (Nr. 165)
☐ 28 Altenburg (Nr. 146) & Kyffhäuser-Denkmal (Nr. 155)
☐ 29 Rudolstadt (Nr. 147) & Aschaffenburg (Nr. 167)
☐ 30 Wittenberg (Nr. 148) & Wützburg (Nr. 168)
☐ 31 Nürnberg Reichsparteitag (Nr. 154) & Wachsenburg (Nr. 157)
☐ 32 Weimar (Nr. 156) & Wasserburg am Bodensee (Nr. 162)
☐ 33 Halberstadt (Nr. 158) & Burg Hohenstein (Nr. 166)
☐ 34 Hameln (Nr. 159) & München (Nr. 161)
☐ 35 Walchensee (Nr. 163) & Burg Saaleck (Nr. 164)
☐ 36 Dinkelsbühl, Tor (Nr. 169) & Hannover (Nr. 170)
☐ 37 Korvey (Nr. 171) & Rothenburg o.T. (Nr. 172)
☐ 38 Gotha (Nr. 173) & Hornberg (Nr. 174)
☐ 39 Nordhausen (Nr. 175) & Stuttgart, Hauptbahnhof (Nr. 176)

☐ 40 Nürnberg, Burg (Nr. 177) & Saarbrükken (Nr. 178)
☐ 41 Stettin (Nr. 179) & Stuttgart (Nr. 180)
☐ 42 Goslar (N4. 181) & Waldeck (Nr. 182)
☐ 43 Burg Bernwartstein (Nr. 183) & Freiburg, Münster (Nr. 184)
☐ 44 Limburg (Nr. 185) & Ludwigshafen (Nr. 186)
☐ 45 Sassnitz (Nr. 187) & Rhodt (Nr. 188)
☐ 46 Dietkirchen (Nr. 189) & Eltville (Nr. 190)
☐ 47 Heppenheim (Nr. 191) & Lüneburger Heide (Nr. 192)
☐ 48 Kropsburg (Nr. 193) & Oberstdorf (Nr. 194)
☐ 49 Gimmeldingen (Nr. 195) & Berchtesgaden (Nr. 196)
☐ 50 Siebengebirge (Nr. 197) & Burg Ehrenbreitstein (Nr. 198)
☐ 51 Madenburg (Nr. 199) & Dreitorspitze Wetterstein (Nr. 200)

☐   —Blank card with no address lines and 4 Pf. (grey-blue) imprinted stamp.

☐   —Berlin-Wilmersdorf, Fritz Paeplow. Five-line sender's imprint on lower left of card. 4 Pf. (grey-blue).

☐ No address lines.

☐ Dr. Ackermann-Mühlhausen imprint.

☐ 1933, Jan.-March—"e" of "Postkarte" with long tail and sender's address with five lines of text. 5 Pf. (light green). Cream or beige-colored stock.

J. Rawlings

☐ 21mm spacing.

☐ 24.5mm spacing.

(See top of next page for details.)

Poſtkarte

—As above but note different spacing between "Absender" lines of text at upper left of card. Far left example is 21mm high and the other is 24.5mm high.

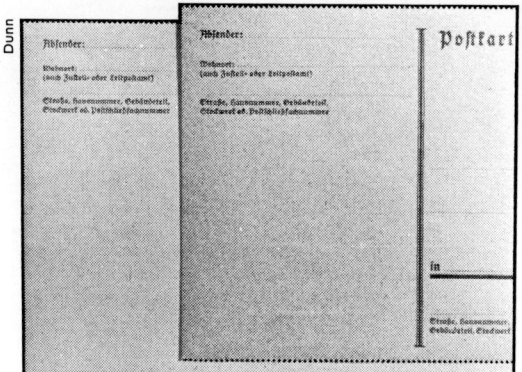

Note: The 21mm variety comes only on cream-colored stock and is a 1932 issue.

☐ 1933, Jan.-March—As above but with perforated edges. 5 Pf. (light green).

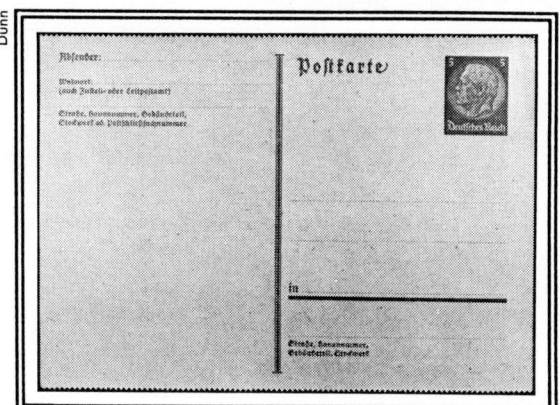

☐ 21mm spacing.

☐ 24.5mm spacing.

☐ 1934, Jan-June—Three lines of sender's text on upper left of card and short tail on "e" of "Postkarte." 5 Pf. (light green). Cream or beige-colored stock.

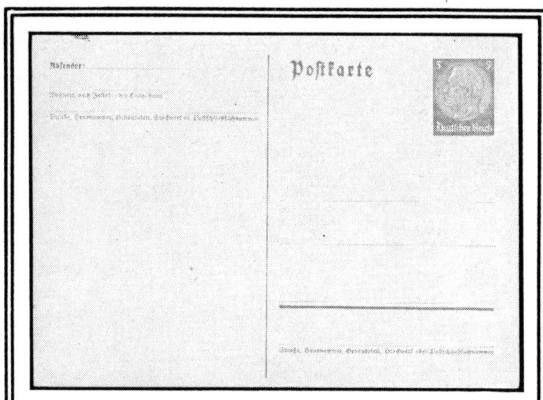

Poſtkarte

□ —Blank card with five address lines (four broken, one solid). Cream-colored stock. 5 Pf. (light green).

□ —Berlin W8, Joseph Rodenstock. The reverse is an acknowledgement concerning eyeglasses. 5 Pf. (light green).

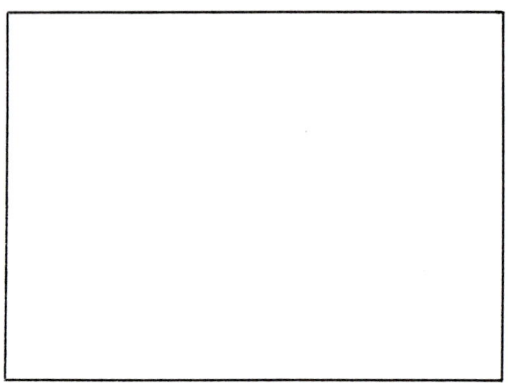

□ —Berlin NO 18, Carl Timner G.m.b.H. 5 Pf. (light Green).

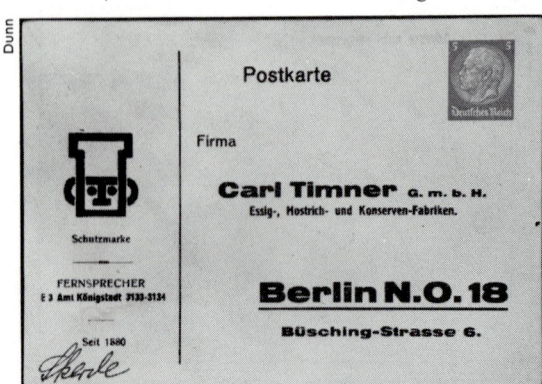

□   —Berlin-Charlottenburg, Georg Gormann. 5 Pf. (light green).

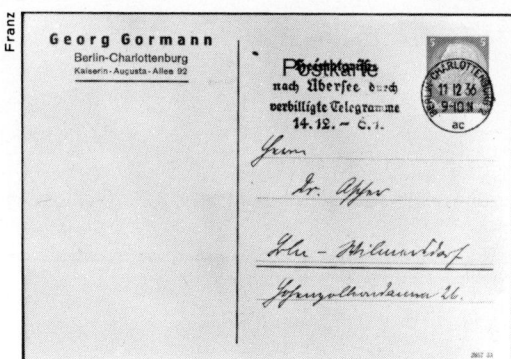

□   —Berlin, Berliner Ganzsachen Sammler Verein Werbestelle. Three versions exist.
5 Pf. (light green).

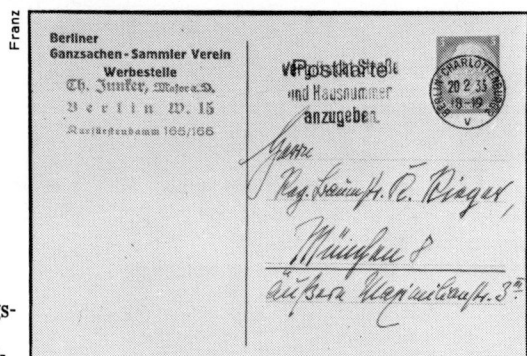

□ Blank
reverse.
□ Reverse
with BGSV
publicity.
8.3. 1934.
□ Rundsendungs-
leiter Dr. O.
Krause, blank
reverse.

□   —Wuppertal, Schuster & Co. 5 Pf. (light green).

☐ 1934, Jan.-June—As above but with perforated edges. 5 Pf. (light green). Cream or beige-colored stock.

☐ 1934, Jan.-June—Two-part card (message and reply) with a short tail on "e" of "Postkarte." 5 & 5 Pf. (light green). Cream or beige-colored stock.

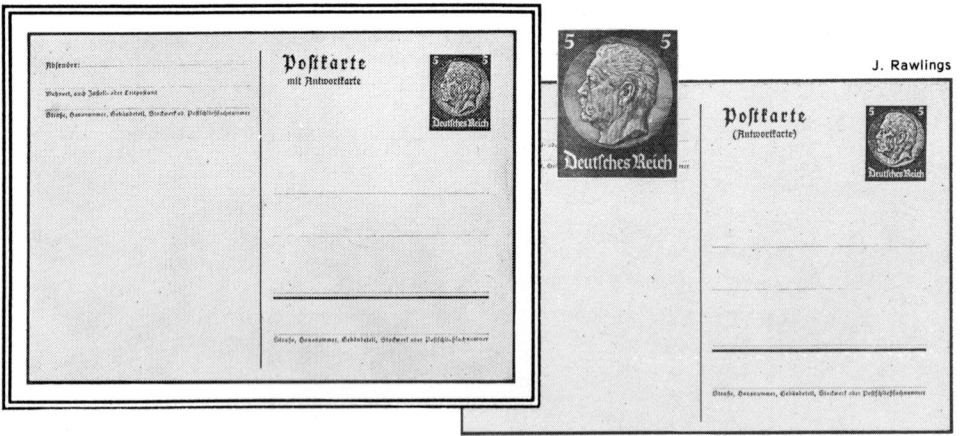

Note:
The proper term used by postal authorities as well as by collectors for the so-called "double-cards" or "two-part cards" is: "unsevered reply cards, while the two portions are called: the "message" card and the "reply" card.

□ 1934, Jan.-June—As above but with perforated edges. 5 Pf. (light green). Cream or beige-colored stock.

□   —Blank card (147 x 105mm), 5 Pf. (light green).

☐ —Berliner Städtische Wasserwerke (Berlin City Water Works).

☐ Sender's address in Grotesque text. Coded: 525.5000. 10.32.

☐ Sender's address in Fraktur text, Coded: 525.5000. 4.35.

☐ —Leipzig C1, Fa. O.H. Meder, facing the old town-hall. 5 Pf. (light green).

☐ —Munich, Residenzmuseum, featuring six portraits by J.K. Stieler. 5 Pf. (light green).

Cards for special exhibitions without exact dates.

Franz

Nr. 1

☐ 1. Anna Hillmeyer (1829)
☐ 2. Nanette Kaula (1829)
☐ 3. Helene Sedlmayr (1831)
☐ 4. Catharina Botzaris (1841)
☐ 5. Marie, Kronprinzessin von Bayern (1843)
☐ 6. Lola Montez (1847)

Franz

Nr. 2

Hanette Kaula
von J. K. Stieler 1829

Franz

Nr. 3

Helene Sellmayr
von J. K. Stieler 1831

Franz

Nr. 4

Catharina Botzaris
von J. K. Stieler 1841

Franz

Nr. 5

Marie, Kronprinzessin von Bayern
von J. K. Stieler 1843

Franz

Nr. 6

Lola Montez
von J. K. Stieler 1847

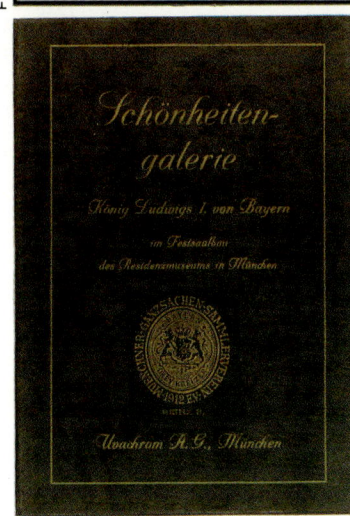

Envelope
which
holds the
museum
set of six
portraits.

☐ 1935—Sixteen picture card series sponsored by the German War Cemetery Service. 5 Pf. (light green). Address: Bez. Unterfranken/Würzburg. This same set exists with a 1 Pf (black) next to a 5 Pf. (light green).

Cemetery in Nazareth for the fallen on the Palestinian front.

Address:

5 Pf.　☐ 1. Gau Bayern/München

　　　　☐ 2. Bez. Oberbayern/München

　　　　☐ 3. Bez. Oberfranken/Bayreuth

　　　　☐ 4. Bez. Unterfranken/Würzburg

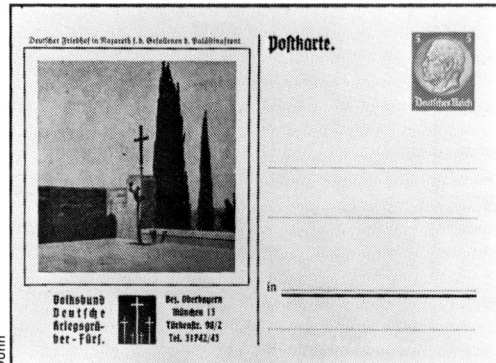

Nr. 1 (5 Pf.)

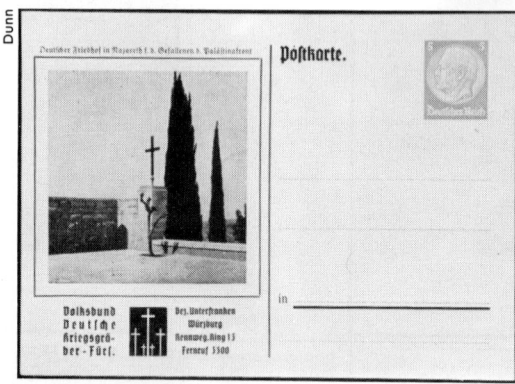

Nr. 4 (5 Pf.)

1 Pf./5 Pf. ☐ 1. Gau Bayern/München

　　　　☐ 2. Bez. Oberbayern/München

　　　　☐ 3. Bez. Oberfranken/Bayreuth

　　　　☐ 4. Bez. Unterfranken/Würzburg

☐ 1935—Address: Bez. Unterfranken/Würzburg.

　　　Vorbruck Cemetery (now Labroque) in the Vogesen (France).

　　　Address:

5 Pf.　☐ 5. Gau Bayern/München

　　　　☐ 6. Bez. Oberbayern/München

　　　　☐ 7. Bez. Oberfranken/Bayreuth

　　　　☐ 8. Bez. Unterfranken/Würzburg

Nr. 8 (5 Pf.)

1 Pf./5 Pf. □ 5. Gau Bayern/München
  □ 6. Bez. Oberbayern/München
  □ 7. Bez. Oberfranken/Bayreuth
  □ 8. Bez. Unterfranken/Würzburg

Nr. 5 (1 Pf./5 Pf.)

□ 1935—Address: Bez. Oberfranken/Bayreuth.
  Cemetery in Vasertal Mieresch-Macarlau (Romania).
  Address:

5 Pf.   □ 9. Gau Bayern/München
  □ 10. Bez. Oberbayern/
       München
  □ 11. Bez. Oberfranken/
       Bayreuth
  □ 12. Bez. Unterfranken/
       Würzburg

Nr. 11 (5 Pf.)

1 Pf./5 Pf. ☐ 9. Gau Bayern/München

    ☐ 10. Bez. Oberbayern/München

    ☐ 11. Bez. Oberfranken/Bayreuth

    ☐ 12. Bez. Unterfranken/Würzburg

Nr. 9 (1 Pf./5 Pf.)

☐ 1935—Address: Bez. Unterfranken/Würzburg.

    Schwabian Cemetery at Salomé near Lille (Northern France).

    Address:

5 Pf.   ☐ 13. Gau Bayern/München

    ☐ 14. Bez. Oberbayern/München

    ☐ 15. Bez. Oberbayern/Bayreuth

    ☐ 16. Bez. Unterfranken/Würzburg

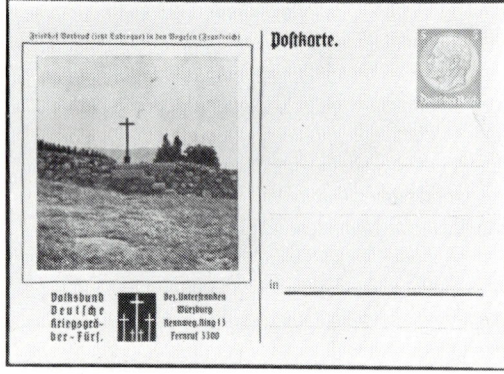

Nr. 16 (5 Pf.)

1 Pf./5 Pf. ☐ 13. Gau Bayern/München

    ☐ 14. Bez. Oberbayern/München

    ☐ 15. Bez. Oberbayern/Bayreuth

    ☐ 16. Bez. Unterfranken/Würzburg

Note:
For 6 Pf. cemetery series, see pp. 128-130.

☐ 1933, Jan.-March—"e" of "Postkarte" with long tail and sender's address with five lines of text. 6 Pf. (grey-green). Cream or beige-colored stock.

☐ 1933, Jan.-March—As above but with perforated edges. 6 Pf. (grey-green). Cream or beige-colored stock.

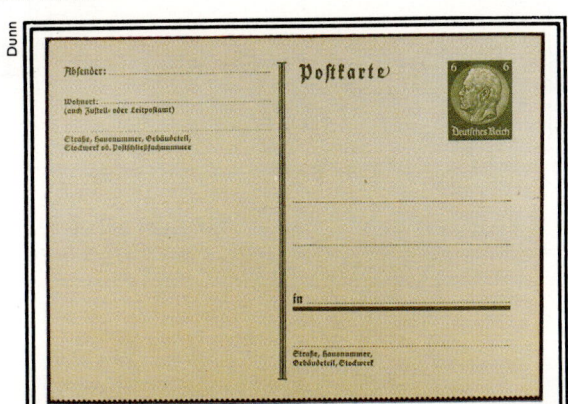

☐ 1933, Jan.-March—Two-part card (message and reply) with long tail on "e" of "Postkarte." 6 & 6 Pf. (grey-green). Cream or beige-colored stock.

☐ Message portion.

☐ Reply portion.

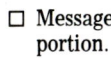

101

☐ 1933, Jan.March—As above but with perforated edges. 6 & 6 Pf. (grey-green). Cream or beige-colored stock.

☐ Message
   portion.
☐ Reply
   portion.

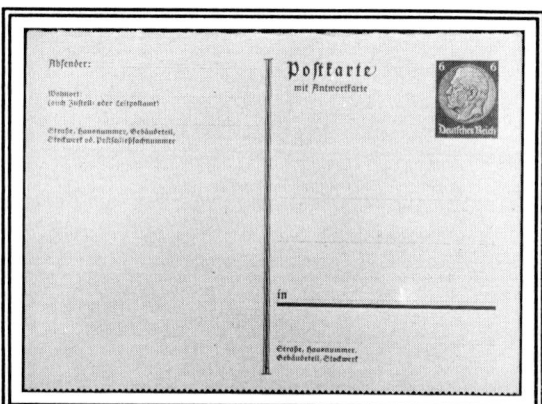

☐ 1934, Jan.-June—6 Pf. (grey-green). "Postkarte" with short tail on "e." Cream or beige-colored stock.

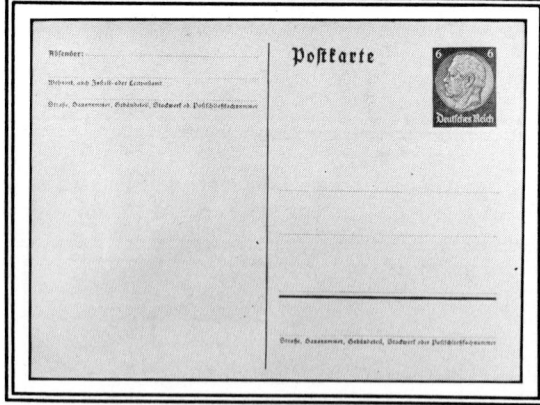

☐ 1934, Jan.-June—As above but with perforated edges. 6 Pf. (grey-green). Cream or beige-colored stock.

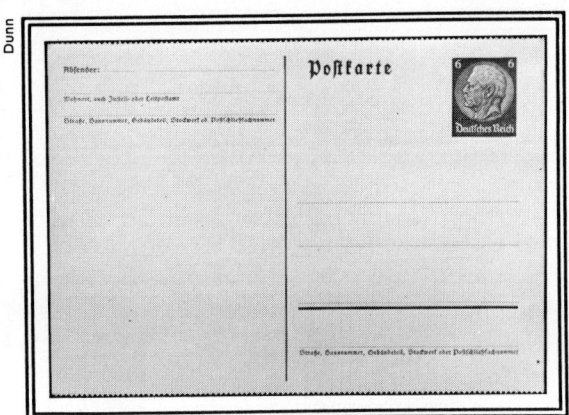

☐ 1934, Jan.-June—Two-part card (question and answer) with short tail on "e" of "Postkarte." 6 & 6 Pf. (grey-green). Cream or beige-colored stock.

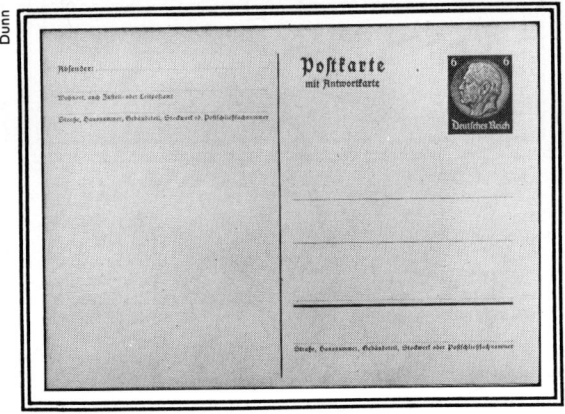

☐ 1934, Jan.-June—As above but with perforated edges. 6 Pf. (grey-green). Cream or beige-colored stock.

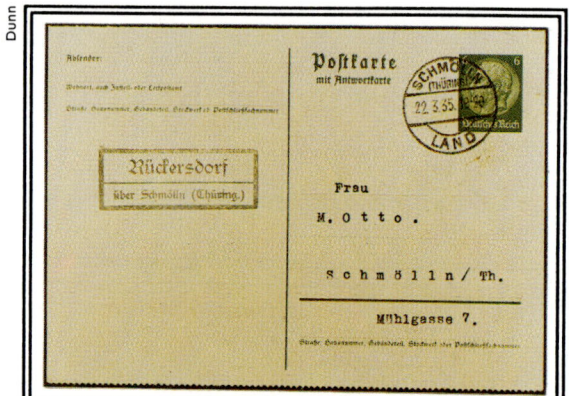

☐ 1933, March—"Get to know Germany" picture series with long tail on "e" in "Postkarte." 78 different photographs in this series. 6 Pf. (dark green).

Nr. 1

Poſtkarte

☐ 1 Ahlbeck (Ostsee)
☐ 2 Altona
☐ 3 Altona-Blankenese
☐ 4 Arendsee, rechts ohne Rutschbahn
☐ 5- rechts mit Rutschbahn
☐ 6 Arnsberg (Sauerland)
☐ 7 Aue (Sachsen)
☐ 8 Baden-Baden,
   Paradies-Anlagen
☐ 9 - Teilansicht
☐ 10 Moorbad Berg-Dievenow
☐ 11 Bielefeld
☐ 12 Bad Brambach
☐ 13 Bremerhaven
☐ 14 Breslau, Rathaus
☐ 15 Bruchsal bei Heidelberg
☐ 16 Chemnitz
☐ 17 Cleve
☐ 18 Coburg
☐ 19 Cottbus
☐ 20 Darmstadt, Porzellan-Museum
☐ 21 - Technische Hochschule
☐ 22 Einbeck
☐ 23 Eisenach

☐ 24 Bad Ems
☐ 25 Essen
☐ 26 Bad Frankenhausen
☐ 27 Friedrichshafen a. Bodensee
☐ 28 Gernrode (Harz)
☐ 29 Göttingen
☐ 30 Guben
☐ 31 Habelschwerdt
   (Grafschaft Glatz)
☐ 32 Hamburger Hafen
☐ 33 Hanau/Main, Handelshafen
☐ 34 - Rathaus
☐ 35 Hannover
☐ 36 Hann. Münden
☐ 37 Karlsruhe, Landestheater
☐ 38 - Schloss
☐ 39 Klessengrund
☐ 40 Königswald bei Dresden
☐ 41 Bad Kösen (Saale)
☐ 42 Konstanz am Bodensee
☐ 43 Krefeld-Uerdingen
☐ 44 Bad Kudowa
☐ 45 Landsberg/Warthe
☐ 46 Langeoog

- ☐ 47 Waldbad Leuna
- ☐ 48 Lindau (Bodensee)
- ☐ 49 Ludwigstein, Ruine Hanstein
- ☐ 50 Luzenau a.d. Mulde
- ☐ 51 Mainz
- ☐ 52 Mannheim
- ☐ 53 Marienwerder
- ☐ 54 Meersburg am Bodensee
- ☐ 55 Misdroy
- ☐ 56 Bad Nenndorf
- ☐ 57 Neuwied
- ☐ 58 Nordhausen, Neues Museum
- ☐ 59 - Stadttheater
- ☐ 60 Nürnberg
- ☐ 61 Oberschlema
- ☐ 62 Regensburg
- ☐ 63 Reinerz

- ☐ 64 Saarbrücken
- ☐ 65 Salzbrunn
  (Bez. Breslau)
- ☐ 66 Gichtbad Salzschlirf
- ☐ 67 Bad Salzungen
- ☐ 68 Bad Schmiedeberg
  (Bez. Halle)
- ☐ 69 Schneidemühl
- ☐ 70 Bad Schwalbach im Taunus
- ☐ 71 Schweinfurt
- ☐ 72 Stettin, Hafenspeicher
- ☐ 73 - Hakenterrasse
- ☐ 74 - Rathaus
- ☐ 75 Thale (Harz
- ☐ 76 Ueckeritz (Insel Usedom)
- ☐ 77 Wittenberg
- ☐ 78 Wyk auf Föhr

☐ 1934, Jan.-June—"Get to know Germany" picture series with tail of "e" in "Postkarte" extended. Nine different photographs in this series. 6 Pf. (dark green). Cream-colored stock.

- ☐ Arendsee, rechts Wald
- ☐ 3 Segelboote
- ☐ Seesteg oben
- ☐ Kurhaus rechts
- ☐ Friedrichroda
- ☐ Bad Ilmenau (Thür.)
- ☐ Bad Mergentheim
- ☐ Pretzsch (Elbe)
- ☐ Rossleben, Klosterschule

□ 1934, March–June—"Get to Know Germany" series with short tail on "e" in "Postkarte." 144 different cards in this series. 6 Pf. (dark green). Note lack of number coding on lower right corner of card.

Nr. 3

Mesturini

Poſtkarte
1.4mm, or

Poſtkarte
0.8mm

- □ 1 Ahlbeck
- □ 2 Altona (Elbe)
- □ 3 Amberg
- □ 4 Andernach (Rhein)
- □ 5 Angerburg
- □ 6 Annaberg (Erzgebirge)
- □ 7 Bansin, Ostseebad
- □ 8 Bendorf (Rhein)
- □ 9 Biedenkopf (Lahn)
- □ 10 Bielefeld (Teutoburger Wald)
- □ 11 Bitterfeld
- □ 12 Blankenburg (Harz)
- □ 13 Bolkenhain
- □ 14 Braubach am Rhein
- □ 15 Rathaus zu Bremen, Roland
- □ 16 Breslau, Jahrhunderthalle
- □ 17 — Rathaus
- □ 18 — Sandinsel
- □ 19 — Sand- und Dominsel
- □ 20 Brunshaupten, Seesteg links
- □ 21 — Walddüne links
- □ 22 — schräger Baum links
- □ 23 Bad Charlottenbrunn
- □ 24 Chemnitz
- □ 25 Darmstadt, Stadion
- □ 26 — Altstadt
- □ 27 Deutsch Krone
- □ 28 Dillenburg
- □ 29 Dinkelsbühl
- □ 30 Düsseldorf
- □ 31 Eisleben
- □ 32 Essen-Ruhrtal
- □ 33 Falkenstein im Vogtland
- □ 34 Bad Flinsberg
- □ 35 Frankfurt (Römer)
- □ 36 Freiberg (Sachsen)
- □ 37 Freilassing
- □ 38 Gera
- □ 39 Glatz
- □ 40 Rügenbad Göhren
- □ 41 Görbersdorf (Schlesien)
- □ 42 Goslar
- □ 43 Göttingen
- □ 44 Grossschönau
- □ 45 Halstenbek
- □ 46 Hameln (Weserbergland)
- □ 47 Hanau, Handelshafen
- □ 48 — Rathaus
- □ 49 Hannover
- □ 50 Hann, Münden
- □ 51 Hersbruck

- □ 52 Bad Hersfeld (Hessen)
- □ 53 Hildesheim
- □ 54 Hirschberg im Riesengebirge
- □ 55 Hof (Saale)
- □ 56 Bad Homburg
- □ 57 Jena (Thüringen)
- □ 58 Insel Juist (Nordsee)
- □ 59 Karlsruhe
- □ 60 Kassel, Wilhelmshöhe
- □ 61 Bad Kissingen
- □ 62 Klotzsche/Königswald bei Dresden
- □ 63 Koblenz
- □ 64 Köln am Rhein
- □ 65 Königsstein (Sächsische Schweiz)
- □ 66 Königstein im Taunus
- □ 67 Krefeld-Uerdingen
- □ 68 Bad Kreuznach, Brückenhäuser
- □ 69 — Elisabeth-Quelle
- □ 70 Bad Kudowa
- □ 71 Landsberg (Warthe)
- □ 72 Lauscha (Thïringer Wald)
- □ 73 Leichingen
- □ 74 Lichtenstein-Callnberg
- □ 75 Bad Liebenwerda
- □ 76 Lindau (Bodensee)
- □ 77 Lüneburg
- □ 78 Lychen (Märkische Seen)
- □ 79 Mannheim
- □ 80 Marburg
- □ 81 Markkleeberg
- □ 82 Meiningen, Querrechteck
- □ 83 — Hochrechteck
- □ 84 Misdroy
- □ 85 Neuenbürg (Schwarzwald)
- □ 86 Neustadt an der Haardt
- □ 87 Neustettin
- □ 88 Neuwied Deichpromenade
- □ 89 Nümbrecht-Homburg
- □ 90 Oberhof in Thüringen
- □ 91 Bad Orb
- □ 92 Osnabrück
- □ 93 Plauen (Vogtland)
- □ 94 Bad Polzin
- □ 95 Ratzeburg
- □ 96 Regensburg
- □ 97 Reichenbach (Vogtland)
- □ 98 Reinerz
- □ 99 Rheinhausen (Niederrhein)
- □ 100 Rheinsberg
- □ 101 Rostock
- □ 102 Rotenburg a.d. Fulda

☐ 1934—Photo postcard series "Get to Know Germany." 6 Pf. (dark green). 36 different cards in this series with number coding on lower right, e.g. 34-49-1-B1.

    34—year

    49—edition

    1—number of printing cylinder

    B1—picture number within the edition

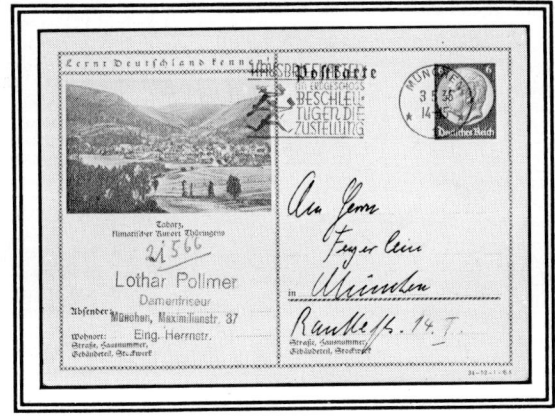

34-52-1-B5

34—49—1—

☐ b 1 Ratibor
☐ B 2 Wuppertal
☐ B 3 Neuzauche
☐ B 4 Bergstadt Gernrode
☐ B 5 Misdroy (Ostseebad)
☐ B 6 Bad Aibling
☐ B 7 Straupitz im Spreewald
☐ B 8 Duisburg-Hamborn
☐ B 9 Bad Eilsen

34—50—1—

☐ B 1 Neuhaus am Rennweg
☐ B 2 Byhlegure (Spreewald)
☐ B 3 Friedrichshafen (Bodensee)
☐ B 4 Andernach (Rhein)
☐ B 5 Langensalza, Schwefelbad
☐ B 6 Spreewaldbahn (Lübben)

☐ B 7 Pössneck (Thüringen)
☐ B 8 Burg, Herz des Spreewaldes
☐ B 9 Bad Homburg

34—51—1—

☐ B 1   Braunsberg (Ostpreussen)
☐ B 2, 3 Karlsruhe
☐ B 4, 9 Rastatt
☐ B 5, 6 Favorite bei Rastatt
☐ B 7, 8 Badenweiler

34—52—1—

☐ B 1, 2 Mannheim
☐ B 3, 4 Schwetzingen
☐ B 5 4 Tabarz
☐ B 6, 7 Bruchsal
☐ B 8, 9 Alt-Heidelberg

☐ 1934—"Get to know Germany." 6 Pf. (dark brown). 999 different photos on 1218 cards in this series with number coding on lower left, e.g., 34-53-1-B1.

34—year

53—edition

1—number of printing cylinder

B1—picture number within the edition

34-53-1-B1

34—53—1—
☐ B 1   Frankfurt (Main)
☐ B 2   Tübingen
☐ B 3   Wildbad (Schwarzwald)
☐ B 4   Offenbach (Rathaus)
☐ B 5   Salzschlirf
☐ B 6   Offenbach, Portal
☐ B 7, 8   — Schloss am Main
☐ B 9   Berchtesgaden

35—54—1—
☐ B 1   Braunschweig, Dom
☐ B 2   —Marktbrunnen
☐ B 3   Wildbad, Häuserfront links
☐ B 4, 5   Elster
☐ B 6, 9   Wildbad
☐ B 7   Angerburg
☐ B 8   Döbeln

35—55—1—

35—55—2—
☐ 1—2—B 1   Stuttgart, Auslands-Institut
☐ 1—2—B 2   — Kursaal Cannstatt
☐ 1—2—B 3   Wittenberg
☐ 1—2—B 4   Löbau
☐ 1—2—B 5   Bad Landeck (Schlesien)
☐ 1—2—B 6   Bad Landeck (Schlesien)
☐ 1—2—B 7   Blankenheim (Eifel)
☐ 1—2—B 8   Landeck (Schlesien)
☐ 1—2—B 9   Landeck (Schlesien)

35—56—1—
☐ B 1   Arendsee, Segelboot am Steg
☐ B 2   Sassnitz
☐ B 3   Friedrichroda
☐ B 4   Arendsee, Strand links
☐ B 5   Eisleben
☐ B 6   Bad Kissingen
☐ B 7   Arendsee, Strand Rechts
☐ B 8   — links Mast mit Flagge
☐ B 9   Grossschönau (Sachsen)

35—57—1—

35—57—2—
☐ 1—2—B 1   Orb, rechts Kurhaus
☐ 1—2—B 2   Tiengen
☐ 1—2—B 3   Hanau, Schleppzug
☐ 1—2—B 4   Orb, links Saline
☐ 1—2—B 5   Malente-Gremsmühlen
☐ 1—2—B 6   Hanau, Rathaus
☐ 1—2—B 7   Zittau
☐ 1—2—B 8   Gottleuba
☐ 1—2—B 9   Mergentheim

35—58—1—
☐ B 1, 4   Soden am Taunus
☐ B 2   Dresden
☐ B 3, 6   Bad Schandau
☐ B 5   Dillenburg
☐ B 7   Liebstadt
☐ B 8   Heringsdorf
☐ B 9   Ahlbeck

35—59—1—
☐ B 1, 2   Hannover
☐ B 3   Bad Wildungen, Badehotel
☐ B 4   — Badeviertel
☐ B 5   Graal
☐ B 6   Burg auf Fehmarn
☐ B 7   Feldberg in Mecklenburg
☐ B 8   Gernrode
☐ B 9   Bielefeld

35—60—1—
☐ B 1, 4   Misdroy
☐ B 2, 5   Leipzig, Peterstrasse
☐ B 3, 6   —Im Messehaus
☐ B 7   —Reichsgericht
☐ B 8   Krefeld—Uerdingen
☐ B 9   Königswinter

35—61—1—

- ☐ B 1 Duisburg
- ☐ B 2 Essen
- ☐ B 3 Stettin
- ☐ B 4 Marktredwitz
- ☐ B 5 Steben
- ☐ B 6 Bodenseefähre
- ☐ B 7 Cochem
- ☐ B 8 Bad Meinberg
- ☐ B 9 Kassel

35—62—1—

- ☐ B 1 Klotzsche
- ☐ B 2 Karlsruhe
- ☐ B 3 Koblenz
- ☐ B 4 Boppard
- ☐ B 5 Rengsdorf
- ☐ B 6 Wenningstedt-Braderup
- ☐ B 7 Bad Segeberg
- ☐ B 8 Osnabrück
- ☐ B 9 Haltern am See

35—63—1—
- ☐ B 1 Osnabrück
- ☐ B 2 Kolberg, Landungssteg mit
    Kurhaus
- ☐ B 3 Brückenau
- ☐ B 4 Andernach, Namedy-Sprudel
- ☐ B 5 Waren
- ☐ B 6 Pforzheim
- ☐ B 7 Kolberg, Parkanlagen
- ☐ B 8 Laboe
- ☐ B 9 Andernach

35—64—1—

- ☐ B 1, 2, 3, 6 Oberschlema
- ☐ B 5 Offenbach, Rathaus
- ☐ B 6 Butzbach
- ☐ B 7 Chemnitz
- ☐ B 8 Offenbach, Technische
    Anstalten
- ☐ B 9 — Schloss am Main

35—65—1—

- ☐ B 1 Düsseldorf
- ☐ B 2 Kaiserslautern
- ☐ B 3 Wuppertal
- ☐ B 4 Mannheim, Strandbad
- ☐ B 5 — Friedrichsplatz
- ☐ B 6 Vegesack
- ☐ B 7 Mannheimer Häfen
- ☐ B 8 — Hafenanlagen
- ☐ B 9 Bad Lippspringe

35—66—1—

- ☐ B 1, 4 Bad Krozingen
- ☐ B 2, 5 Baden-Baden, Parkanlagen
- ☐ B 3, 6 — Heisse Quellen
- ☐ B 7 Karlsruhe
- ☐ B 8 Müllheim (Baden)
- ☐ B 9 Ettlingen

36—67—1—

- ☐ B 1, 2, 3, 4 Karlsruhe
- ☐ B 5, 6 Köln
- ☐ B 7 Schönlanke, Ostbahn
- ☐ B 8 Viersen
- ☐ B 9 Weissstein

36—68—1—

- ☐ B 1 Greiz
- ☐ B 2 Hildburghausen
- ☐ B 3 Kaisermühle (Viersener Höhen)
- ☐ B 4 Radolfzell (Mettnau)
- ☐ B 5 Elzach
- ☐ B 6 Friedrichroda
- ☐ B 7 Ötigheim
- ☐ B 8 Bad Dürrheim
- ☐ B 9 Meersburg

36—69—1—

- ☐ B 1 Offenbach,
    Technische Anstalten
- ☐ B 2, 3, 5, 6 Radiumbad Landeck
- ☐ B 4 Petersdorf
- ☐ B 7 Sooden-Allendorf
- ☐ B 8 Offenbach, Schloss a. Main
- ☐ B 9 — Rathaus

36—70—1—

- ☐ B 1 Hohen Neuendorf
- ☐ B 2 Marburg
- ☐ B 3, 4 Heidelberg
- ☐ B 5 Bad Kissingen
- ☐ B 6 Preetz
- ☐ B 7, 8 Schandau
- ☐ B 9 Festung Königstein

36—71—1—

- ☐ B 1 Gaggenau
- ☐ B 2 Tiengen
- ☐ B 3 Aschaffenburg
- ☐ B 4 Bad Sulva
- ☐ B 5 Rengsdorf
- ☐ B 6 Bad Segeberg
- ☐ B 7 Eckernförde
- ☐ B 8 Arnstadt
- ☐ B 9 Thum

36—72—1—

- ☐ B 1 Grossschönau (Sachsen)
- ☐ B 2 Butzbach
- ☐ B 3 Waldsieversdorf
- ☐ B 4 Gernrode
- ☐ B 5 Bühl
- ☐ B 6 Langenargen
- ☐ B 7 Stadt Achern
- ☐ B 8 Kreis Hildburghausen
- ☐ B 9 Kassel-Wilhelmshöhe

36—73—1—

- ☐ B 1, 4 Rudolstadt
- ☐ B 2 Potsdam
- ☐ B 3, 6 Heidelberg, Kultur-
    veranstaltung
- ☐ B 5 Darmstadt
- ☐ B 7 Kampen auf Sylt
- ☐ B 8 Darmstadt
- ☐ B 9 Wenningstedt-Braderup

36—74—1—

- ☐ B 1 Kolberg, hinten die Ostsee
- ☐ B 2 Salzwedel
- ☐ B 3 Braunschweig
- ☐ B 4 Salzbrunn
- ☐ B 5 Kolberg, Parkanlagen
- ☐ B 6 Reutlingen
- ☐ B 7 Bad Schwalbach
- ☐ B 8 Osterode
- ☐ B 9 Heidenheim

36—74a—1—
☐ B 1, 2, 3, 4, 5, 6, 7, 8, 9 Leipzig,
Juristentage

36—75—1—

☐ B 1   Birkenfeld
☐ B 2   Hirsau
☐ B 3, 6, 9 Schömberg, Rundblick
☐ B 4   Liebenzell
☐ B 5   Schömberg, Spielwiese
☐ B 7   Unterreichenbach
☐ B 8   Herrenalb

36—76—1—
☐ B 1   Löbau
☐ B 2   Luckenwalde
☐ B 3, 6   Hannover
☐ B 4   Görbersdorf
☐ B 5   Halle
☐ B 7   Timmendorfer Strand
☐ B 8   Boppard
☐ B 9   Neuzelle

36—77—1—

☐ B 1   Görlitz
☐ B 2   Krefeld-Uerdingen
☐ B 3   Schlangenbad
☐ B 4   Königswinter
☐ B 5   Hornberg
☐ B 6   Brückenau
☐ B 7   Kaiserslautern
☐ B 8   Sülze
☐ B 9   Leipziger Zoo

36—78—1—

☐ B 1   Chemnitz
☐ B 2   Küstrin
☐ B 3   Essen
☐ B 4   Langensalza
☐ B 5   Wuppertal
☐ B 6   Freudenstadt
☐ B 7   Karlsruhe
☐ B 8   Kirn
☐ B 9   Brieg

36—79—1—

☐ B 1   Essen-Mülheim
☐ B 2   Schneidemühl
☐ B 3   Neustadt a. d. fr. Saale
☐ B 4   Düsseldorf, Kunstmuseum
☐ B 5   Bad Überkingen
☐ B 6   Ahlbeck
☐ B 7   Düsseldorf, Schloss Jägerhof
☐ B 8   Bad Tainach
☐ B 9   Wittenberg

36—80—1—

☐ B 1   Osnabrück
☐ B 2   Coburg
☐ B 3   Glotterbad
☐ B 4   Frankfurt (Main), Blick auf Dom
☐ B 5   Sigmaringen
☐ B 6   Pforzheim
☐ B 7   Säckingen
☐ B 8   Frankfurt (Main), Römer
☐ B 9   Neustadt a. d. Weinstrasse

37—81—1—

37—81—2—

☐ 1—2—B 1 Breisach
☐ 1—2—B 2 Singen (Hohentwiel)
☐ 1—2—B 3 Müllheim (Baden)
☐ 1—2—B 4 Freiburg/Breisgau,
rechts Turm

☐ 1—2—B 5 Badenweiler, Markgrafenbad
☐ 1—2—B 8 —Markgrafenbad
☐ 1—2—B 6 —Blick von Burgruine
☐ 1—2—B 9 — Blick von Burgruine
☐ 1—2—B 7 Freiburg/Breisgau,
vorn links Bäume

37—82—1—

☐ B 1   Blieskastel
☐ B 2   Landstuhl
☐ B 3   Bad Mergentheim
☐ B 4   Tholey
☐ B 5   Rothenburg ob der Tauber
☐ B 6   Greifswald
☐ B 7   Löwenberg
☐ B 8   Magdeburg, Kaiser-Otto-
Denkmal
☐ B 9   — Der Dom

37—83—1—

☐ B 1   Bad Orb, Wandelhalle
☐ B 2   Halle
☐ B 3   Sulzbach (Saar)
☐ B 4   Bad Orb, Badehaus
☐ B 5   Garmisch—Partenkirchen
☐ B 6   Dillingen (Saar)
☐ B 7   Hof
☐ B 8   Langenargen
☐ B 9   Birkenfeld (Nahe)

37—84—1—
☐ B 1   Essen
☐ B 2   Dudweiler
☐ B 3   Darmstadt
☐ B 4   Bad Münster am Stein
☐ B 5   Schweinfurt
☐ B 6   Bad Kreuznach
☐ B 7   Wenningstedt (Sylt)
☐ B 8   Forst
☐ B 9   Leipziger Zoo

37—85—1—

☐ B 1   Pfalzel (Mosel)
☐ B 2   Schweidnitz
☐ B 3   Kolberg, Blick auf Ostsee
☐ B 4   Rodalben
☐ B 5   Festung Königstein
☐ B 6   Kolberg, Parkanlagen
☐ B 7   Füssen-Faulenbach
☐ B 8   Traunstein
☐ B 9   Elbing

37—86—1—

☐ B 1   Saarbrücken
☐ B 2   Ahlbeck
☐ B 3   Butzbach
☐ B 4   Löbau
☐ B 5   Weiskirchen
☐ B 6   Marburg
☐ B 7   Sooden-Allendorf
☐ B 8, 9   Königswinter

37—87—1—

☐ B 1   Breslau, Dom
☐ B 2, 3   Landeck, Hallenschwimmbad
☐ B 4   — Bänke im Vordergrund
☐ B 5   — Kuppelbau
☐ B 6   Breslau, Rathaus
☐ B 7   — Jahrhunderthalle
☐ B 8   Görlitz
☐ B 9   Breslau, Sandinsel

37—88—1—
- ☐ B 1, 2, 3, 4 Oberschlema
- ☐ B 5 Bruttig (Mosel)
- ☐ B 6 Darmstadt
- ☐ B 7 Hagen (Westfalen)
- ☐ B 8 Kassel-Wilhelmshöhe
- ☐ B 9 Eller (Mosel)

37—89—1—
- ☐ B 1, 2 Quedlinburg
- ☐ B 3 Bad Neuenahr
- ☐ B 4 Neustadt an der Weinstrasse
- ☐ B 5 Bad Mergentheim
- ☐ B 6 Birkenfeld (Württemberg)
- ☐ B 7 Soden am Taunus
- ☐ B 8 Gohrisch
- ☐ B 9 Brieg

37—90—1—
- ☐ B 1 Helgoland, Lange Anna
- ☐ B 2 — Düne
- ☐ B 3 — Gesamtansicht
- ☐ B 4 — Abendstimmung
- ☐ B 5 — Königin Luise von Backbord
- ☐ B 6 — dto. von Steuerbord
- ☐ B 7 Helgoland, Cobra
- ☐ B 8 — Reede
- ☐ B 9 — Bild ähnlich B 1

37—91—1—
- ☐ B 1, 2 Schömberg
- ☐ B 3 Wuppertal
- ☐ B 4 Heilbrunn (Oberbayern)
- ☐ B 5 Valwig
- ☐ B 6 Geising
- ☐ B 7 Wittenberg
- ☐ B 8 Salzhausen
- ☐ B 9 Gernrode

37—92—1—
- ☐ B 1 Bad Hönningen
- ☐ B 2 Bendorf-Sayn
- ☐ B 3 Allenstein
- ☐ B 4 Mühldorf am Inn
- ☐ B 5 Remagen
- ☐ B 6 Potsdam
- ☐ B 7 Weinort Ernst
- ☐ B 8 Manderscheid-Eifel
- ☐ B 9 Klotten (Mosel)

37—93—1—
- ☐ B 1 Bad Niederbreisig, Gesamtansicht
- ☐ B 2 Hameln
- ☐ B 3 Bad Niederbreisig, Rheinterrassen
- ☐ B 4 Ansbach
- ☐ B 5 St. Goar
- ☐ B 6 Kirkel
- ☐ B 7 Bad Bertrich, Kurhaus
- ☐ B 8 — Schwimmbad
- ☐ B 9 Stolpen

37—94—1—
- ☐ B 1 Kaiserslautern
- ☐ B 2 Ediger
- ☐ B 3 Niederbreisig
- ☐ B 4 Coswig (Anh.)
- ☐ B 5 Stassfurt
- ☐ B 6 Hanau (Main)
- ☐ B 7 Morbach (Hunsrück)
- ☐ B 8 Salzwedel (Altmark)
- ☐ B 9 Jastrow

37—95—1—
- ☐ B 1 Leipzig, Gohliser Schlösschen
- ☐ B 2 Hardenburg
- ☐ B 3 Ludwigsburg
- ☐ B 4 Leipzig
- ☐ B 5 Eberswalde
- ☐ B 6 Rheinhausen
- ☐ B 7 Bad Soden am Taunus
- ☐ B 8 Karden
- ☐ B 9 Treis

37—96—1—
- ☐ B 1 Offenbach, Technische Anstalten
- ☐ B 2 — Schloss am Main
- ☐ B 3 — Rathaus
- ☐ B 4 Neidenburg
- ☐ B 5 Wadern
- ☐ B 6 Bad Bodendorf
- ☐ B 7 Langen (Hessen)
- ☐ B 8 Burg Eltz (Mosel)
- ☐ B 9 Berus

37—97—1—

This series has a 5 Pf. (green) imprinted stamp and was issued for local postal traffic, additional postage was required for farther distances. See 1937 for illustration.

37—98—1—
- ☐ B 1, 2 Gera
- ☐ B 3 Arnstadt
- ☐ B 4, 5 Rudolstadt
- ☐ B 6 Greiz
- ☐ B 7 Hildburghausen
- ☐ B 8 Kyffhäuser-Denkmal
- ☐ B 9 Friedrichroda

37—99—1—
- ☐ B 1, 2 Stettin
- ☐ B 3 Kiel
- ☐ B 4 Bernburg
- ☐ B 5 Dessau
- ☐ B 6 Tangermünde
- ☐ B 7 Pforzheim
- ☐ B 8 Dortmund
- ☐ B 9 Nidda

37—100—1—
- ☐ B 1 Düsseldorf
- ☐ B 2 Waldmohr
- ☐ B 3 Oberhausen (Rheinland)
- ☐ B 4 Westerwald
- ☐ B 5 Homburg
- ☐ B 6 Ruhrberg
- ☐ B 7 Blieskastel
- ☐ B 8 Otzenhausen
- ☐ B 9 Ueckermünde

37—101—1—
- ☐ B 1, 2 Hannover
- ☐ B 3 Weiskirchen
- ☐ B 4 Niederbreisig
- ☐ B 5 Weisswasser
- ☐ B 6 Bertrich
- ☐ B 7 Würzburg
- ☐ B 8 Beuthen
- ☐ B 9 Düsseldorf-Benrath

37—101a—1—

☐ B 1, 2, 3, 4, 5, 6, 7, 8, 9 Bad
Reichenhall

37—102—1—

☐ B 1 Tauberbischofsheim
☐ B 2 Farchant
☐ B 3 Rodalben
☐ B 4 Karden
☐ B 5 Sehma
☐ B 6 Treis
☐ B 7 Osnabrück
☐ B 8 Chemnitz
☐ B 9 Morbach

37—103—1—

☐ B 1 Stolp
☐ B 2 Waldmohr
☐ B 3 Ruhrberg
☐ B 4 Rothenfelde
☐ B 5 Burg Eltz (Mosel)
☐ B 6 Wadern
☐ B 7 Manderscheid
☐ B 8 Belzig
☐ B 9 Hönningen

38—104—1—

38—104—2—

☐ 1—2—B 1 Münster (Westfalen)
☐ 1—2—B 2 Berus
☐ 1—2—B 3 Birkenfeld (Nahe)
☐ 1—2—B 4 Bad Mergentheim
☐ 1—2—B 5 Landstuhl
☐ 1—2—B 6 Forst (Rheinpfalz)
☐ 1—2—B 7 Sankt Goar
☐ 1—2—B 8 Oppeln
☐ 1—2—B 9 Kreuznach

38—105—1—

☐ B 1 Wächtersbach
☐ B 2 Hanau
☐ B 3 Bernburg
☐ B 4 Bad Orb, Parkanlagen
☐ B 5 — Badehaus I
☐ B 6 Remagen
☐ B 7 Langenargen
☐ B 8 Nonnweiler
☐ B 9 Nohfelden

38—106—1—

☐ B 1 Eisleben
☐ B 2 Kirn
☐ B 3 Lähn
☐ B 4 Warmbrunn
☐ B 5 Bad Peterstal
☐ B 6 Bad Salzuflen
☐ B 7 Freudenburg
☐ B 8 Hellenthal-Hollerath
☐ B 9 Sooden-Allendorf

38—107—1—

☐ B 1 Burghausen a. d. Sulzach
☐ B 2 Enkenbach
☐ B 3 Halle
☐ B 4 Bad Bodendorf
☐ B 5 Bad Münster am Stein
☐ B 6 Hardenburg
☐ B 7 Ludwigsburg

☐ B 8 Potsdam
☐ B 9 Jastrow

38—108—1—

☐ B 1 Miltenberg
☐ B 2, 3 Königswinter
☐ B 4 Hilbringen
☐ B 5 St. Ingbert
☐ B 6 Altenahr
☐ B 7 Ürzig
☐ B 8 Hermeskeil
☐ B 9 Schömberg

38—109—1—

☐ B 1, 2 Weimar
☐ B 3 Arnstadt
☐ B 4 Wachsenburg
☐ B 5 Gera
☐ B 6 Finsterbergen
☐ B 7 KyffhäuserDenkmal
☐ B 8 Friedrichroda
☐ B 9 Langensalza

38—110—1—

☐ B 1 Halberstadt, Rathaus
☐ B 2 — Holzmarkt
☐ B 3 — Roland
☐ B 4 Butzbach
☐ B 5 Essen
☐ B 6 Tangermünde
☐ B 7 Elgersberg
☐ B 8 Stolpen
☐ B 9 Salzelmen

38—111—1—

☐ B 1 Breslau, Sandinsel
☐ B 2 — Rathaus
☐ B 3 — Sportfeld
☐ B 4 — Jahrhunderthalle
☐ B 5 Landeck, Kuppelbau
☐ B 6 — Hallenschwimmbad
☐ B 7 — Hecken im Vordergrund
☐ B 8 — Fernblick
☐ B 9 Krummhübel

38—112—1—

☐ B 1, 2, 3, 4, 5, 6 Heidelberg
☐ B 7 Wildgrund
☐ B 8 Wuppertal
☐ B 9 Altheide

38—113—1—

☐ B 1 Bad Salzbrunn
☐ B 2 Schweidnitz
☐ B 3 Aschersleben
☐ B 4 Blieskastel
☐ B 5 Berlinchen (Neumark)
☐ B 6 Schandau
☐ B 7 Neustadt a. d. Weinstrasse
☐ B 8 Saarbrücken
☐ B 9 Homburg (Saar)

38—114—1—

☐ B 1, 2, 3, 4 Oberschlema
☐ B 5 Leisnig
☐ B 6 Waldheim (Sachsen)
☐ B 7 Glauchau, Eingang
zum Tal
☐ B 8 — Buntweberei
☐ B 9 Borna

38—115—1—

☐ B 1, 2 Quedlinburg
☐ B 3   Weinheim a. d. badischen
         Weinstrasse
☐ B 4   Filzteich bei Neustädtel
☐ B 5   Bad Mergentheim
☐ B 6   Eppstein (Taunus)
☐ B 7   Wenningstedt (Sylt)
☐ B 8   Brieg
☐ B 9   Salzwedel

38—116—1—

☐ B 1   Mülheim (Ruhr), Brücke
☐ B 2   — Stadthalle
☐ B 3   Landau (Südpfalz)
☐ B 4   Rüdesheim am Rhein
☐ B 5   Thalkirchdorf (Allgäu)
☐ B 6   Gernrode (Harz)
☐ B 7   Gelnhausen
☐ B 8   Illingen (Saar)
☐ B 9   Erbeskopf

38—117—1—

☐ B 1, 2, 3, 4 Bad Nenndorf
☐ B 5   Dürrheim (Schwarzwald)
☐ B 6   Darmstadt, Landestheater
☐ B 7   — Monument
☐ B 8   Magdeburg, Kaiser-Otto
☐ B 9   — Dom

38—118—1—

☐ B 1   Offenbach, Kunstgewerbeschule
☐ B 2   — Schloss am Main
☐ B 3   — Rathaus
☐ B 4   Kudowa, Fürstenhof
☐ B 5   — Schloss
☐ B 6   Wasserburg (Bodensee)
☐ B 7   Bad Salzhausen
☐ B 8   Wangen (Allgäu)
☐ B 9   Magdeburg

38—119—1—

38—119—2—

☐ 1—2—B 1 Seligenstadt
☐ 1—2—B 2 Kaiserslautern
☐ 1—2—B 3 Wertingen
☐ 1—2—B 4 Neu-Isenburg
☐ 1—2—B 5 Bad Wimpfen am Neckar
☐ 1—2—B 6 Mainburg
☐ 1—2—B 7 Immenstadt (Allgäu)
☐ 1—2—B 8 Ladenburg
☐ 1—2—B 9 Garmisch-Partenkirchen

38—120—1—

☐ B 1   Thannhausen (Schwaben)
☐ B 2   Kaiserslautern
☐ B 3   Neuenbürg (Schwarzwald)
☐ B 4   Ludwigshafen
☐ B 5   Sulzbach (Saar)
☐ B 6   Grossenhain
☐ B 7   Diez (Lahn)
☐ B 8   Nidda
☐ B 9   Rohrbach (Saar)

38—121—1—

☐ B 1   Dessau
☐ B 2   Hachenburg

☐ B 3   Dudweiler
☐ B 4   Emden, Rathaus
☐ B 5   — Werften
☐ B 6   Alsfeld
☐ B 7   Todtmoos
☐ B 8   Kirchheimbolanden
☐ B 9   Meersburg

38—122—1—

☐ B 1   Weiskirchen
☐ B 2   Rossleben
☐ B 3   Igls bei Innsbruck
☐ B 4, 5 Siebengebirge
☐ B 6   Oberwiesenthal
☐ B 7   Bunzlau
☐ B 8   Schwetzingen, Theater
☐ B 9   — Schloss und Park

38—123—1—

☐ B 1, 2 Steyr
☐ B 3   Gallspach
☐ B 4   Nonnenhorn am Bodensee
☐ B 5   Velden am Wörthersee
☐ B 6   Blaibach-Ettensberg
☐ B 7   Neuburg (Donau)
☐ B 8   Mariazell (Steiermark)
☐ B 9   Höchstädt

38—124—1—
☐ B 1   Leipzig, Völkerschlachtdenkmal
☐ B 2   — Deutsche Bücherei
☐ B 3   Planitz, Park
☐ B 4   — Liegestühle
☐ B 5   Potsdam
☐ B 6   Donauwörth
☐ B 7   Hall in Tirol
☐ B 8   Süchteln
☐ B 9   Rheinhausen

38—125—1—

☐ B 1, 2 Stettin
☐ B 3, 4 Swinemünde
☐ B 5   Altmünster am Traunsee
☐ B 6   Bad Gleichenberg (Steiermark)
☐ B 7   Flattnitz (Kärnten)
☐ B 8   Wasserburg am Bodensee
☐ B 9   Pörtschach am Wörthersee

39—126—1—

☐ B 1   Lechbruck
☐ B 2   Rodalben
☐ B 3   Bad Bodendorf
☐ B 4   Jastrow
☐ B 5   Bad Münster am Stein
☐ B 6   Waldmohr
☐ B 7   Forst (Rheinpfalz)
☐ B 8   Bad Sulza (Thüringen)
☐ B 9   Ehrwald in Tirol

39—127—1—

☐ B 1, 2 Weimar
☐ B 3   Arnstadt
☐ B 4   Wachsenburg
☐ B 5   Finsterbergen
☐ B 6   Bad Berka
☐ B 7   Eisenach
☐ B 8   Gera
☐ B 9   Friedrichroda

39—128—1—

- ☐ B 1, 2, 3 St. Joachimsthal
- ☐ B 4 Dortmund
- ☐ B 5 Bregenz
- ☐ B 6 Belzig
- ☐ B 7 Hellenthal-Holleroth
- ☐ B 8 Glauchau
- ☐ B 9 Gelnhausen

39—129—1—

- ☐ B 1, 2 Salzschlirf
- ☐ B 3 Sagan
- ☐ B 4 Wächtersbach
- ☐ B 5 Langenbrücken (Baden)
- ☐ B 6 Ruhrberg (Eifel)
- ☐ B 7 Fünf Odenwaldstädtchen
- ☐ B 8 Hanau
- ☐ B 9 Soden bei Salmünster

39—130—1—

- ☐ B 1 Karlsbad, Rundblick
- ☐ B 2 — Mühlbrunnpromenade
- ☐ B 3 St. Wolfgang (Salzkammergut)
- ☐ B 4 Lienz (Osttirol)
- ☐ B 5 Elgersburg
- ☐ B 6 Weinheim a. d. Bergstrasse
- ☐ B 7 Bad Orb, Badehaus
- ☐ B 8 — Quellen-Schwimmbad
- ☐ B 9 Sooden-Allendorf

39—131—1—

- ☐ B 1 Wertingen
- ☐ B 2 Salzelmen
- ☐ B 3 Kaufbeuren
- ☐ B 4 Stolpmünde
- ☐ B 5 Rohrbach (Saar)
- ☐ B 6 Kirkel-Neuhäusel
- ☐ B 7 Landstuhl (Saarpfalz)
- ☐ B 8 Berus
- ☐ B 9 Mariahütte

39—132—1—

- ☐ B 1 Remagen
- ☐ B 2 Bad Bertrich
- ☐ B 3 Bad Hönningen
- ☐ B 4 Birkenfeld (Nahe)
- ☐ B 5 Wadern
- ☐ B 6 Moselkern, Burg Eltz
- ☐ B 7 Erbeskopf
- ☐ B 8 Treis
- ☐ B 9 Morbach (Hunsrück)

39—133—1—

- ☐ B 1 Salzwedel
- ☐ B 2 Enkenbach
- ☐ B 3 Hardenburg
- ☐ B 4 Landau (Südpfalz)
- ☐ B 5 Saarbrücken
- ☐ B 6 Niederbreisig
- ☐ B 7 Neuenahr
- ☐ B 8 Nohfelden (Nahe)
- ☐ B 9 Manderscheid (Eifel)

39—134—1—

- ☐ B 1, 2, 3, 4, 5, 6 Heidelberg
- ☐ B 7 Eckernförde
- ☐ B 8 Rotenburg an der Fulda
- ☐ B 9 Krummhübel

39—135—1—

- ☐ B 1 Kaiserslautern, Museum
- ☐ B 2 — Ausstellungspark
- ☐ B 3 Grossschönau (Sachsen)
- ☐ B 4 Bad Kreuznach
- ☐ B 5 Karden (Mosel)
- ☐ B 6 Ehrang (Mosel)
- ☐ B 7 Ürzig (Mosel)
- ☐ B 8 Halle
- ☐ B 9 Altenahr

39—136—1—

- ☐ B 1, 2 Kudowa
- ☐ B 3 Tangermünde
- ☐ G 4 Franzensbad
- ☐ B 5 Oppeln (Oberschlesien)
- ☐ B 6 München
- ☐ B 7 Aschersleben
- ☐ B 8 Taben (Saar)
- ☐ B 9 St. Goar

39—137—1—

- ☐ B 1, 2 Wismar
- ☐ B 3 Chemnitz
- ☐ B 4 Filzteich
- ☐ B 5 Magdeburg, Dom
- ☐ B 6 — Altstadt
- ☐ B 7 — Kaiser-Otto
- ☐ B 8 Kaaden (Sudetengau)
- ☐ B 9 Ziegenhals

39—138—1—

- ☐ B 1, 2 Königswinter
- ☐ B 3 Pirmasens, Brücke
- ☐ B 4 — Stadtbild
- ☐ B 5 Au in der Hallertau
- ☐ B 6 Northeim
- ☐ B 7 Osnabrück
- ☐ B 8 Bielefeld
- ☐ B 9 Blieskastel

39—139—1—

- ☐ B 1, 2 Hannover
- ☐ B 3 Grossenhain
- ☐ B 4 Stolpen (Sachsen)
- ☐ B 5 Bad Mergentheim
- ☐ B 6 Garmisch-Partenkirchen
- ☐ B 7 Bad Schandau
- ☐ B 8 Schwäbisch Gmünd
- ☐ B 9 Bad Schwartau

39—140—1—

- ☐ B 1 Bernburg
- ☐ B 2 Neustadt a. d. Weinstrasse
- ☐ B 3 Heidenheim
- ☐ B 4 Coburg
- ☐ B 5 Kühlungsborn, Bäume vorn
- ☐ B 6 — Bäume hinten
- ☐ B 7 Bautzen
- ☐ B 8 Badenweiler, Überblick
- ☐ B 9 — Sportbad

39—141—1—

- ☐ B 1 Innsbrucker Nordkettenbahn
- ☐ B 2 Trier
- ☐ B 3 Reutlingen
- ☐ B 4 Wittenberg
- ☐ B 5 Kandel

☐ B 6 Heilbrunn (Oberbayern)
☐ B 7 Igls-Patscherkofel
☐ B 8 Schkeuditz

39—142—1—

☐ B 1 Breslau, Sportfeld
☐ B 2 — Sandinsel
☐ B 3 — Jahrhunderthalle
☐ B 4 — Dom
☐ B 5 — Rathaus
☐ B 6 Reinerz
☐ B 7 Weisswasser
☐ B 8 Beuthen

39—143—1—

☐ B 1, 2 Karlsruhe
☐ B 3 Salzhausen
☐ B 4 Meersburg
☐ B 5 Marienbad
☐ B 6 Ladenburg
☐ B 7 Wenningstedt
☐ B 8 Seligenstadt

39—144—1—

☐ B 1 Schwarzenberg
☐ B 2 Mainburg
☐ B 3 Nidda
☐ B 4 Dudweiler
☐ B 5 Homburg (Saarpfalz)
☐ B 6 Gelnhausen
☐ B 7 Nördlingen
☐ B 8 Rohrbach (Saar)

39—145—1—

☐ B 1 Germersheim
☐ B 2 Wächtersbach
☐ B 3 Bad Flinsberg, Winterzauber
☐ B 4 — Hasenstein
☐ B 5 Böhlitz-Ehrenberg, Waldbad
☐ B 6 — Platz
☐ B 7 Recklinghausen
☐ B 8 Erbeskopf

39—146—1—

☐ B 1 Offenbach, Isenburger Schloss
☐ B 2 — Rathaus
☐ B 3 Nohfelden
☐ B 4 Offenbach, Ledermuseum
☐ B 5 Bad Hall, Brunnenhaus
☐ B 6 Bad Oeynhausen
☐ B 7 Rastatt
☐ B 8 Bad Hall, Wandelhalle

39—147—1—

☐ B 1, 2 Halle (Saale, Giebichenstein
☐ B 3, 4 — Händeldenkmal
☐ B 5, 6 Moritzburg
☐ B 7 — Hallorengruppe
☐ B 8 Marienkirche

39—148—1—

☐ B 1 Halle (Saale), Giebichenstein
☐ B 2 — Marienkirche
☐ B 3 Augsburg
☐ B 4 Markt Pongau (St. Johann i. P.)
☐ B 5 Hagen (Westfalen)
☐ B 6 Neuenahr

☐ B 7 Sooden-Allendorf
☐ B 8 Karlsbrunn (Ost-Sudetenland)

40—149—1—

☐ B 1 Innsbruck
☐ B 2 Wekelsdorf
☐ B 3 Soden bei Salmünster
☐ B 4 Altenahr
☐ B 5 Ürzig (Mosel)
☐ B 6 Bludenz
☐ B 7, 8 Salzschlirf

40—150—1—

☐ B 1 Dillingen a. d. Donau
☐ B 2 Mainburg
☐ B 3 München
☐ B 4 Hall in Tirol
☐ B 5 Innsbrucker Nordkettenbahn
☐ B 6 Kandel
☐ B 7 Landau (Südpfalz)
☐ B 8 Forst (Rheinpfalz)

40—151—1—

☐ B 1 Bad Salzungen
☐ B 2 Finsterbergen
☐ B 3 Bad Berka
☐ B 4 Bad Sulza
☐ B 5 Elgersburg
☐ B 6 Sondershausen
☐ B 7 Tabarz
☐ B 8 Friedrichroda

40—152—1—

☐ B 1 Bad Mergentheim
☐ B 2 Au in der Hallertau
☐ B 3 Ehrwald
☐ B 4 Wertingen
☐ B 5 Nördlingen
☐ B 6 Heilbrunn (Oberbayern)
☐ B 7 Stadtroda
☐ B 8 Lindau

40—153—1—

☐ B 1 Forst (Lausitz), Neissebrücke
☐ B 2 — Rosengarten
☐ B 3 Magdeburg, Altstadt
☐ B 4 — Kaiser-Otto
☐ B 5 — Dom
☐ B 6 Bad Aibling
☐ B 7 Passau
☐ B 8 Chemnitz
☐ B 9 Dornbirn

40—154—1—

☐ B 1 Franzensbad
☐ B 2 Karlsbad, Sprudelbrunnen
☐ B 3 — Mühlbrunnkolonade
☐ B 4 Marienbad, Kreuzbrunnen
☐ B 5 — Rundblick
☐ B 6 Konstantinsbad
☐ B 7 München
☐ B 8 Zoppot
☐ B 9 Halle

40—155—1—

☐ B 1 Steinschönau
☐ B 2 Danzig, Rathaus
☐ B 3 — Blick auf Hafen
☐ B 4, 5, 6 Bad Nauheim,
rechts Ziegeldach

☐ B 7, 8, 9 — ohne Ziegeldach

40—156—1—

☐ B 1   Wismar
☐ B 2, 3 Kudowa
☐ B 4   Wittenberg
☐ B 5   Kühlungsborn, Strand rechts
☐ B 6   — Strand links
☐ B 7   Ratzeburg
☐ B 8   Pfänderbahn, Bregenz
☐ B 9   Salzburg

40—157—1—

☐ B 1, 2, 3, 4, 5, 6, 7 Oberschlema
☐ B 8 Görbersdorf
☐ B 9 Nieder-Lindewiese

40—158—1—

☐ B 1, 2, 3, 4 Baden bei Wien
☐ B 5   Bad Vöslau, Brunnen
☐ B 6   — Teich
☐ B 7   Bad Brückenau
☐ B 8   Augsburg
☐ B 9   Freiwaldau-Gräfenberg

40—159—1—

☐ B 1   Spindelmühle, Luftkurort
☐ B 2   — Wintersportplatz
☐ B 3   Oberwiesenthal, Überblick
☐ B 4   — vorn Tannen
☐ B 6   Brüx
☐ B 6   Ingolstadt
☐ B 7   Ehrwald
☐ B 8, 9 Frankfurt (Main)

40—160—1—

☐ B 1, 2 Saaz
☐ B 3   Hofgastein, links Gebüsch
☐ B 4   — Vorn Heustadel
☐ B 5   — Skiläufer
☐ B 6   Innsbruck, Nordkettenbahn
☐ B 7   Eberswalde
☐ B 8, 9 Wekelsdorf

40—161—1—

☐ B 1, 2 Posen, Grosses Haus
☐ B 3, 4 — Universität
☐ B 5, 6 — Rathaus
☐ B 7   Marienburg, Südostecke
☐ B 8   — Blick v. d. Nogat
☐ B 9   Zahnradbahn Brannenburg-
            Wendelstein

40—162—1—

☐ B 1   München, Deutsches Museum
☐ B 2   — Schloss Nymphenburg
☐ B 3   Mayrhofen, vorn Häuser
☐ B 4   — vorn Tannen
☐ B 5   Reichenhall, Florianplatz
☐ B 6   — Kurgarten
☐ B 7   Brixlegg
☐ B 8   Lindau
☐ B 9   Heilbrunn

41—163—1—

☐ B 1   Elbing
☐ B 2   Hall (Tirol)
☐ B 3   Wiessee

☐ B 4   Donauwörth
☐ B 5   Dornbirn
☐ B 6   Mainburg
☐ B 7   Pongau (St. Johann i.P.)
☐ B 8   Bregenz
☐ B 9   Salzburg

41—164—1—

☐ B 1   Kitzbühel (Tirol)
☐ B 2   Rottach-Egern
☐ B 3   Füssen-Faulenbach
☐ B 4   Galtür (Tirol)
☐ B 5   Kufstein (Tirol)
☐ B 6   Landeck (Tirol)
☐ B 7   Schliersee, Überblick
☐ B 8   — Tennisplätze
☐ B 9   Boppard

41—165—1—

☐ B 1, 2, 3, 4, 5, 6, 7, 8, 9 Bad Salzuflen

41—166—1—

☐ B 1, 2, 3, 4, 5, 6, 7, 8, 9 Oberschlema

41—167—1—

☐ B 1, 2, 3 Bad Eilsen
☐ B 4   Reichenhall, Predigtstuhlbahn
☐ B 5, 6   Bad Salzuflen
☐ B 7   Wertingen
☐ B 8   Badgastein
☐ B 9   Oberschlema

41—168—1—

☐ B 1   Joachimsthal, Badehaus
☐ B 2   — Kurhaus
☐ B 3   — Fenblick
☐ B 4   Bad Elster, Pergola
☐ B 5   — Marienquelle
☐ B 6, 7   Brambach
☐ B 8   Eberswalde
☐ B 9   Bad Nauheim

41—169—1—

☐ B 1, 2, 3, 4, 5, 6, 7, 8, 9 Bad Nauheim

41—170—1—

☐ B 1   Kattowitz, Hochofen
☐ B 2   — Parkanlage
☐ B 3   — Theater
☐ B 4   — Strasse
☐ B 5   Franzensbad, Blick durch Säulen
☐ B 6   — Kurhaus
☐ B 7   Danzig, Marienkirche
☐ B 8   — Krantor
☐ B 9   Diez

41—171—1—

☐ B 1   Karlsbad, Überblick
☐ B 2   — Mühlbrunnkolonade
☐ B 3   — Sprudel
☐ B 4   Bad Lippspringe, Gebäude
☐ B 5   — Freibad
☐ B 6   Chemnitz
☐ B 7   Saybusch
☐ B 8   Krummhübel
☐ B 9   Bad Neuenahr

41—172—1—

☐ B 1   Zwickau
☐ B 2   Freiwaldau-Gräfenberg

ADVERTISING WITH POSTAL STATIONERY

The National Postal Advertising Company used the above picture postcards to encourage associations, chambers of commerce, and local governments to use postcards and cancels in their publicity campaigns.

With the slogan "Get to Know Germany" the German Reichspost printed to order picture postcards for various municipalities. Private business advertising was not permitted. The minimum order was 50,000 postcards, and a very large distribution was assured. The sender of the postcard as well as the recipient would notice the beauty of the promoted town. The cost for this advertising was RM225 for 50,000 picture postcards, an amount that even small communities could afford, because it benefited all community members through increased tourism.

The postal cancel with its comparatively small cost was especially suitable for communities, officials, and associations to advertise. The publicity cancel carried the message of meetings, exhibitions, and resorts to all parts of the world. The cost was based on the actual number of cancellations in close relationship to the results achieved. Communities and organizations received full details concerning costs.

Examples from the previously listed "Get to Know Germany" series:

37-93-1-B1

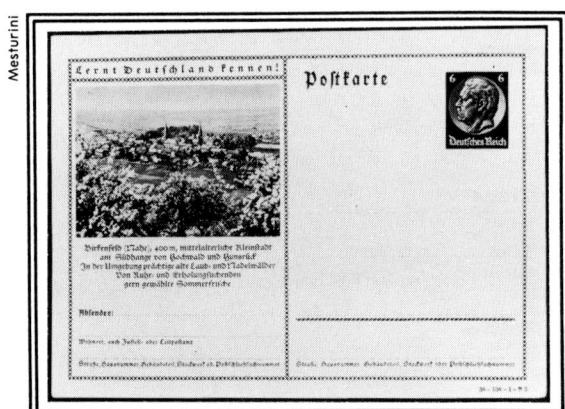

Mesturini

38-104-1-B3

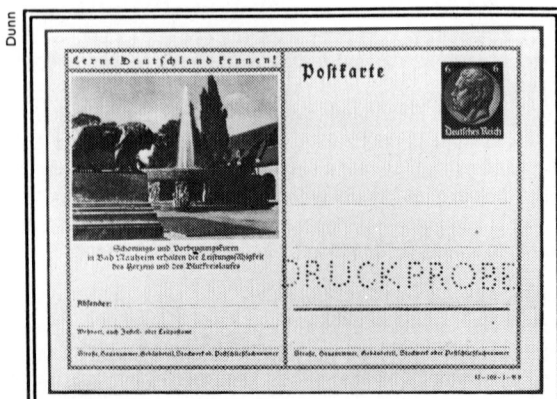

Dunn

Note printer's proof or "specimen" ("Druckprobe") mark.

41-169-1-B9

☐ —Blank card with five address lines. 6 Pf. (green).

☐ —Blank card with wavy line border and four address lines. 6 Pf. (green).

☐ —Berlin NW7, an order card for a chemical company (Stickstoff-Syndikat). 6 Pf. (green).

119

☐ —Dresden-A. 1, Firma Gustav Gericke. On reverse are two broken lines for "Konto-Nr." (accent nr.) and "name." 6 Pf. (green).

☐ —Gütersloh/Westf., Mielewerke, Miele Staubsauger. Perforated on top and bottom. 6 Pf. (green).

☐ —Hannover, advertising card for J.W. Sältzer, a clothier and outfitter in Hannover. 6 Pf. (green). Five known varieties exist.

☐
Nr. 1

Ziegelhofer

□
Nr. 2

Dunn

□
Nr. 3

Dunn

□
Nr. 4

Dunn

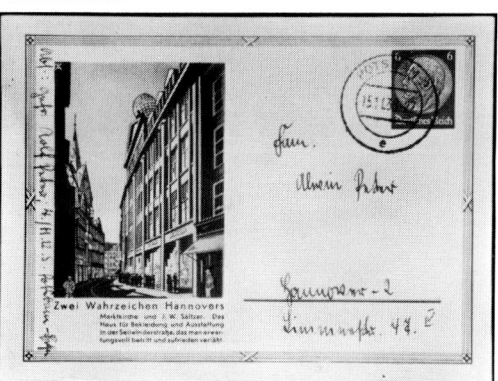

□
Nr. 5

☐ —Landshut i. Bayern, Landshuter Kunstmühle, obverse has ordering imprint. 6 Pf. (green).

☐ —Leipzig C1, Evers & Kornemann. 6 Pf. (green). Printing number 75/15/3.34.
Reverse is blank.

☐ As above, but with printing number 405/133/12.34.

☐ As above, but with text line on reverse. Printing number 668/133/3.35.

☐ As above. Printing number 863/133/7.35.

Printing number 405/133/12.34.

Printing number 863/133/7.35.

122

—Leverkusen, Behringwerke. Available with "Wichtige Präparate" or "Besonders empfehlenswerte Präparate" on upper left of card, a list of products and different imprinted addresses. 6 Pf. (green).

Printed "Drucksache"

- [ ] 1. Nabburg, M. Spiegler (2294/0)
- [ ] 2. Straubing, Jul. Münich (2294/0)
- [ ] 3. Stuttgart, Behringwerke (2294/0)

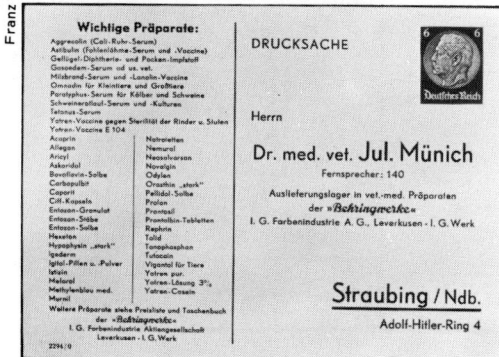 

Nr. 2

Printed "Postkarte"

- [ ] 4. Without address imprint (2550/0)
- [ ] 5. Berlin W15, Behringwerke (1676/9)
- [ ] 6. Frankfurt/M., Behringwerke (802/1)
- [ ] 7. Freiburg/B., Wwe. Karbach (487/0)
- [ ] 8. Freiburg/B., Dr. Leimenstoll (802/6)
- [ ] 9. Freiburg/B., Dr. Leimenstoll (1463/33)
- [ ] 10. Görlitz, Dr. Theiler (980/33)
- [ ] 11. Halle/S., Tiergesundheitsamt (802/6)
- [ ] 12. Hannover, Bayer-Meister Lucius
- [ ] 13. Hochheim a.M., without name (351/9)
- [ ] 14. Idar/Nahe, Dr. Zipp (351/9)
- [ ] 15. München 2, Behringwerke (487/0)
- [ ] 16. Straubing, Jul. Münich (487/0)
- [ ] 17. Straubing, Jul. Münich (2550/0)
- [ ] 18. Stuttgart, Behringwerke (351/9)
- [ ] 19. Stuttgart, Behringwerke (1215/7)
- [ ] 20. Wien 1, Bayer (351/9)
- [ ] 21. Stuttgart, Behringwerke (176/5)
- [ ] 22. As 13, Dr. Med. Vet. W. Schaaf (351/9)
- [ ] 23. Furstena/Hann., Dr. Hustede (2294/0)

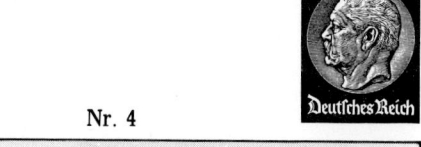

Nr. 4

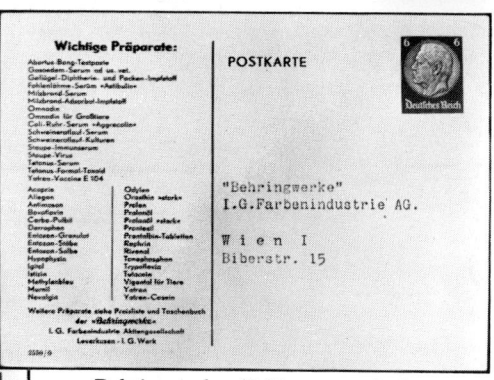

Behringwerke (Addressographed, not imprinted).

Nr. 15

Nr. 16

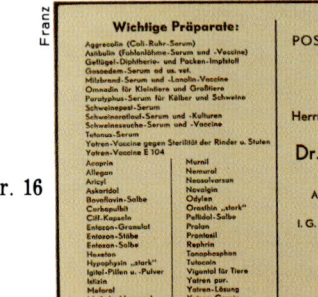

Nr. 17

Nr. 20

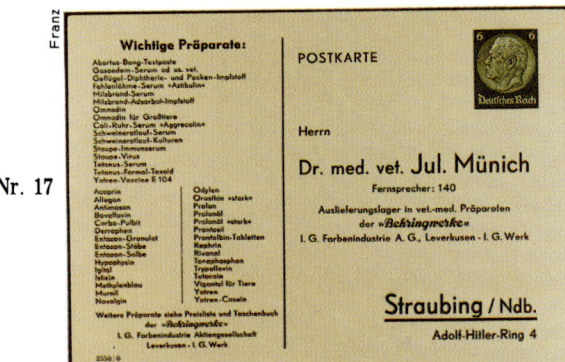

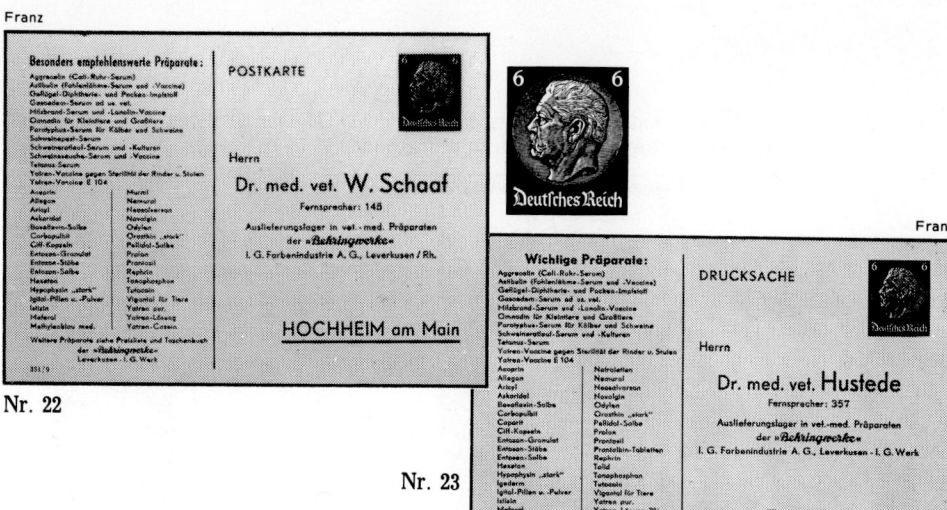

Nr. 22

Nr. 23

☐ —Nürnberg-O, Adolf Schneider; Kautschulpflaster "Elbaplast." Reverse has ordering imprint. 6 Pf. (green).

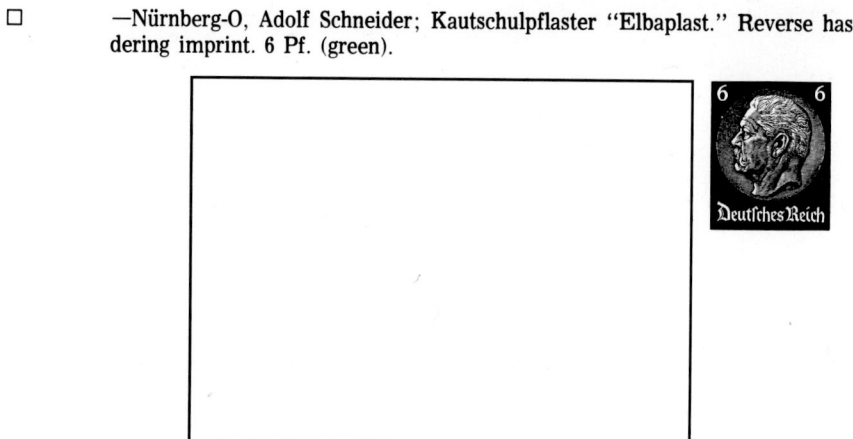

☐ —Stassfurt-Leopoldshall, C.W. Adam & Sohn; Bleche (sheet-metal), etc. Reverse carries an ordering imprint. 6 Pf. (green).

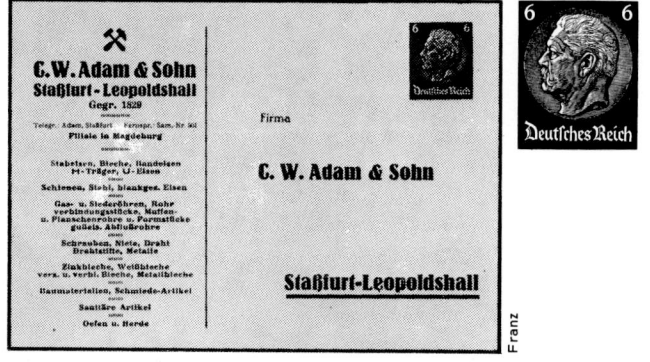

125

□   —Miele Waschmaschinen (washing machines). The same card exists perforated on top and bottom and with an imprinted address. 6 Pf. (green).

□ With perforated top and bottom,
   and with imprinted address.

□   —Wuppertal, Walter Götze. 6 Pf. (green).

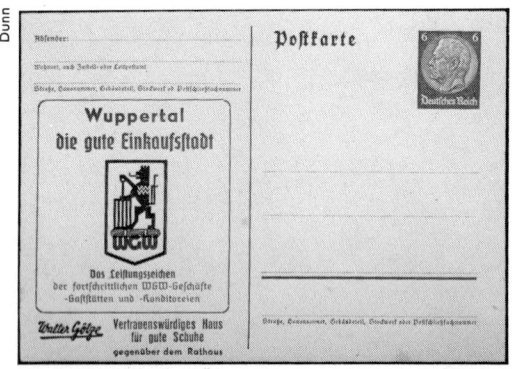

☐ —A six-card series commemorating Richard Wagner Year. This series depicts, through oil paintings, various themes from Wagner's operas. 6 Pf. (green).

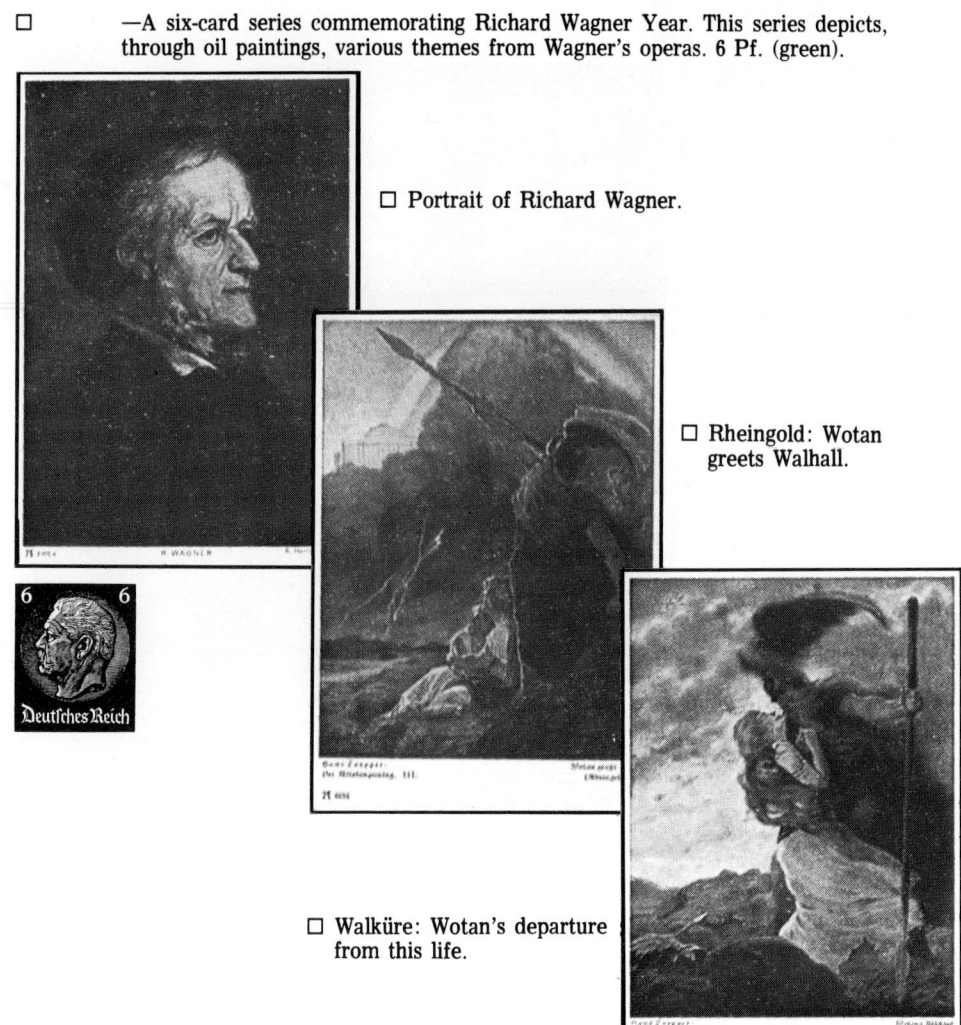

☐ Portrait of Richard Wagner.

☐ Rheingold: Wotan greets Walhall.

☐ Walküre: Wotan's departure from this life.

☐ Siegfried: Siegfried and Mime.

☐ Siegfried: Siegfried in the forest.

☐ Götterdämmerung: Hagen slays Siegfried.

☐ 1935—Twenty-four picture card series sponsored by the German War Cemetery Administration. 6 Pf. (green). Address: Bez. Unterfranken/Würzburg.

Cemetery at Mondidier (Somme/France).

Address:

☐ 1. Bay Bayern/München
☐ 2. Bez. Oberbayern/München
☐ 3. Bez. Oberfranken/ Bayreuth
☐ 4. Bez. Unterfranken/ Würzburg

Nr. 3 (6 Pf.)

Mesturini

Vitolj Cemetery (earlier known as Monastir) in Yugoslaiva.

Address:

☐ 5. Gau Bayern/München
☐ 6. Bez. Oberbayern/München
☐ 7. Bez. Oberfranken/Bayreuth
☐ 8. Bez. Unterfranken/Würzburg

Nr. 8 (6 Pf.)

Connantre Cemetery in France.

Address:

☐ 9. Gau Bayern/München
☐ 10. Bez. Oberbayern/Munchen
☐ 11. Bez. Oberfranken/Bayreuth
☐ 12. Bez. Unterfranken/Würzburg

Nr. 11 (6 Pf.)

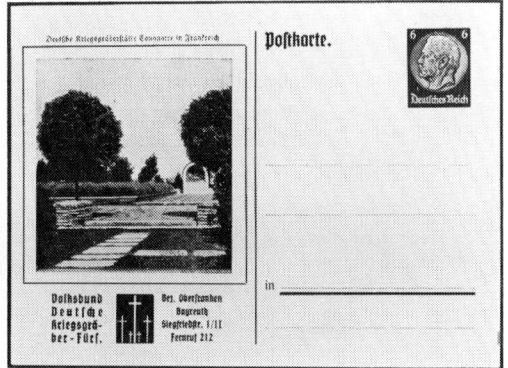

Rousselaere "De Ruyter" Cemetery in Flanders.

Address:

☐ 13. Gau Bayern/Munchen
☐ 14. Bez. Oberbayern/München
☐ 15. Bez. Oberfranken/Bayreuth
☐ 16. Bez. Unterfranken/Würzburg

Nr. 13 (6 Pf.)

1935 heroes' memorial at the Feldherrnhalle in Munich.

Address:

- ☐ 17. Gau Bayern/München
- ☐ 18. Bez. Oberbayern/München
- ☐ 19. Bez. Oberfranken/Bayreuth
- ☐ 20. Bez. Unterfranken/Würzburg

Nr. 20 (6 Pf.)

Mesturini

Cemetery in the Dolomites on the Pordoijoch (Italy).

Address:

- ☐ 21. Gau Bayern/München
- ☐ 22. Bez. Oberbayern/München
- ☐ 23. Bez. Oberfranken/Bayreuth
- ☐ 24. Bez. Unterfranken/Würzburg

Note:
For 5 Pf. & 1 Pf., and 5 Pf. cemetery series, see pp. 98-100.

Franz

Nr. 21 (6 Pf.)

Franz

Nr. 22 (6 Pf.)

☐ 1935—München 13, Bezirk Oberbayern, two-part card (question and answer). 6 & 6 Pf. (green).

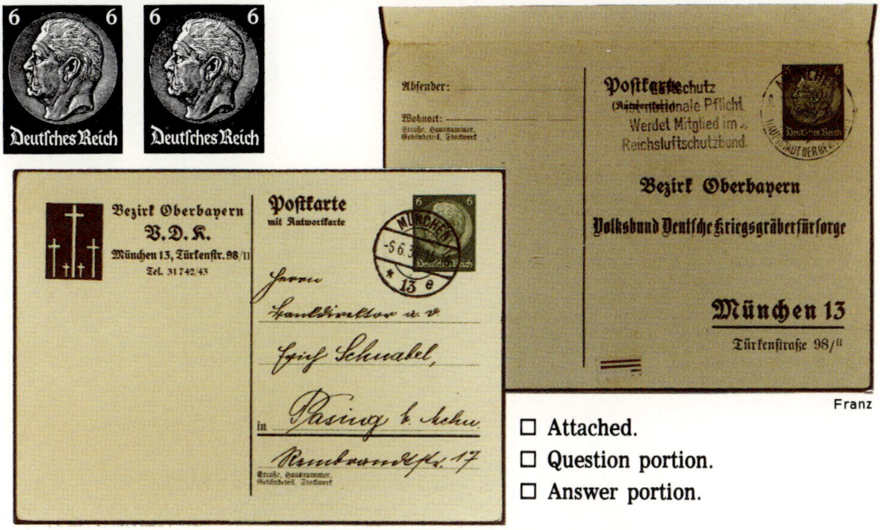

Franz

☐ Attached.
☐ Question portion.
☐ Answer portion.

☐   —blank card with no address lines or text. 10 Pf. (brown).

☐   —Return and address lines, no text. 10 Pf. (brown).

☐ With text.

131

☐   —Blank card with five address lines (four broken, one solid). 10 Pf. (brown).

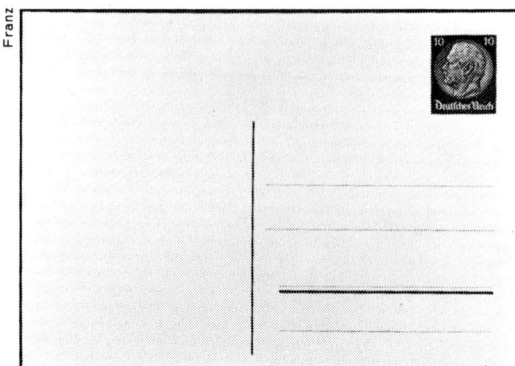

☐ 1933, Jan.-March—"E" of "Postkarte" with long tail and sender's address with five lines of text. 15 Pf. (carmine). Cream or beige-colored stock.

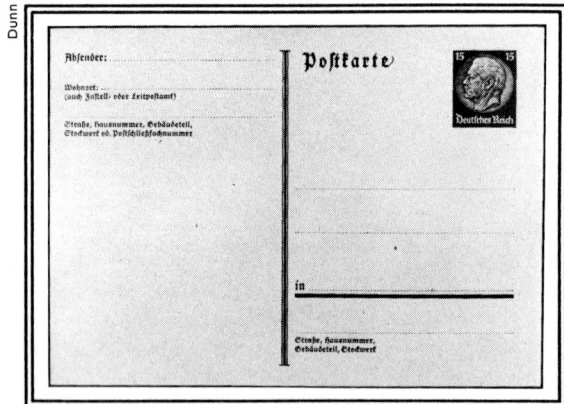

Poſtkarte

☐ 1933, Jan.-March—As above but with perforated edges. 15 Pf. (carmine). Cream or beige-colored stock.

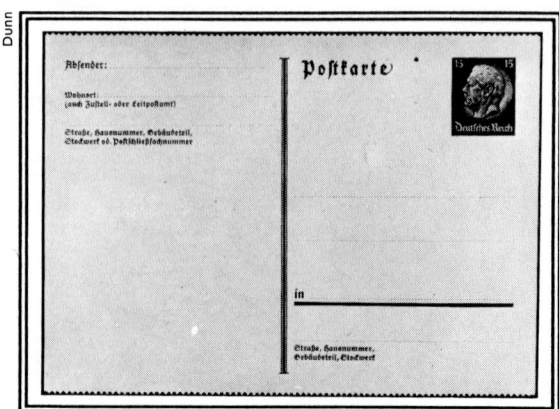

□ 1933, Jan.-March—"e" of "Postkarte" with long tail and with five lines of sender's text (upper left). 15 Pf. (brownish-lilac—note change of color from carmine). Beige-colored stock.

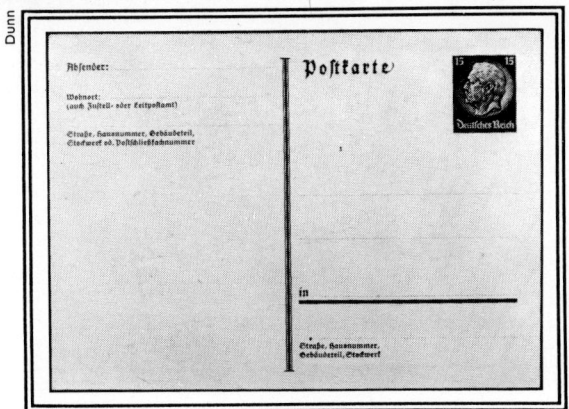

□ 1933, Jan.-March—Two-part card (question and answer) with short tail on "e." 15 & 15 Pf. (brownish-lilac—note change of color from carmine). Beige-colored stock.

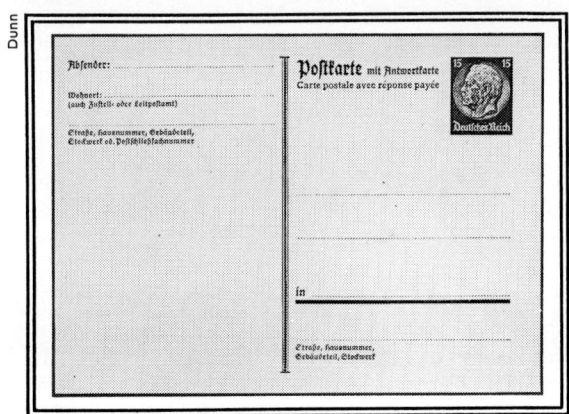

□ Attached.
□ Question portion.
□ Answer portion.

□ 1934, Jan.-June—15 Pf. (brownish-lilac). "Postkarte" with short tail on "e." Beige-colored stock.

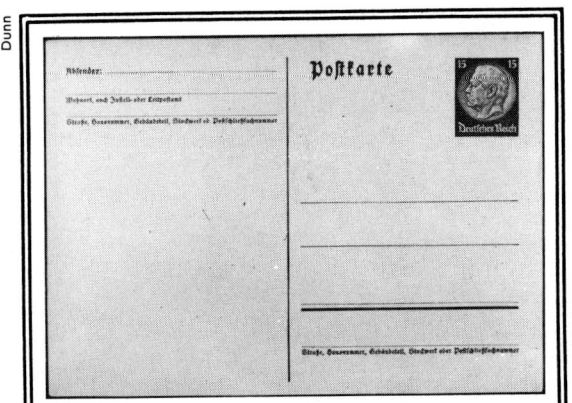

☐ 1934, Jan.-June—As above but with perforated edges. 15 Pf. (brownish-lilac). Beige-colored stock.

☐ 1934, Jan.-June—Two-part card (question and answer) with short tail on "e" of "Postkarte." 15 & 15 Pf. (brownish-lilac). Beige-colored stock.

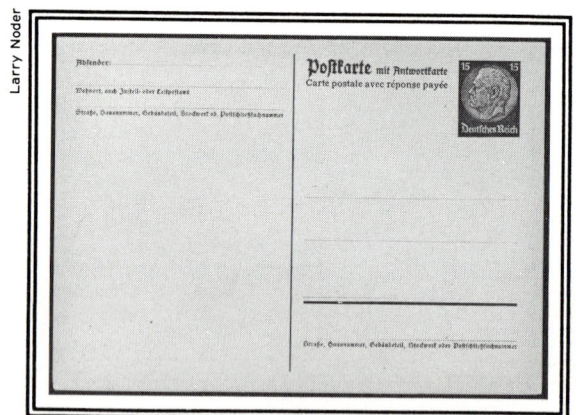

☐ Attached.
☐ Question portion.
☐ Answer portion.

☐ 1934, Jan.-June—As above but with perforated edges. 15 Pf. (brownish-lilac). Beige-colored stock.

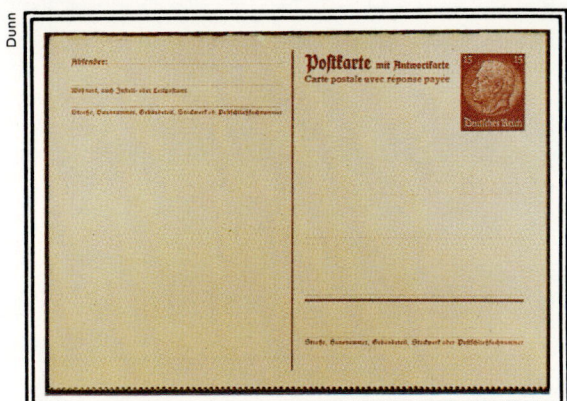

☐ —Blank card with five address lines (four broken, one solid. 15 Pf. (brown-violet).

☐ 1934, 21 Jan.—Blank card with only the imprinted 5 Pf. Luftpost stamp (green). 147x-104mm, cream-colored stock.

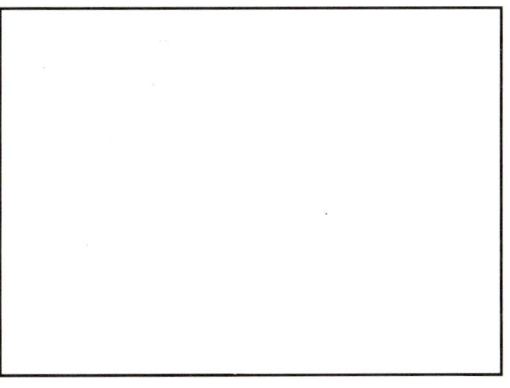

☐ 1934, 21 Jan.—As above, but with five address lines (green). 5 Pf. Luftpost (green).

☐ 1934, 21 Jan.—5 Pf. Luftpost (green). Black printing.

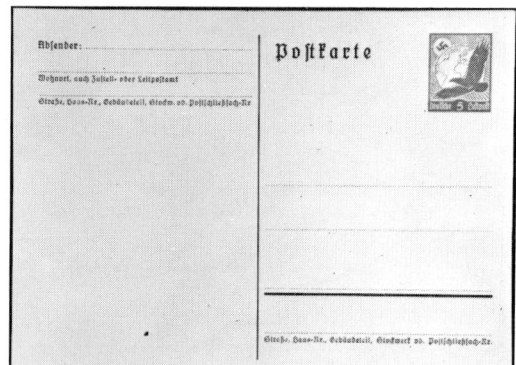

☐ 1934, 21 Jan.—Mampe Berlin, the original home of Mampe-Halb und Halb. 5 Pf. Luftpost (green).

□ 1934, 21 Jan.—Königsberg, Dr. Gruber. 5 Pf. Luftpost (green).

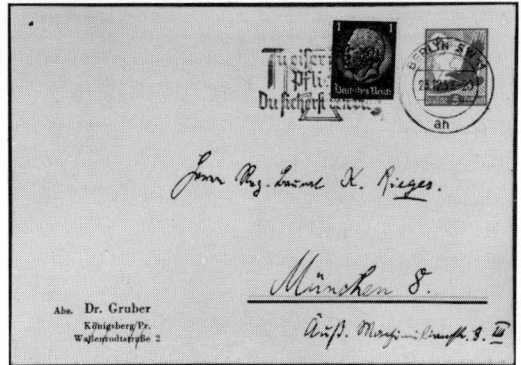

□ 1934, 21 Jan.—Mühlausen i. Thür., Dr. Ackermann Zahnarzt (dentist), four address lines. 5 Pf. Luftpost (green).

□   — ''Mein Lommatzsch'' 5 Pf. Luftpost (green) with an adhesive 1 Pf. (black). Approximately 1000 specimens were produced.

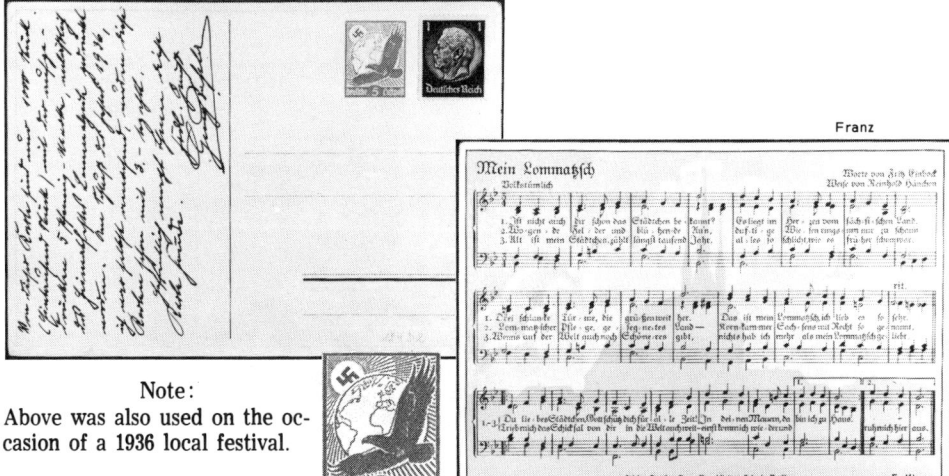

Note:
Above was also used on the occasion of a 1936 local festival.

☐ 1934—Rohrpostkarte (mail system by penumatic tube). 55 Pf. (vermillion).

Undated patriotic cards introduced sometime in 1933.

☐ 1933—Germany has awakened!

☐ 1933—Best Birthday Wishes
and German Greetings.

☐ 1933—Hail Germany!

No. 8231

Ziegelhofer

☐ 1933—True German Greetings.

Ziegelhofer

☐ 1933—Hail Germany!

Ziegelhofer

☐ 1933—True German Birthday Wishes.

☐ 1933—Heil Hitler!

Ziegelhofer

☐ 1933—German Greetings. Publ.: H. Straub, Heilbronn-Böckingen. This patriotic card illustrates the flag of the Weimar Republic, a "Deutsche Turnerschaft" banner, and the National Socialist flag.

Nr. 1718

☐ 1933—German Greetings
and Best Birthday
Wishes.

☐ 1933—True German
Birthday wishes.

☐ 1933—German Birthday
Greetings.

☐ 1933—Never will the Reich be destroyed when you are united and true.

Ziegelhofer

Nr. 1811

Nr. 1800/01

Ziegelhofer

Deutsche Grüße und beste Wünsche
zum Geburtstage

Ziegelhofer

☐ 1933—Birthday greetings
and best wishes.

☐ 1933—Best Good Luck Wishes
and German Greetings
on your Birthday.

Ziegelhofer

☐ 1933—Hindenburg

□ 1933—"To a new Germany." Publ.:
N.S. Kunstverlag Fr. Königsdorf & Co., Braunschweig.

□ 1933—Göring

□ 1933, Jan.—"Forward—we have succeeded before." Text on reverse: "We Germans fear
God, and nothing else in the world," a quote from Bismarck. Publ.: E. Buch v.
Griesheim, Leipzig.

□ 1933—"Kampf Heil! Deutschland erwache!" (Fight
Heil! Germany awake!) Note identical design with the 1931 card.

☐ 1933, 27 Jan.—Commemorating the 10 year anniversary of the first Parteitag (Party Rally) in 1923 (27-29 January) at Nürnberg. The photo is of Hitler and Julius Streicher. Publ.: Verlag Photo-Hoffmann, München. Nr. 498.

☐ 1933, 30 Jan.—Commemorating Hitler's accession to power. Friedrich the Great, Bismarck and Hitler are depicted. Publ.: Verlag Bayerl, München. Nr. 1.

☐ 1933, 30 Jan.—Commemorating Hitler's accession to power. Friedrich the Great, v. Hindenburg and Hitler are depicted. Titled: "Germany's Awakening." Publ.: R.N.K. Verlag, Berlin.

143

Hengstey-See Brücke

☐ 1933, 30 Jan.—Commemorating Hitler's accession to power.

This is part of a series. Verified views are:
☐ Altena/Westfalen
☐ Dortmund
☐ Hengstey-See Brücke

☐ 1933, 30 Jan.—Commemorating Hitler's accession to power. The Iron Chancellor, Bismarck, and Hitler are depicted.

☐ 1933, 30 Jan.—"Hitler's prayer for Germany." Publ.: Harry Rothenberg, Breslau.

☐ 1933, 30 Jan.—The historic day: Hitler's assumption of power. Publ.: Karl Kropp, Berlin-Schöneberg.

☐ 1933, 30 Jan.—Commemorating Hitler's assumption of power. Depicted are Reichspräsident v. Hindenburg, Chancellor Hitler, and members of his cabinet, Dr. Wilhelm Frick, Hermann Göring, Dr. Josef Goebbels, Alfred Hugenberg, Franz von Papen and Franz Seldte.

☐ 1933, 30 Jan.—Commemorating Hitler's assumption of power.

☐ 1933, 30 Jan.—"The new course." This card with rotating photos also depicts Seldte, Dr. Frick and Göring. Publ.: Dr. Trenkler, Leipzig.

☐ 1933, 30 Jan.—The song, "Reichskanzler Hitler," written to commemorate Hitler's assumption of power. Sang to the melody of "Hast du dem Lied der alten Eichen..."

☐ 1933, 30 Jan.—Commemorating the assumption of power by Adolf Hitler.

☐ 1933, 30 Jan.—Two-part card produced at the time of Hitler's assumption of power. Work and bread is promised.

☐ 1933, 30 Jan.—"Young Germany, awaken." American-produced card urging a common struggle against foreign oppression of Germans everywhere. Publ.: Freunde des neuen Deutschland, Milwaukee, Wis.

☐ 1933, 30 Jan.—Hitler and his representatives. "The Reich will never be destroyed, if you are united and loyal."

☐ 1933, 30 Jan.—"The Saviours of the Nation" (Hitler and v. Hindenburg). Commemorating Hitler's accession to power.

☐ 1933, 30 Jan.—Commemorating Hitler's accession to power. "What the king conquered, what the sovereign shaped, what the field marshal defended, the soldier rescued and unified."

☐ 1933, 30 Jan.—Commemorating Hitler's accession to power. Friedrich the Great (he fought), Bismarck (he unified), v. Hindenburg (he protected) and Hitler (he rescued) are depicted. Publ.: Rex-Verlag, Potsdam. Nr. 172.

☐ 1933, 30 Jan.—Card showing the honor plaque produced to commemorate Hitler's accession to power. Publ.: Wilhelm v. Kaminietz, Berlin-Wittenau.

Es ist erreicht!

☐ 1933, 30 Jan.—"It is achieved!"
    (i.e. national leadership).

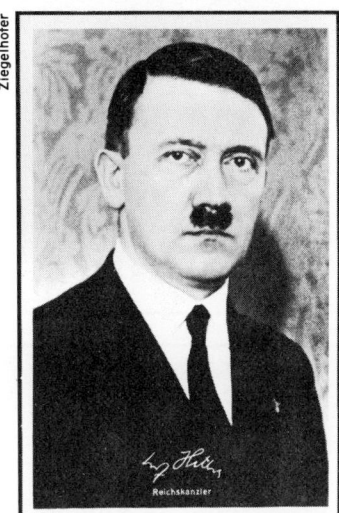

Ziegelhofer

Reichskanzler

☐ 1933, Feb.—Hitler, after the first cabinet meeting.
    Publ.: K.W.K. Nr. 1.

Ausgebrannte Kuppel

Plenar-Saal

Ziegelhofer

☐ 1933, 27 Feb.—Commemorating the burning of the
    Reichstag Building.

Ziegelhofer

☐ 1933, March—For People and Fatherland. Publ.:
    Schwarz-Weiss-Kunst, Stuttgart.

☐ 1933, 5 March—Commemorating the accomplishment at the March 5 Reichstag (parliaments) election.

☐ 1933, 5 March—Commemorating the National Socialist victory during the vote for Reichstag members.

☐ 1933, 11-26 March—Essen, commemorating the German Air Sports Exhibition.

☐ 1933, 21 March—The Kroll Opera House in Berlin, meeting place of the Reichstag after the Reichstag building was burned on 27 February 1933.

Ziegelhofer

150

☐ 1933, 21 March—Commemorating the opening festivities of the 1933 Reichstag, held at the Garrison Church at Potsdam. Hitler, Friedrich the Great and v. Hindenburg are shown.

☐ 1933, 21 March—Commemorating the opening festivities of the 1933 Reichstag, held at the Garrison Church at Potsdam. Publ.: Hoffmann und Kirchner, Potsdam.

Webb

☐ 1933, 21 March—Commemorating the opening festivities of the 1933 Reichstag, held in the Garrison Church at Potsdam. Publ.: Franz Hanfstaengl, München.

Ziegelhofer

☐ 1933, 21 March—Commemorating the opening festivities of the 1933 Reichstag, held in the Garrison Church at Potsdam. Designed by Fritz Heublein, Frankfurt a.M.

☐ 1933, 21 March—Commemorating the opening festivities of the 1933 Reichstag. "Speech of Reichskanzler Hitler in the Garrison Church."

☐ 1933, 21 March—Commemorating the opening festivities of the 1933 Reichstag, held in the Garrison Church at Potsdam. Photo by Heinrich Hoffmann.

☐ 1933, 21 March—Commemorating the opening festivities of the 1933 Reichstag. Hitler and v. Hindenburg are illustrated.

☐ 1933, 21 March—Commemorating the opening festivities of the 1933 Reichstag, held in the Garrison Church at Potsdam. Publ.: Kunstverlag Wentz & Co., GmbH, Berlin.

☐ 1933, 21 March—Potsdam, march-by of the Reichswehr.

Ziegelhofer

Ziegelhofer

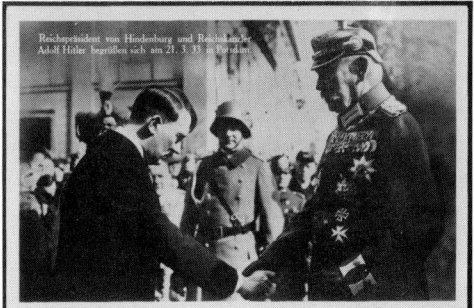

☐ 1933, 21 March—Commemorating the opening festivities of the 1933 Reichstag, held in the Garrison Church at Potsdam. Publ.: Kunstverlag Robert Hügel, Berlin.

☐ 1933, 21 March—Commemorating the opening festivities of the 1933 Reichstag, held in the Garrison Church at Potsdam.

Mesturini

153

□ 1933, 21 March—Reminiscence of that date when the opening festivities of the 1933
Reichstag were held at Potsdam. Publ.: Spannagelt Caesar, Lüdenscheid.

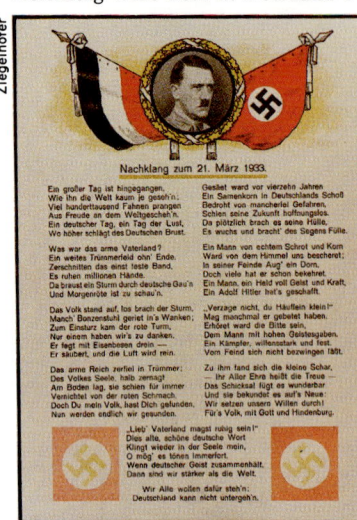

Ziegelhofer

Ziegelhofer

□ 1933, 21 March—Commemorating the opening
festivities of the 1933 Reichstag, held in
the Garrison Church at Potsdam.

□ 1933, 21 March—Commemorating the opening
festivities of the 1933 Reichstag.

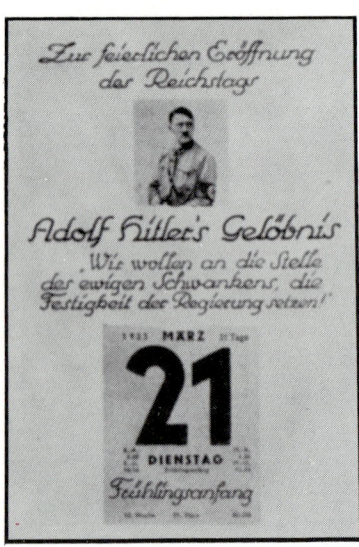

Ziegelhofer

□ 1933, April—Commemorating the NSDAP Gau Day "Bayerische Ostmark." Publ.:
Neumeister, Bayreuth. Ritter von Epp (left) and Hans Schemm (right) are illustrated with three Bavarian memorials.

☐ 1933, April—"German honor." Showing German and Austrian solidarity. Publ.: Verlag für nationale Bildkunst, R. Bischoff, München. Designed by A.v. Meitzl. Nr. 26.

D. Geary

Webb

☐ 1933, April—Commemorating a German Easter.

☐ 1933, April—German Easter greetings.

155

□ 1933, 1-2 April—Berlin, commemorating the postal exhibition, "Markoposta," sponsored by the Mars-Berlin club and the association of colonial postal collectors. 3 Pf. (brown ((Ebert)) and 5 Pf. (light green).

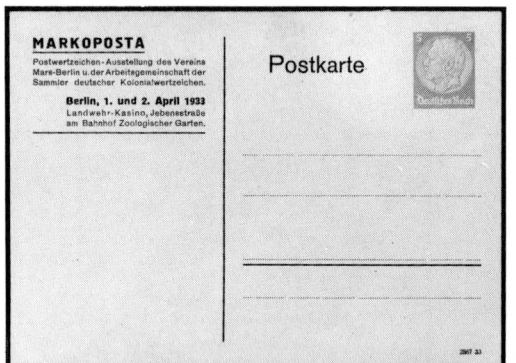

□ 1933, 8-18 April—Dresden, commemorating the 1933 postage stamp show. 3 Pf. (brown). Ⓢ Briefmarkenschau/Dresden (Ausstellung).

Note: Also available with a special, red pre-paid rubber stamping assigning a higher value of 5 Pf.

□ —Reverse of above with red pre-paid rubber stamping (Nr. 1004).

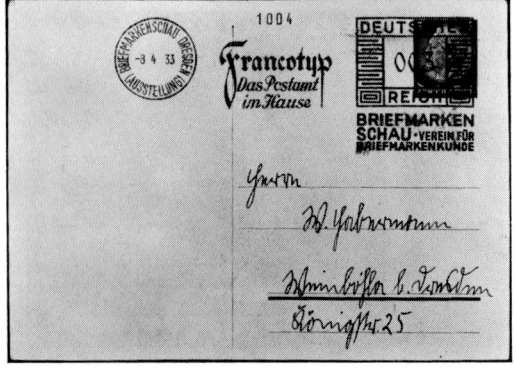

Webb

☐ 1933, 8-18 April—Dresden, commemorating the 1933 postage stamp
show. 3 Pf. (brown).

   Ⓢ Briefmarkenschau/Dresden
(Ausstellung).

☐   —Reverse of above with
red pre-paid rubber
stamping (Nr. 4487).

☐ 1933, 12 April—Commemorating the Opening of the Reichstag in Potsdam on 21 March
1933. 6 Pf. (dark green).

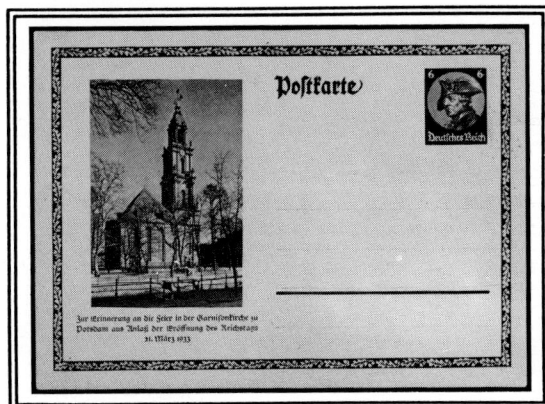

Valid until
31 Dec. 1935.

☐ 1933, 15 April—Mannheim, official postcard for the unveiling of the Carl Benz memorial. Designed by Prof. M. **Laeuger** and printed by Scherl Verlag, **Berlin. 6 Pf. (green).**

☐ 1933, 20 April—Commemorating Hitler's **44th** birthday. Publ.: Wilhelm Schütze, Würzburg.

☐ 1933, 1 May—Commemorating the Day of National Labor (May Day). Publ.: Militär-Kunstverlag "Ares," F. Mittelbach, Berlin-Steglitz.

Imprinted on obverse.

☐ 1933, 1 May—Commemorating the Day of National Labor (May Day), 1 May 1933. "Labor ennobles."

☐ 1933, 1 May—Commemorating the Day of National Labor (May Day), 1 May 1933. This one-color card features a gold foil seal in place of the v. Hindenburg/Hitler plaque on the full-color version. Bild Nr. 43.

☐ 1933, 1 May—Commemorating the Day of National Labor (May Day), 1 May 1933 (Publ.: Verlag Krüger und Lindenberg, Berlin). Designed by Felix Albrecht.

☐ 1933, 1 May—Bad Kreuz-
   nach, commem-
   orating May Day.

☐ 1933, 1 May—Commemorating the
   Day of National Labor (May
   Day).

☐ 1933, 1 May—Berlin, commemorating the day of National Labor (May Day). Hitler is
   shown speaking to German youth in the Lustgarten.

Mesturini

☐ 1933, 1 May—The National Day of Labor is commemorated. "German Youth honor their Reichskanzler. Publ.: K.W.W. Nr. 115.

☐ 1933, 1 May—Commemorating the Day of National Labor.

☐ 1933, 1 May—Commemorating the Day of National Labor, 1 May 1933. Reich President v. Hindenburg and Reich Chancellor Hitler on their way to the Lustgarten.

☐ 1933, 1 May—Commemorating the Day of National Labor (May Day), 1 May 1933. Publ.: H.P. Münchhosen, Berlin. Artist: Hanns Haas.

Berlin-Tempelhof Field.

Ziegelhofer

☐ 1933, 1 May—Commemorating the Day of National Labor, 1 May 1933. Reich President v. **Hinden**burg speaks to the youth in the Lustgarten.

☐ 1933, 1 May—"The Struggle and Freedom Song" on a card commemorating the 1933 Day of National Labor (May Day).

☐ 1933, 1 May—Card featuring a song "To the German Worker."

Ziegelhofer

☐ 1933, 8 May—Dormagen, to commemorate the Day of the German Cavalry, and to honor Field Marshal von Mackensen.

Talacko

Ziegelhofer

□ 1933, 18 May—Commemorating the Prussian legislature. Göring reviews the honor guard.

Ziegelhofer

□ 1933, 26 May—Düsseldorf, commemorating the 10th anniversary of Schlageter being executed by French occupation troops.

□ 1933, 20-28 May—Berlin, commemorating the 39th 4-H Fair (agricultural organization established to instruct young rural people in modern farming methods).

Mesturini

1953, 31 May-7 June—Cologne, commemorating the 42nd 4-H Fair. This postcard is included as a point of interest since the card's art is almost identical to that for the 1933 Berlin fair.

Mesturini

Mesturini

□ 1933, 21 May—The "Freedom Sun" (swastika)) is shown rising behind the new Reich Chancellor, Adolf Hitler.

□ 1933, 25 May—Iburg, commemorating the National Frontier Lands Day.

□ 1933, 26 May—Postcard from "German Heroes Series II," commemorating the 10th anniversary of Albert Leo Schlageter's death. Schlageter was an early sympathizer who was executed in 1923 by the French for blowing up a bridge.

Schlageter was a member of Freikorps Rossbach in the Ruhr region who fought against the French.

Ziegelhofer

164

☐ 1933, 28 May—"Danzig is National Socialist."

☐ 1933, 31 May-11 June—Nuremberg, commemorating German Week.

☐ 1933, June—Fund-raising card of the VDA (Volksbund für Deutschtum in Ausland) on the occasion of the Whitsun holidays (Pfingsttagung) in Klagenfurt. Overprint on bottom of card indicates the convention in Klagenfurt was moved to Passau.

□ 1933, June—Schönau, commemorating the 10th anniversary of Albert Schlageter's execution by the French on 26 May 1923 in Düsseldorf. Publ.: Alleinverlag von Wilh. Wetzel, Schönau.

□ 1933, June—Fund-raising card for the VDA (Volksbund für Deutschtum im Ausland) on the occasion of the relay race to the German border. Publ.: Verlag des VDA, Dresden.

□ 1933, 3-11 June—Bautzen, commemorating the one week celebration of the city being 1000 years old.

□ 1933, 8-11 June—Munich, commemorating the 1st German Apprentice Day.

166

☐ 1933, 17-18 June—Kolberg, commemorating the 1st District meeting of the Pomeranian Hitler Youth.

☐ 1933, 18 June—Calw, commemorating German Day.

Gogolinski

☐ 1933, 24-25 June—Spandau, commemorating Day of the "Old Guard" of the NSDAP.

☐ 1933, 1-3 July—Düsseldorf, commemorating the 3rd Anniversary of Weapons Day/i.e., annual reunion of the cavalry.

☐ 1933, 15-23 July—Frankfurt/M., commemorating the 18th Bowling Association tournament.

□ 1933, 22-30 July—Stuttgart, ten card set commemorating the 15th German Gymnastics Display. Publ.: Kunstanstalt Schuler, Stuttgart. 6 Pf. (green).
    Ⓢ Stuttgart/15./deutsches/Turnfest/Stuttgart 1933 (marching cancel).
    Ⓢ Stuttgart/15./Deutsches Turnfest (hand cancel).

□ Nr. 1

□ Nr. 2

□ Nr. 3

□ Nr. 4

☐ Nr. 5

☐ Nr. 6

☐ Nr. 7

 ☐ Nr. 8

☐ Nr. 9

☐ Nr. 10

☐ 1933, 22-30 July—15th German Gymnastic Competition in Stuttgart (Publ.: D.T.-Geschäftsstelle, Stuttgart). D.T. stands for Deutsche Turnerschaft (German Gymnastic Association).

☐ 1933, 22-30 July—Stuttgart, commemorating the 15th German Gymnastic Competition.

☐ 1933, 22-30 July—Stuttgart, commemorating the 15th German Gymnastic Competition.

☐ 1933, 22-30 July—Commemorating the 15th German Gymnastic Competition in Stuttgart. The reverse has a small head smoking a cigar, an advertisement for "Villinger Stumpen" (the brand of cigar). "Mild and Good!"

Kaiser

Webb

☐ 1933, 22-30 July—Stuttgart, commemorating the 15th German gymnastic displays.

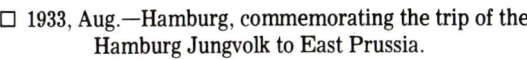

☐ 1933, 22-25 July—Ellwangen, commemorating the 700th anniversary of the collegiate church.

☐ 1933, Aug.—Hamburg, commemorating the trip of the Hamburg Jungvolk to East Prussia.

Kaiser

☐ 1933, 11-13 Aug.—Berlin, commemorating the 1st SS inspection of Group East. Artist: Ludwig Hohlwein.

☐ 1933, 12-27 Aug.—Hamburg, commemorating the German Aviation Exhibition.

☐ 1933, 19-21 Aug.—Aschersleben, commemorating the postage stamp exhibition. 3 Pf. (brown), 5 Pf. (light green), 6 Pf. (green) and 15 Pf. (violet).

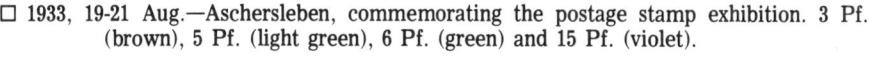

Talacko

Ⓢ Aschersleben/Brief-marken-Ausstellung, etc.

+12 Pf. meter   +1Pf. metter

Aschersleben, 5 Pf. (green) plus 1 Pf. meter (see below left).

☐ 1933, 20 Aug.—Büren, commemorating German Day.

☐ 1933, 26 Aug.-3 Sept.— Rosenheim, commemorating the autumn festival.

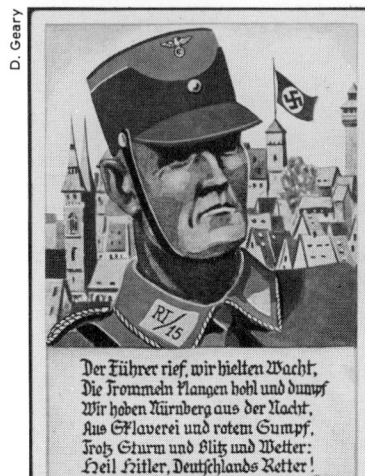

☐ 1933, 30 Aug.-3 Sept.—SA motif card commemorating the 1933 Reichsparteitage.

☐ 1933, 30 Aug.—Fund-raising card for the furthering of German sports. Von Tschammer, the sports leader is illustrated. Nr. 4. Publ.: Reichssportverlag GmbH, Berlin.   173

Kaiser

☐ 1933, 30 Aug.-4 Sept.—Commemorating the 1933 Reichsparteitage.

D. Gloster

☐ 1933, 30 Aug.-3 Sept.—Commemorating the 1933 Reichsparteitage.

☐ 1933, 1-3 Sept.—Official Nürnberg Reich Party Rally Days postcards. Publ.: Franz Eher Verlag, München.

Kaiser

Designed by Siegmar von Suchodolski.

"United the People, Strong the Nation."

174

The following is a sampling of the numerous cards produced by various publishers for the 1933 Reichsparteitage.

☐ 1933, 1-3 Sept.—Commemorating the 1933 Reichsparteitage. Publ.: H. Hunsinger, Nürnberg. Designed by Gustav Goetschel.

☐ 1933, 1-3 Sept.—Commemorating the 1933 Reichsparteitage. Publ.: Photo-Hoffmann, München, P. Nr. 45 and Nr. 410).

☐ 1933, 1-3 Sept.—Commemorating the 1933 Reichsparteitage. Publ.: Photo-Hoffmann, München.

□ 1933, 1-3 Sept.—Unofficial cards commemorating the 1933 Reichsparteitage. Publ.: Verlag Wilhelm Serz, Nürnberg.

☐ 1933, 1-3 Sept.—Commemorating the 1933 Reichsparteitage. Publ.: F. Willmy, Nürnberg-Fürth.

☐

Webb

Webb

Webb

☐ 1933, 1-3 Sept.—Commemorating the 1933 Reichsparteitage.

☐ 1933, 2-4 Sept.—Geringswalde, card commemorates the 700 year anniversary of the city's founding. Publ.: Paul Grumms, Geringswalde.

□ 1933, 8-10 Sept.—Illustrated is the shooting prize of Reich Chancellor Hitler which was awarded for the first time on this date at this automated small caliber target range. Publ.: H. Klee G.m.b.H., Hannover.

Ziegelhofer

Ziegelhofer

□ 1933, 9 Sept.—"Hitlerjunge Quex." Promotional card on this film which opened in all UFA theaters on 22nd September.

□ 1933, 9-17 Sept.—Tangermünde, commemorating the 1000 year anniversary of the city. Publ.: Gebr. Walter, Magdeburg-N.

☐ 1933, 10-24 Sept.—Fund-raising card for the VDA (Volksbund für Deutschtum in Ausland). "Protect the German schools abroad."

☐ 1933, 23 Sept.—Commemorating the start of the national Autobahn construction. This photo was also used on a postal card, September 21, 1936.

☐ 1933, 16-18 Sept.—Karlsruhe, commemorating the 60th anniversary of the Baden veterans' association.

☐ 1933, 23-24 Sept.—Hannover, commemorating the Stahlhelm's (veterans' association) national leader day. Publ.: Der Stahlhelm.

179

☐ 1933, Oct.—Fund-raising card for the 1933/34 Winterhilfswerk programs in the Gau Great Berlin area.

☐ 1933, Oct.—Fund-raising card for the 1933/34 Winterhilfswerk programs in the Gau Mecklenburg-Lübeck area. Note different text below eagle and placement of pins.

☐ 1933, Oct.—Winterhilfswerk fund-raising card stressing no portion of the German people will go hungry, especially those in the southeast portion of the Reich.

☐ 1933, Oct.—The Thanks of the Fatherland extended to the Heroes of the Great World War.

Note: This wounded hero is humiliated after losing the war and seeing his country in ruins. Only the SA can show him the way!

□ 1933, 1 Oct.—Fund-raising cards for the 1933/34 Winterhilfswerk programs. Publ: N.S. Volkswohlfahrt, Berlin.

Webb

□ "Admiral Ritter von Hipper."

□

Webb

"Gustav Simon, Gauleiter of Koblenz-Trier."

□

Mesturini

□

The WHW leaders (Hilgenfeldt, Janowsky and Lemme) are pictured.

Mesturini

□

"Sereth front. In a mortar emplacement."

Webb

Reich Minister
Goebbels is
pictured.

Mesturini

Mesturini

Mesturini

☐ 1933, 1 Oct.—Fund-raising card for the 1933/34 Winterhilfswerk programs. "Nürnberg 1923." Publ.: Heinrich Hoffmann, Munich.

☐ 1933, 1 Oct.—Festival card commemorating the 1933 Harvest Thanksgiving Festival at Bückeberg. Publ.: Verlag Frz. Nacht, München.

☐ 1933, 1 Oct.—Commemorating the Harvest Thanksgiving Festival at Bückeberg. Publ.: Nordd. Städte-Verkehrs-Werbung, Hannover-Hainholz. Two different printings exist. Note reverse variations.

☐   This is for 1933.

Einzige offizielle
     Erntedanktag-Postkarte

☐   This is for 1934.

Erntedankfest (Bückeberg)

ben ....

☐ 1933, 1 Oct.—Bückeberg, commemorating the Harvest Thanksgiving Festival. Note portraits of Hitler and National Food Minister, Walter Darré.

184

□ 1933, 1 Oct.—Commemorating the Harvest Thanksgiving Festival at Bückeberg.

Ziegelhofer

□ 1933, 1-2 Oct.—Potsdam, commemorating the 1st
   National Socialist Youth Day.   Designed
   by Ludwig Hohlwein.

□ 1933, 7-9 Oct.—Gablonz a.N., commemorating
   the 14th German Stamp Collectors' Day.

□ 1933, 14-22 Oct.—Breslau, commemorating the
   Great Silesian Brown Fair.

185

☐ 1933, 15 Oct.—Official postcard commemorating the Day of German Art and ground laying ceremonies for the House of German Art. Nr. 2. Publ.: Jos. E. Huber, Diessen v München.

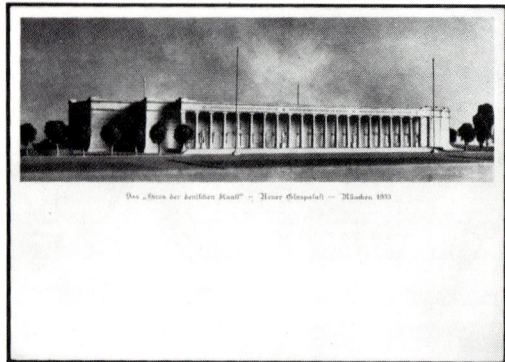

☐ 1933, 15 Oct.—Munich, commemorating the ground-laying ceremonies for the House of German Art (Haus der Deutschen Kunst). Publ.: Gauleitung München-Oberbayern der NSDAP, München.

☐

Kaiser

1933, 22 Oct.—"A marvel of nature as a sign of our time." Note swastika on the forehead of this calf born in Wrist in Holstein on the farm of Max Granzow. Publ.: Hans Andres, Hamburg.

☐

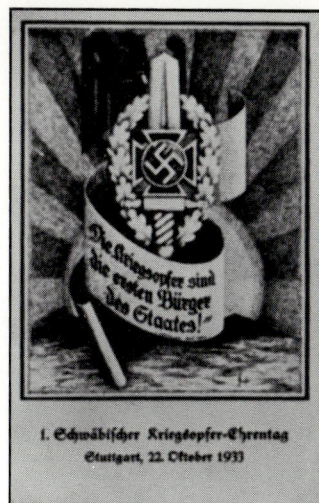

☐ 1933, 22 Oct.—Stuttgart, commemorating the 1st Schwabish War Wounded Day.

☐ 1935, 28-29 Oct.—Chemnitz, commemorating Brigade Ehrhard meeting.

☐ 1933, 1 Nov.—Special card for the German Emergency Service. 6 & 4 Pf. (green). The card is entitled ''Honor your German Masters.''

Ⓢ ''Bayreuth/Festspielhügel''

Valid until 30 Sept. 1934.

☐ 1933, 4 Nov.—Commemorating the 450th birthday of Dr. Martin Luther. 6 Pf. (black). Ⓢ "Eisleben/Dr. Martin Luthers/Geburtsstadt"/1483-1933-10.11.1933.

☐ 1933, 9 Nov.—Honoring the fallen of 9 November 1923 during the Munich Putsch. Publ.: H. Hunsinger, Nürnberg. Designed by Gustav Goetscherl. For sale until 31 August 1937.

☐ 1933, 9 Nov.—Commemorating the 10th anniversary of the 9 November 1923 Munich Putsch. Publ.: Photo-Hoffmann, München. Nr. 358.

☐ 1933, 9 Nov.—Commemorating the 10th anniversary of the 9 November 1923 Munich Putsch. Publ.: Photo-Hoffmann, München. Nr. 401.

☐ 1933, 9 Nov.—Commemorating the 10th anniversary of the 9 November 1923 Munich Putsch. Publ.: Verlag Uvachrom AG., München.

☐ 1933, 9 Nov.—Commemorating the 10th anniversary of the Munich Putsch. The photo was found in the Party Archives of the NSDAP in Munich and depicts the start of the historic march. In actuality, no photos exist of the Putsch leaders near the Feldherrnhalle and this photo was re-enacted to fill the gap of photographic coverage of this historic event.

189

☐ 1933, 9 Nov.—Honoring the fallen of 9 November 1923 during the Munich Putsch (Publ.: Gu-Gö-Verlag, Nürnberg). "And you have nevertheless been victorious."

☐ 1933, 9 Nov.—Commemorating the 16 fallen heroes of the aborted 9 November 1923 Putsch in Munich. Publ.: Verlag Bayern, München. Nr. 5.

☐ 1933, 9 Nov.—Commemorating the 10 year anniversary of the 1923 Putsch in Munich. Illustration by Ludwig Johst. Publ.: Verlag Hermann A. Wiechmann, München.

☐ 1933, Dec.—Fund-raising card for the 1933/34 Winterhilfswerk programs. Publ.: Hauser-presse (Hans Schaefer), Frankfurt am Main.

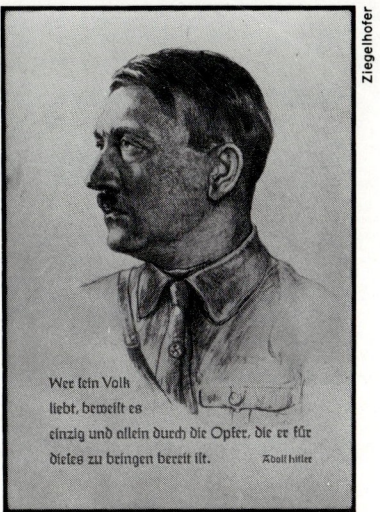

Ziegelhofer

☐ 1933, Dec.—Kreisgruppe St. Pölten, commemorating the association of German postal collectors in that area. Note the design at left of card was imprinted on a standard postcard printed in December 1933.

Mesturini

Ziegelhofer

☐ 1933, Dec.—Fund-raising card for the 1933/34 Winter hilfswerk programs. Publ.: Hanns Reindl, München.

191

☐ 1933, Dec.—1933/34 Bavarian officials' emergency fund-raising card for the Winterhilfswerk.

☐ 1933, Dec.—1933/34 Bavarian officials' emergency fund-raising card for the Winterhilfswerk.

☐ 1933, Dec.—Postcard wishing blessed New Year's greetings for 1934.

Exact date of issuance not known on the following card.

☐ 1933—Breslau, commemorating the meeting of the Silesian SA.

1934

□ 1934, 1 Jan.—German New Year greetings. Publ.: C. Jungmann, Leipzig.

Geary

□ 1934, 30 Jan.—Commemorating one year of power by the National Socialists.

□ 1934, 29 Jan.—In remembrance of Hitler's accession to power (30 Jan. 1933). 6 Pf. (brown). Valid until 31 Dec. 1935.

□ 1934, Feb.—Postcard depicitng the labor successes of Hitler's first year in office, and with everyone's help, the unemployment problems will be won in the Pfalz area during his second year.

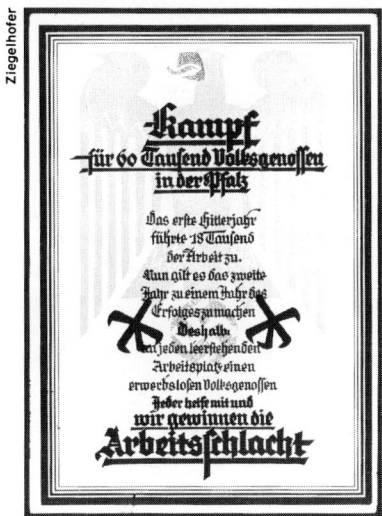

□ 1934, 7-12 Feb.—Berchtesgaden, commemorating the German and Army Ski Championships.

☐ 1934, 14, 16 & 17 Feb.—Announcing a mid-term party by university students.

☐ 1934, 24-25 Feb.—Commemorating Gau Day in Mecklenburg-Lübeck and the swearing-in of Political Leaders.

☐ 1934, 24-25 Feb.—Gau Baden, commemorating the 14th Annual Party Foundation day.

☐ 1934, March—Fund-raising card for the 1933/34 Winterhilfswerk programs. This coat-of-arms made from 18,000 sponsored nails raised RM 12,500 for the WHW. Publ.: Ehler & Hander, Hannover.

196

☐ 1934, 3-18 March—Hannover, commemorating the German Aviation Exhibition.

Pechy

☐ 1934, 8-18 March—Berlin, commemorating the International Automobile and Motorcycle Exhibition.

Ziegelhofer

☐ —As above.

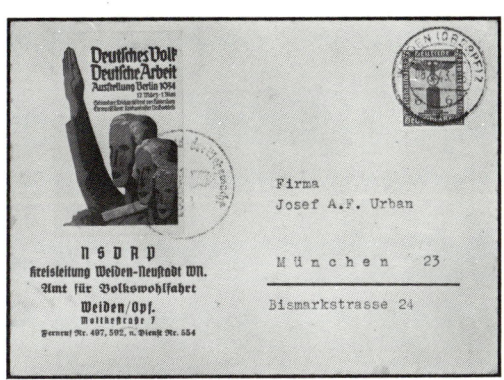

☐ 1934, 17 March-1 May—Berlin, commemorating the German People/German labor exhibition. Consists of an exhibition sticker mounted on an NSDAP postcard for Kreisleitung Weiden-Neustadt.

□ 1934, 24-25 March—Dresden, commemorating the meeting of the SA from Saxony.

□ 1934, 8 April—Berlin, commemorating the "Germanoposta" exhibition of postal items of the Teutonic States. 3Pf. (brown) and 5 Pf. (green).

Ⓢ Berlin W62/Germanoposta.

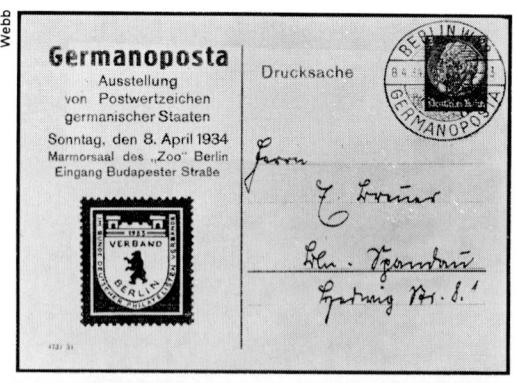

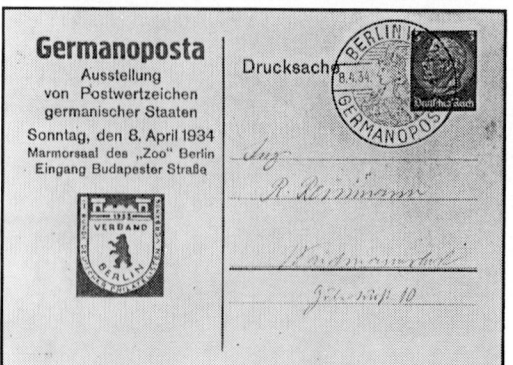

☐ 1934, 8 April—Hamburg, commemorating the meeting of the Hitler Youth. Publ.: Lichtbildwerkstatte "Niedersachsen," Hamburg.

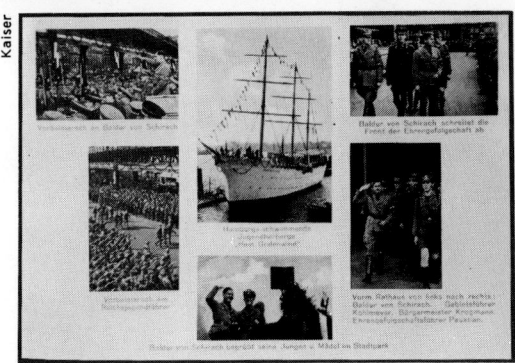

☐ 1934, April—Hemau, a contribution receipt for funds collected to build a memorial for M. Faust, killed during the 9 November 1923 attempted Putsch.

☐ 1934, April—Saarbrücken, fund-raising card commemorating the VDA convention.

Ziegelhofer

☐ 1934, 21-22 April—Munich, commemorating the 1st Bavarian Farmers' day.

☐ 1934, 21 April-3 June—Berlin, commemorating the German People/German Work exhibition.

☐ 1934, 28-30 April—Neumark SA commemorating the 10th anniversary of the NSDAP.

☐ 1934, 30 April—Commemorating the Day of National Labor, 1 May 1934. 6 Pf. (brown).

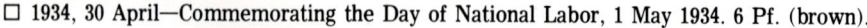

Valid until 31 Dec. 1935.

☐ 1934, May-Sept.—Oberammergau, commemorating the 300th year of the Passion Play.

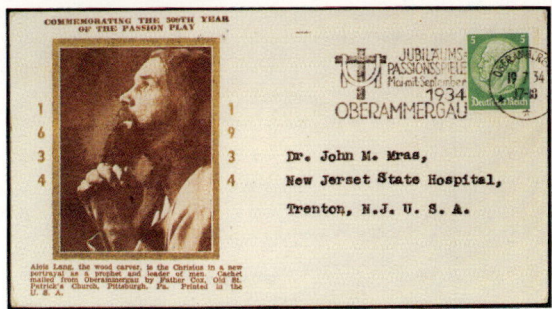

☐ 1934, 1 May—Official postcard commemorating May Day, the day of national labor. Publ.: Zentralverlag der NSDAP Frz. Eher, München.

☐ 1934, 1 May—Commemorating the Day of Labor. Publ.: Photo-Hoffmann, München.

☐ 1934, 1 May—Postcard commemorating May Day, 1934, the day of labor. A copper-foil medallion is on the front.

☐ 1934, 1 May—Königsberg, commemorating the Day of National Labor (May Day).

☐ 1934, 29 May-3 June—Erfurt, commemorating the 1st Agricultural Producers Exhibit at the Reichsbahn building.

☐ 1934, 27 May-3 June—Dresden, commemorating the 1st National Theater Week.

☐ 1934, 29 May-3 June—"We invite you to the 1st National Agricultural Producers' Exhibition in Erfurt."

☐ 1934—Commemorating the finishing of studies at the Kempten non-classical secondary school.

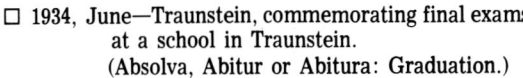

☐ 1934, June—Traunstein, commemorating final exams at a school in Traunstein.
  (Absolva, Abitur or Abitura: Graduation.)

□ 1934, 9-10 June—Commemorating the march of NSKK-Brigade 43 to Meiningen.

□ 1934, 9-11 June—Dresden, commemorating the 125th anniversary of the "Black Brigade."

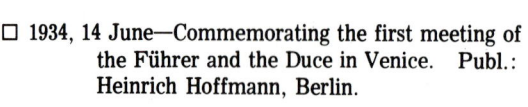

□ 1934, 9-24 June—Bremen, commemorating the Brown Hansa Fair, which featured products and commerce from Northwestern Germany.

□ 1934, 14 June—Commemorating the first meeting of the Führer and the Duce in Venice. Publ.: Heinrich Hoffmann, Berlin.

□

Nr. I1.

Ziegelhofer

□ 1934, 14 June—Commemorating the first meeting
of the Führer and the Duce in Venice.
Publ.: R. Schlothauer, Leipzig.

□ 1934, 16-17 June—Gera, commemorating the district Party day in Gera (Thuringia). Publ.:
J. Sommermann, Gera. "Swear on the fiery alter to be true."

J. Rawlings

Ziegelhofer

☐ 1934, 20-21 June—Commemorating the SA meeting at Heidelberg. Publ.: Druckerei Winter, Heidelberg.

Mesturini

☐ 1934, 21 June—Celebrating the summer solstice. Publ.: Max Hartmann, München.

☐ 1934, 23-24 June—Frankfurt/O., commemorating the Hitler Youth district meeting.

Ziegelhofer

☐ 1934, 23-30 June—Regensburg, commemorating the Hitler Youth craft show. Publ.: Oberpfalz-Verlag, Kallmünz.

□ 1934, 1 July-2 Sept.—Cologne, commemorating the German Colonial Exhibition.

□ 1934, 6-8 July—Munich, commemorating the 4th anniversary of Weapons Day/reunion of the cavalry.

Ziegelhofer

□ 1934, 7 July—"The Saar is German." Part of the propaganda campaign to return the Saar to Germany.

☐ 1934, 7-9 July—Kassel, official postcard commemorating the 5th German War Veterans Day, 1934.

Note: This card is overprinted on its obverse with "6.-8. Juli 1935," in red, indicating it was an excess card which was used the following year.

☐ 1934, 7-9 July—Kassel, commemorating the 5th German War Veterans' Day, 1934.

Note: This card is overprinted on its reverse with "Verlegt auf den 6.-8. Juli 1935," indicating it was an excess card which was used the following year.

☐ 1934, 7-9 July—Commemorating the 5th National Veterans' Day in Kassel.

□ 1934, 14-15 July—Weimar, commemorating German Pharmacist Day.

□ 1934, 20-22 July—Commemorating the 18th Bavarian Gymnastic Trials (20-22 July) and the National Competition (23-29 July) in Nuremberg. Publ.: Zerreiss & Co., Nürnberg. Designed by H. Kannegiesser.

☐ 1934, 20-22 July—Festive card for the 18th Bavarian National Gymnastic Competition in Nuremberg. This serial numbered card was issued to participants and allowed them entry to all events plus free restive insignia and booklets.

Ziegelhofer

feftkarte
18.Bayerisches
Landesturnfest
NÜRNBERG
20.-22.HEUETS 1934

Kaiser

☐ 1934, 20-22 July—Commemorating the 18th Bavarian Sports Festival in Nürnberg.

Der Festzug in
der Königstrasse

☐ 1934, 23-29 July—Nürnberg, official postcard commemorating the military tournament of the Reichsheer.

Pechy

Deutsche
Kampfspiele
Nürnberg
1934

☐ 1934, 23-29 July—Nürnberg, commemorating the German military tournament held at Nürnberg. Publ.: W. Tümmels Buchdruckerei, Nürnberg.

☐ 1934, 23-29 July—Nürnberg, official postcard commemorating the German Sports Competitions. Publ.: W. Tümmels Buchdruckerei, Nürnberg.

☐ 1934, August—President von Hindenburg's final resting place.

☐ 1934, 2 Aug.—Commemorating the death of Reich President v. Hindenburg. He is shown shaking hands with Hitler on 30 January 1933.

☐ 1934, 2 Aug.—Commemorating the death of Reich President Paul von Hindenburg. Publ.: Heinrich Hoffmann Verlag, national sozialistischer Bilder, Berlin.

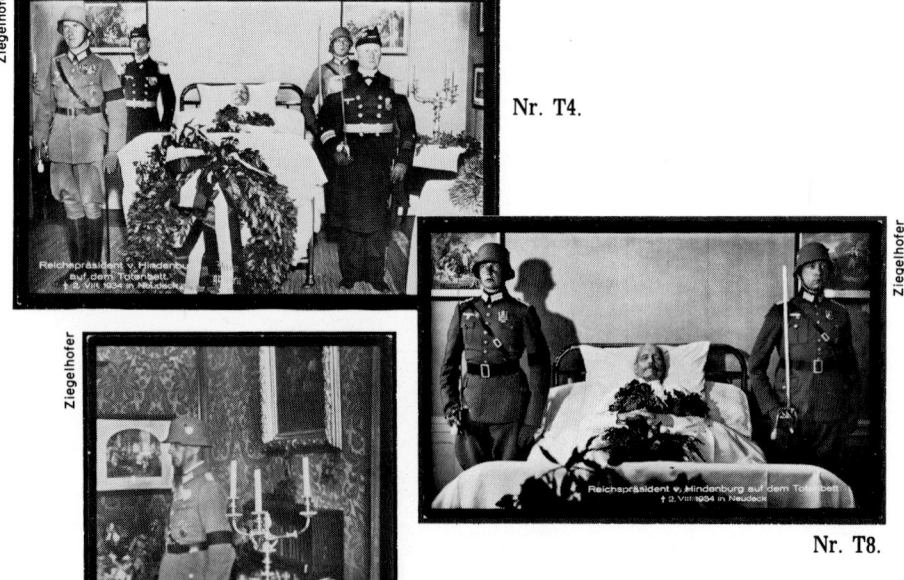

Nr. T4.

Nr. T8.

Note:
There appears to be a total of 17 cards in this "Death ("Tod") of von Hindenburg" series, several of which are illustrated.

Nr. T11.

Nr. T16.

Nr. T17.

Check-off list for the von Hindenburg
death series.

☐ Nr. T1   ☐ Nr. T7   ☐ Nr. T13
☐ Nr. T2   ☐ Nr. T8   ☐ Nr. T14
☐ Nr. T3   ☐ Nr. T9   ☐ Nr. T15
☐ Nr. T4   ☐ Nr. T10   ☐ Nr. T16
☐ Nr. T5   ☐ Nr. T11   ☐ Nr. T17
☐ Nr. T6   ☐ Nr. T12

☐ 1934, 3-5 Aug.—Frankfurt/M., commemorating the
   National Socialist Teachers Association
   Convention.

213

□ 1934, 10-19 Aug.—Leipzig, commemorating the World Championship Bicycle Races.

□ 1934, 11-26 Aug.—Amberg, commemorating the 900th anniversary of that city's founding.

□ 1934, 19-21 Aug.—Munich, commemorating the 1st area meeting of the Hitler Youth from Gebiet "Hochland."

 □

 □

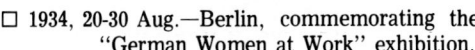

☐ 1934, 19-22 Aug.—Königsberg, commemorating the 22nd Eastern Fair, featuring technical, hand-made and agricultural products.

☐ 1934, 20-30 Aug.—Berlin, commemorating the "German Women at Work" exhibition.

☐ 1934, 26 August—Demonstration of Solidarity with the Saar, Koblenz-Ehrenbreitstein.

☐ 1934, 1 Sept.—Commemorating the 1934 Reichsparteitag. 5 Pf. (dark brown). Official Issue.
Ⓢ "Nürnberg/Reichsparteitag der NSDAP in Nürnberg."

Valid until
31 Dec. 1935.

Note this card was shipped by the airship "Graf Zeppelin" on 27 September 1934.

Larry Smith

□ 1934, 4 Sept.—Commemorating the Death of Paul von Hindenburg. 5 Pf. (light green) and 6 Pf. (greyish-green). Both are available on beige and cream colored stock.

Valid until 31 Dec. 1935.

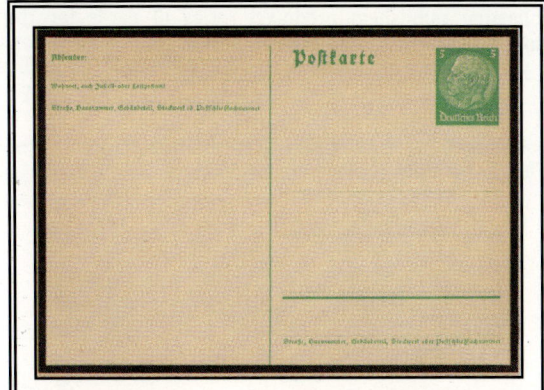

□ Beige, 5 Pf.   □ Beige, 6 Pf.
□ Cream, 5 Pf.   □ Cream, 6 Pf.

□ 1934, 5-10 Sept.—Official 1934 Reichsparteitage postcard (Publ.: Verlag Franz Eher, München). Designed by Richard Klein.

□ 1934, 5-10 Sep.—Official 1934 Reichsparteitage postcard (Publ.: Verlag Franz Eher, München). Designed by Siegmar von Suchodolski.

The following publishers produced series of cards for the 1934 Reichsparteitage. Illustrated are samples of prominent series to acquaint you with the style and design of the various publishers.

☐ 1934. 5-10 Sept.—Commemorating the 1934 Reichsparteitage. Publ.: Photo-Hoffmann, Nr. P. 21. This Party rally series contains 24 cards.

☐ 1934, 5-10 Sept.—Commemorating the 1934 Reichsparteitage. Publ.: Bruno Panzer, Nürnberg.

☐ 1934, 5-10 Sept.—Commemorating the 1934 Reichsparteitage. Publ.: W. Serz, Nürnberg.

☐ 1934, 5-10 Sept.—Commemorating the 1934 Reichsparteitage. (Publ.: Verlag Wilhelm Serz, Nürnberg).

□ 1934, 5-10 Sept.—Commemorating the 1934 Reichsparteitage. Publ.: Sturmer Verlag, Nürnberg.

□ 1934, 4-10 Sept.—Commemorating the 1934 Reichsparteitage. Publ.: Paul F. Weber, Leipzig.

Note: All 1934 Willmy cards have a red cachet on the reverse.

□ 1934, 5-10 Sept.—Commemorating the 1934 Reichsparteitage. Publ.: Verlag F. Willmy. Nürnberg. Note red imprinted rally motive on reverse.

J. Rawlings

Mesturini

J. Rawlings

J. Rawlings

J. Rawlings

J. Rawlings

DER FÜHRER UND STABSCHEF LUTZE NEHMEN DEN VORBEIMARSCH AB

EINZUG DER BLUTFAHNE

SA-FAHNEN AN DER SEBALDUSKIRCHE

DER FÜHRER SPRICHT ZUR SA.U.SS.

VORBEIMARSCH DER SA.u.SS.

DER APPELL DER POLITISCHEN LEITER

DER FÜHRER BEI DER TOTENEHRUNG

J. Rawlings

BLICK AUF DIE EHRENTRIBÜNE

TEILANSICHT DER EHRENTRIBÜNE

☐ 1934, 5-10 Sept.—Commemorating
the 1934 Reichsparteitage.

Capparelli

Reichsparteitag
der N·S·D·A·P·
Nürnberg
5-10. September
1934

DIE FAHNE HOCH / DIE REIHEN DICHT GESCHLOSSEN!

☐ 1934, 5-10 Sept.—Commemorating
the 1934 Reichsparteitage.

☐ 1934, 9 Sept.—Soest, commemorating the Great Rally of the German Labor Front.

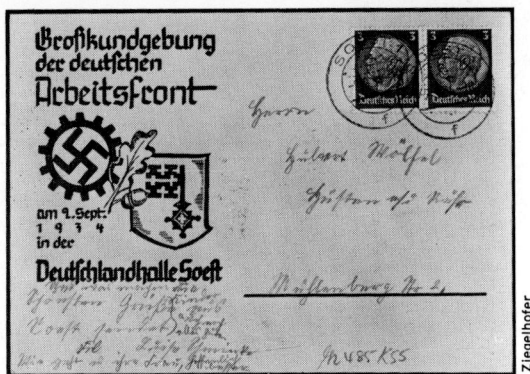

☐ 1934, 30 Sept.—Commemorating the Harvest Thanksgiving Festival at Bückeberg. Publ.: Verlag Paul F. Weber, Leipzig.

☐ 1934, 30 Sept.—Munich, commemorating that city's October Fest.

☐ 1934, Oct.—Munich, fund-raising card for the 1934/1935 WHW programs.

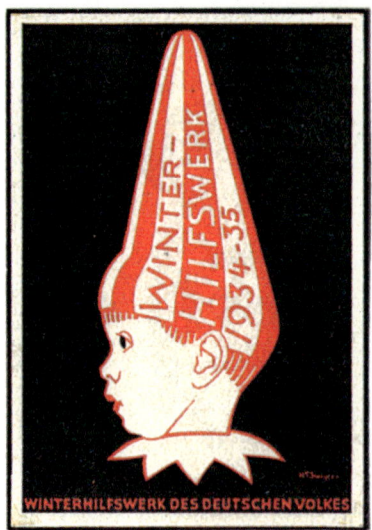

☐ 1934, Oct.—Fund-raising drive of the Schornstein-feger (chimney-sweepers) to assist the WHW programs.

Kaiser

☐ 1934, 1 Oct.—Commemorating the Harvest Thanksgiving Festival. Publ.: H. Drögehopp, Berlin.

Ziegelhofer

☐ 1934, 4-7 Oct.—Saxony, commemorating the meeting of the "Old Fighters."

☐ 1934, Oct.—Fund-raising card for the 1934/1935 WHW programs. "Help fight against hunger and cold." Designed by Ludwig Hohlwein.

☐ 1934, 7 Oct.—Commemorating the dedication of the memorial of fallen sons from the city of Burg. Publ.: Foto u. Verlag Fritz Schmidt, Burg b.M.

Gogolinski

☐ 1934, 12-14 Oct.—Köln, commemorating the Gau Party convention (Gau Köln-Aachen).

☐ 1934, 12-13 Oct.—Munich, commemorating the Gau level convention of German lawyers.

225

☐ 1934, 14 Oct.—Chemnitz, commemorating the 1st War Casualty Day. Publ.: Lauschke & Thiele, Leipzig.

☐ 1934, 5 Nov.—Special card for the German Emergency Service. 6 & 4 Pf. (green).

Valid until 31 Dec. 1935.

☐ 1934, 8 Nov.—Commemorating the 1st anniversary of the start of the national Autobahn.

☐ 1934, 9 Nov.—Austrian Party members honor the 13 heroes who died during the 1934 Putsch against the Austrian government of Dolfuss.

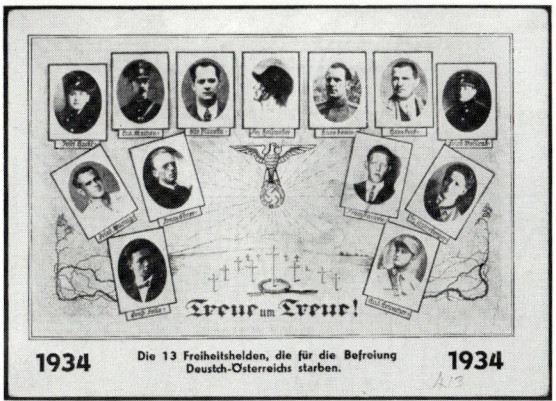

☐ 1934, Dec.—Fund-raising card issued by the Office for Social Welfare, Gau Hamburg.

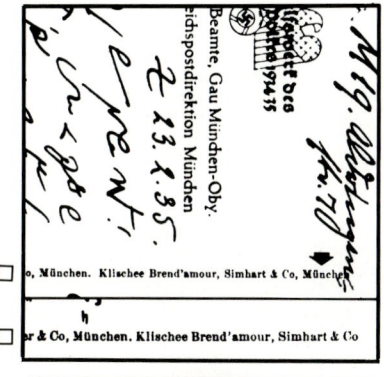

Note: Two printings exist - with and without "München" on the credit line (see upper right).

☐ 1934, 18-23 Dec.—Fund-raising card for the Winterhilfswerk (WHW), Gau Munich, 1934/-1935 3 Pf. (brown).

☐ 1934, 29 Dec.—Fund-raising card series for the Winterhilfswerk (WHW lottery (1934/35)). 6 Pf. (dark green). The series consists of 199 different photo cards depicting various locations in Germany.

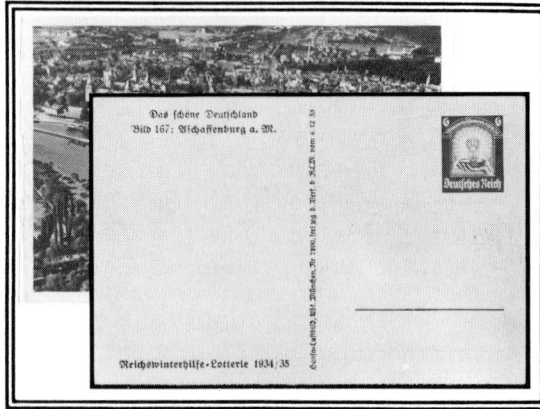

Valid until 31 Dec. 1935.

A double picture postcard was enclosed with each lottery ticket purchased, on which only one of the cards had an imprinted stamp. These double cards were not permitted for postal use, but some did, however, make it through the postal system and are more desireable. The following numbered postcards have imprinted stamps.

☐ 1 Potsdam, Stadtschloss
☐ 2 Roland und Kurfürstenhaus/in Brandenburg
☐ 4 Niedersächsisches Bauernhaus
☐ 5 Lüneburger Heide bei Wilsede
☐ 9 Marienburg, Ordensschloss
☐ 12 Quedlinburg, Schloss- und Stiftskirche
☐ 13 Braunschweig, alte Waage
☐ 14 Hildesheim/Knochenhauer Amtshaus
☐ 15 Paderborn, Rathaus
☐ 16 Marburg
☐ 17 Veste Coburg
☐ 18 Nürnberg, Dürer-Haus
☐ 19 Rothenburg o. Tauber, Markustor
☐ 20 Bayrischer Wald
☐ 21 München, Frauenkirche

☐ 22 Kloster Ettal
☐ 23 Danzig, Marienkirche
☐ 24 Tannenberg-Denkmal
☐ 26 Schloss Sigmaringen
☐ 27 Leipzig, Völkerschlachtdenkmal
☐ 28 Schloss Linderhof
☐ 29 Alpspitze
☐ 30 Rindalphorn (Allgäu)
☐ 32 Brieg, Piastenschloss
☐ 34 Kirche in Göhren, Rügen
☐ 35 Frankfurt a. Main., Römerhöfchen
☐ 39 Erfurt, Augustiner-Kloster
☐ 40 Detmold, Schloss
☐ 41 Der Harkortsee (Ruhr)
☐ 44 Die Loreley

Mesturini

An example of a double card; (left) Nr. 160 Zugspitze, and (right) Nr. 142 Neu-Leiningen bei Grünstadt (Rupf.).

Note: Of the 199 numbered cards, 84 are without an imprinted stamp. Additionally, 30 cards exist with and without an imprinted stamp.

Nr. 132 Landsberg am Lech, Bayerntor.

☐ 1934, 29 Dec.-March 1935—"Beautiful Germany" picture double card series of 102 different numbers. Privately produced for the 1934/35 WHW lottery. 3 Pf. (brown).

☐ 1 Sylt/Strand (Nr. 7)
☐ 2 Paderborn (Nr. 15)
☐ 3 München, Frauenkirche (Nr. 21)
☐ 4 Schloss Linderhof (Nr. 28)
☐ 5 Magdeburg, Domhauptportal (Nr. 45)
☐ 6 Beilstein, Zehnthaus (Nr. 59)
☐ 7 Wolfachtal (Nr. 65)
☐ 8 Schloss Egg bei Metten (Ndby.) (Nr. 66)
☐ 9 Sächs. Schweiz, Basteibrücke (Nr. 75)
☐ 10 Burg Eltz (Nr. 76)
☐ 11 Bad Ems (Nr. 109)
☐ 12 Ostseebad Warnemünde, Hafen (Nr. 110)
☐ 13 Engen im Hegau m. Hohenhöwen (Nr. 111)
☐ 14 Potsdam, Marmorpalais am heiligen See (Nr. 112)
☐ 15 Bolkenhain mit Bolkeburg (Ndsch.) (Nr. 113)
☐ 16 Poppelsdorfer Schloss (Nr. 114)
☐ 17 Dinkelsbühl (Nr. 115)
☐ 18 Berneck im Schwarzwald (Nr. 116)
☐ 19 Burg Runkel, Lahnstein (Nr. 117)
☐ 20 Monreal in der Eifel (Nr. 118)
☐ 21 Saarburg und die Burg Brz. Trier (Nr. 119)
☐ 22 Harburg a.d. Wörnitz (Nr. 120)
☐ 23 Die Trifels-Burgengruppe bei Annweiler (Nr. 121)
☐ 24 Kreuzeck bei Garmisch, Wettersteinwand (Nr. 122)
☐ 25 Stralsund (Nr. 123)
☐ 26 Trier, Römische Kaiserthermen (Nr. 124)
☐ 27 Klosterruine Limburg bei Bad Dürkheim (Nr. 125)
☐ 28 Schloss Hellenstein, Schwäb. Alb (nr. 126)
☐ 29 Bernsteinbergwerk Palmnicken (Nr. 127)
☐ 30 Rothenburg o.T., Burgtor (Nr. 128)
☐ 31 Balingen, Am Zollernschloss (Nr. 129)

☐ 32 Aachen, Münster (Nr. 130)
☐ 33 München, Mahnmal in der Feldherrnhalle (Nr. 131)
☐ 34 Landsberg am Lech, Bayerntor (Nr. 132)
☐ 35 Insel Reichenau im Bodensee, Münster (Nr. 133)
☐ 36 Abend im Spreewald (Nr. 134)
☐ 37 Ruine Trifels bei Annweiler (Nr. 135)
☐ 38 Kynsburg überm Schlesiertal im Eulengebirge (Nr. 136)
☐ 39 Schneekoppe überm grossen Teich (Nr. 137)
☐ 40 Tübingen (Nr. 138)
☐ 41 Lindau im Bodensee, der alte Leuchtturm (Nr. 139)
☐ 42 Der Rhein bei Speyer (Nr. 140)
☐ 43 Das historische Hambacher Schloss bei Neustadt a. Hadt. (Nr. 141)
☐ 44 Neu-Leiningen bei Grünstadt (Rhpf.) (Nr. 142)
☐ 45 Leuchtenburg b. Kahla a. Saale (Nr. 143)
☐ 46 Wernigerode, Harz (Nr. 144)
☐ 47 Zeitz a. Elster, Moritzburg (Nr. 145)
☐ 48 Altenburg (Thür.), Schloss (Nr. 146)
☐ 49 Rudolstadt a. Saale (Nr. 147)
☐ 50 Wittenberg a. Elbe, Schlosskirche (Nr. 148)
☐ 51 Berlin, Brandenburger Tor (Nr. 149)
☐ 52 Goslar, Kaiserpfalz (Nr. 150)
☐ 53 Hitzacker a. Elbe (Nr. 151)
☐ 54 Quedlinburg, Dom (Nr. 152)
☐ 55 Schloss Ettersburg b. Weimar (Nr. 153)
☐ 56 Nürnberg, 5. Reichsparteitag (Nr. 154)
☐ 57 Kyffhäuser-Denkmal (Nr. 155)
☐ 58 Weimar, Schloss (Nr. 156)
☐ 59 Wachsenburg b. Arnstadt (Thür.) (Nr. 157)
☐ 60 Halberstadt (Nr. 158)
☐ 61 Hameln a. Weser (Nr. 159)

☐ 1934—Artist-relief postcard featuring a foil medallion of Horst Wessel and the words of the "Horst-Wessel-Lied" (Die Fahne hoch). Publ.: Kunstler-Reliefkarte D.R.G.M.

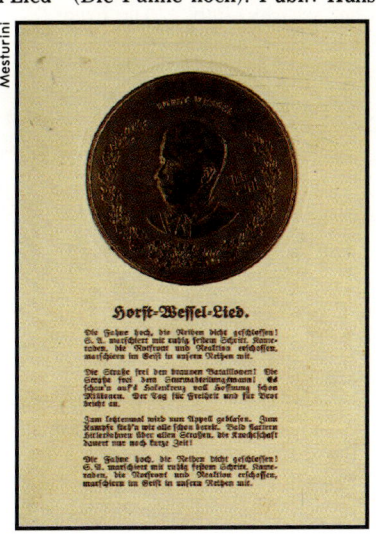

☐ 1934—Commemorating "The Front" exhibition. Card stresses the fact that 3800 heavy pieces of artillery are pointed at Germany while Germany is allowed no heavy artillery at all.

☐ 1934,—English-language propaganda card depicting how the one-sided disarmament of Germany affects her security. Publ.: "Die Front."

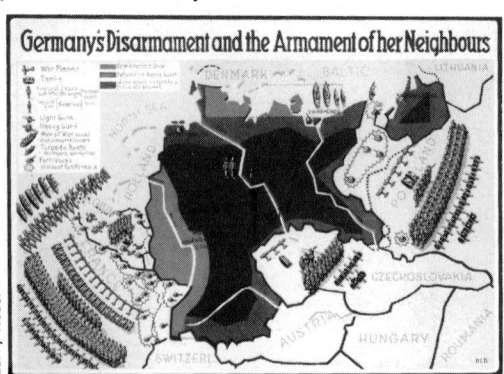

Cards also known to exist in the following languages:
- ☐ German
- ☐ French
- ☐ Spanish
- ☐ Dutch

Exact date of issuance not known on the following cards.

☐ 1934—Commemerating the 20th German shooting competition at Leipzig.

1935

☐ 1935, Jan.—The determination of the people of the Saar: Return to the Reich! Issued to bring attention to the upcoming vote of returning the Saar to Germany (13 January 1935). Publ.: Gebr. Hofer A.-G., Saarbrücken.

Catella

Des Saarvolks Wille:
Zurück zum Reich!

SAARLAND

☐ 1935, Jan.—Issued to bring attention to the upcoming vote on 13 January 1935 for the return of the Saar to Germany. "Hands off the German Saar!"

☐ 1935, Jan.—Issued to bring attention to the upcoming vote on 13 January 1935 for the return of the Saar to Germany.

☐ 1935, Jan.—Remember the upcoming vote on 13 January 1935 for the return of the Saar to Germany. The poem outlines the criminality of the Versailles Treaty.

☐ 1935, Jan.—The Saar Vote in 1935. Issued to bring attention to the upcoming vote on 13 January 1935 for the return of the Saar to Germany.

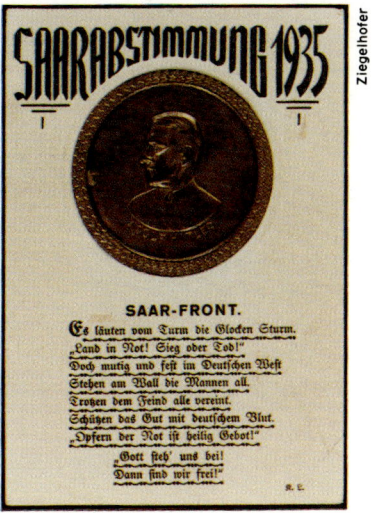

☐ 1935, 13 Jan.—Commemorating the people's vote to return the Saar to Germany.

1935, Jan.— Sarcastic "Obituary Notice" listing the political parties that will die if the 13 January 1935 vote results in the return of the Saar to Germany (i.e., Sep...tists, Socialists, etc.).

☐

☐

Note: Published by the NSDAP office of Commissioner Bürckel after the vote results had been released.

□ 1935, 13 Jan.—Commemorating the people's vote to return the Saar to Germany. "We died for you! And you will betray us?" Publ.: Gebr. Hofer Ag., Saarbrücken.

□ 1935, 13 Jan.—Commemorating the people's vote to return the Saar to Germany. "We died for you! And you?" Publ.: F. Maas & Sohn AG, Saarbrücken. This card has the special red wax commission seal on the reverse.

☐ 1935, 13 Jan.—Commemorating the people's vote deciding if the Saar should be returned to Germany. Publ.: Ferd. Bayer, Wiesbaden.

☐ 1935, 13 Jan.—"German Greetings." Saarbrücken, commemorating the return of the Saar to Germany.

☐ 1935, 13 Jan.—Commemorating the return of the Saar to Germany.

☐ 1935, 13 Jan.—Commemorating the return of the Saar to Germany. "The day of our freedom has come"

☐ 1935, 13 Jan.—Commemorating the return of the Saar to Germany. The walls of oppression (symbolizing the border of Germany) are depicted being torn down.

☐ 1935, 13 Jan.—"The Saar is German and free!"

Note Voting Commission wax seal and national colors ribbon.

☐ 1935, 13 Jan.—Commemorating the people's vote deciding if the Saar should be returned to Germany. "The Saar is free." Publ.: Th. Klein, Saarbrücken. Card comes in two forms: one with stamps in full color and the other in black and white.

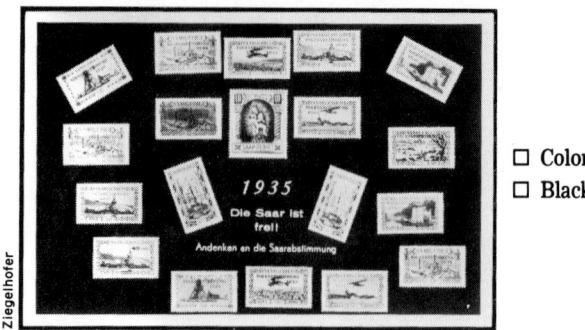

☐ Color
☐ Black/white

☐ 1935, 13 Jan.—Commemorating the return of the Saar to Germany. The stamps of the Saar from 1918-1935 are depicted. Publ.: Verlag von Emil Hartmann, Mannheim.

☐ 1935, 13 Jan.—Commemorating the return of the Saar to Germany.

240

Ziegelhofer

SAARABSTIMMUNG 1935

☐ 1935, 13 Jan.—Commemorating the vote to return the Saar to Germany. "The Saar is always German."

☐ 1935, 13 Jan.—Commemorating the liberation of the Saar.

☐ 1935, 13 Jan.—Commemorating the people's vote to return the Saar to Germany. "Return to the Fatherland." Publ.: Verlag Bernt Zander, Saarbrücken.

Ziegelhofer

☐ 1935, 13 Jan.—Commemorating the people's vote for the return of the Saar to Germany. Publ.: Verlag F. Stahl, Saarbrücken.

Ziegelhofer

□ 1935, 13 Jan.—"The Saar is forever German!" Publ.: Bund der Saarvereine, "Geschäftsstelle" Saar-Verein.

□ 1935, 13 Jan.—Commemorating the people's vote to return the Saar to the German Reich. Publ.: Germann Sonntag & Co., München.

□ 1935, 13 Jan.—Saarbrücken, commemorating the freeing of the Saar through the people's vote. Publ.: Th. Klein, Saarbrücken.

Die Saar ist frei! Saarbrücken, 13. Januar 1935

☐ 1935, 16 Jan.—Commemorating the return of the Saar to Germany at Saarbrücken (Publ.: Verlag Th. Klein, Saarbrücken).

Mesturini

☐ 1935, 16 Jan.—Saarbrücken, commemorating the return of the Saar to Germany.

Ziegelhofer

Saarbrücken. Rathaus u. Sparkasse in Festbeleuchtung

☐ 1935, 16 Jan.—Saarbrücken, commemorating the return of the Saar to Germany.

☐ 1935, 16 Jan.—Fund-raising card for the Winterhilfswerk (1934/35) commemorating the return of the Saar to Germany. "The Saar is free!" Issued in Gau Westfalen-Nord.

Frei ist die Saar!

☐ 1935, 16 Jan.—Fund-raising card for the Saar Winterhilfswerk (1934/35) and to commemorate the return of the Saar to Germany. Publ.: Heist & Unger, Homberg-Saar.

John D. Griffin

☐ 1935, 16, Jan.—"The Saar is German forever."

☐ 1935, 16 Jan.—Saarbrücken, the D.K.O.V. (German War Casualty Assistance Organization) of the Saar commemorating the return of the Saar to Germany. Publ.: Gebr. Hofer A.-G., Saarbrücken.

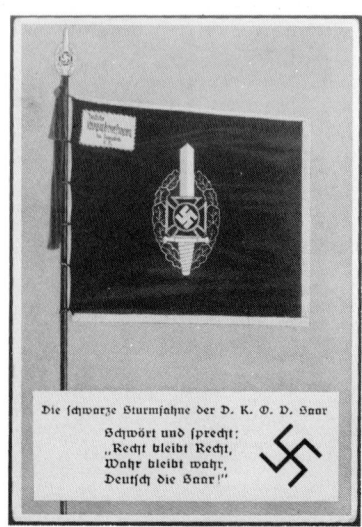

☐ 1935, 8 Feb.-20 March—Berlin, commemorating the Olympic Exhibition.

☐ 1935—Commemorative card honoring Hitler Youth member, Otto Blöcker who was shot on 26 February 1933 in Hamburg by a member of the Red Front.

☐ 1935, 28 Feb.—Sarcastic postcard showing the resting place of the Governing Commission of the Saar area, whose death is attributed to the 13 January 1935 vote.

□ 1935, 1 March—"The Saar is and will remain German." Commemorating the successful 13 January 1935 vote to reunite the Saar with Germany. Publ.: Otto Hoppe Verlag, Berlin. Nr. 36.

Pechy

□ 1935, 1 March—Commemorating the return of the Saar to the Reich.

J. Rawlings

□ 1935, 1 March—Commemorating the freeing of the Saar after 15 years of foreign domination. Publ.: Robert Grub, Saarbrücken.

Mesturini

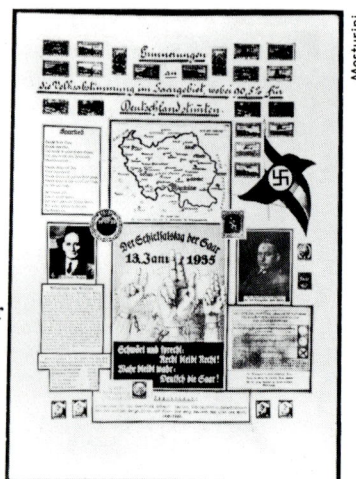

□ 1935, 1 March—Commemorating the vote in the Saar (13.1.35) which was a overwhelming victory (90.5%) to be returned to the Reich.

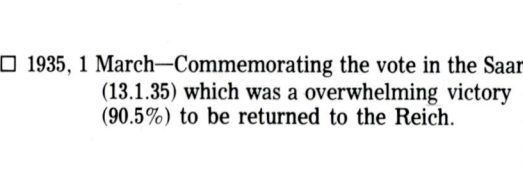

☐ 1935, 1 March—Symbolic representation of the bond between the Saar and the German Reich, a result of the successful 13 January 1935 vote to reunite the Saar with Germany.

☐ 1935, 1 March—Commemorating the successful 13 January 1935 vote to reunify the Saar with Germany.

☐ 1935, 1 March—Commemorating the successful 13 January 1935 vote to reunite the Saar with Germany. "The Saar is free!"

☐ 1935, 1 March—Commemorating the successful 13 January 1935 vote to reunite the Saar with Germany. This is a folded two-part card.

247

□ 1935, 16 March—Military District Command in Amberg commemorating the discarding of the Versailles Treaty, enlargement of the army and the reintroduction of national conscription.

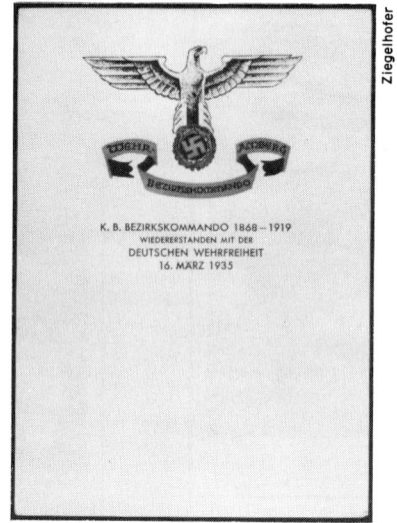

□ 1935, April—The Saar: Home within the Reich at Easter time.

□ 1935, 9 April—Commemorating General Ludendorf's 70th birthday. On this date Hitler gave him the title of "Field Lord" (Feldherr).

☐ 1935, 26-28 April—Frankfurt/M., commemorating the 1st World Exhibition for all Dog Breeders.

☐ 1935, 1 May—Commemorating German May Day.

☐ 1935, 4-10 May—Regensburg, commemorating the 1st Brown Austrian Fair, featuring German week.

Mesturini

☐ 1935, 5 May—Baustein, commemorating the 1st National Mothers convalescent home in Gau Schwabia.

Webb

☐ 1935, 11-19 May—Hannover, commemorating the Postage Stamp Exhibition in that city. 3 Pf. (brown) and 6 Pf. (green).

☐ 1935, 11-12 May—Leipzig, commemorating the 2nd Saxon Field Comerads (Veterans) convention.

☐ 1935, 16-19 May—Breslau, commemorating the 61st Farm Machinery Market/Rural Exhibiton/28th Breeding Cattle Market at the Southeast Exhibition. Publ.: Breslauer Messe- und Ausstellungs-Gesellschaft, Breslau.

☐ 1935, 24-26 May—Dresden, commemorating the 1935 Party meeting in Saxony.

☐ 1935, 26-30 May—Bautzen, official postcard commemorating the festival of Lausitz.

☐ 1935, 1-2 June—Braunschweig, commemorating the 50th anniversary of that city's postage-stamp collectors' club. 3 Pf. (brown) and 6 Pf. (green).

Ⓢ Braunschweig/50 Jahre Verein, etc.

 ☐

 ☐

☐ 1935, June—Neuburg, commemorating graduation day. "Germany must become free."

☐ 1935, 1-2 June—Darmstadt, commemorating the district (Gau) Party Day of the NSDAP.

☐ 1935, 1-2 June—Erfurt, commemorating the district (Gau) Party Day of the NSDAP.

☐ 1935, 1-2 June—Jessnitz, commemorating the district (Kreis) meeting of the NSDAP.

☐ 1935, 1-3 June—Meeting of the German War Blind in Stuttgart. Publ.: Chr. Belser AG, Stuttgart.

☐ 1935, 11-16 June—Kiel, commemorating Navy week. Design by Hugo Fischer, Kiel. Publ.: Kieler Zeitung, Kiel.

Kaiser

☐ 1935, 15-16 June—Frankfurt a/M, commemorating National Handiwork Day. "The whole world is our sphere."

☐ 1935, 15-17 June—Hattingen, Reunion of old Party members at Hattingen, Gau Westfalen-Süd. Commemorating the first visit of Hitler to the Ortsgruppe of Hattingen (Ruhr area) in June 1926.

Angolia

Ziegelhofer

☐ 1935, July-Aug.—Commemorating the world meeting of Hitler Youth members. Design by Ludwig Hohlwein.

☐ 1935, 6-8 July—Kassel, official postcard commemorating the 6th German War Veterans Day. This card was left over from the 1934 conference and overprinted "6.-8. Juli 1935."

Ziegelhofer

Webb

☐ 1935, 13-21 July—Leipzig, commemorating the sports competitions at the Gau Saxony Festival.

☐ 1935, 21-28 July—Karlsruhe, commemorating the high school sports competitions during the Gau festival (Gau 14-Baden).

☐ 1935, 28 July-6 Aug.—Card available to Hitler Youth members of Gebiet 21 Baden, during their encampment near Offenburg.

☐ 1935, 2-4 Aug.—Commemorating district (Gau) day in Essen (also the 10th anniversary of the NSDAP in that district).

☐ 1935, 11 Aug.—Commemorating the Front Soldiers and Wounded Veterans Day in Tübingen. Publ.: Nationalsozialistische Kriegsopfer-Versorgung, Stuttgart.

☐ 1935, 16-19 Aug.—Mainz and Wiesbaden, 41st German Philatelic Day, 12th Mainz Club Day, Postage-Stamp Exhibition in Wiesbaden. 3 Pf. (brown), 5 Pf. (green) and 6 Pf. (dark green).

Ⓢ Mainz/41. Philatelistentag, 12. Bundestag.

Ⓢ Wiesbaden/Briefmarken-Ausstellung.

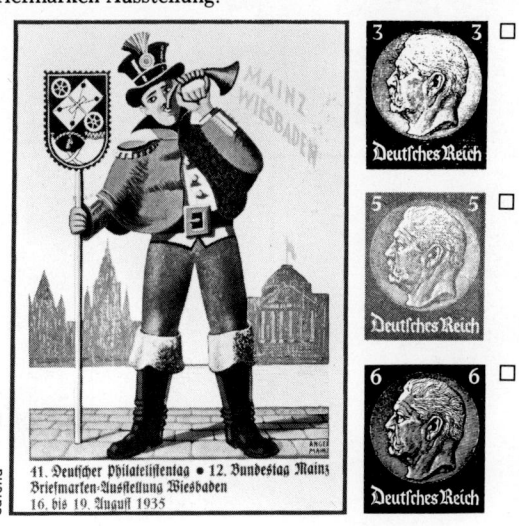

41. Deutscher Philatelistentag • 12. Bundestag Mainz
Briefmarken-Ausstellung Wiesbaden
16. bis 19. August 1935

☐ 1935, 17 Aug.—Wiesbaden, part of a twelve card artist series depicting various parts of Germany. Designed by W. Lenz.

☐ Nr. 1
☐ Nr. 2
☐ Nr. 3
☐ Nr. 4
☐ Nr. 5
☐ Nr. 6
☐ Nr. 7
☐ Nr. 7
☐ Nr. 8
☐ Nr. 9
☐ Nr. 10
☐ Nr. 11
☐ Nr. 12

Nr. 4 Memel, Mole-Leuchtturm

□ 1935, 18-25 Aug.—Commemorating the 1935 Reichenberg Fair.

Mesturini

Kaiser

□ 1935, 18-25 Aug.—Saarbrucken, commemorating the 1st Southwest Gau Festival of the National League of Gymnastics.

□ 1935, 24 Aug.-8 Sept.—Frankfurt/M., commemorating the Great Exhibition of the Rhine-Main Economy.

☐ 1935, 15-17 June—Frankfurt a/M commemorating National Handicraft Day.

Pechy

☐ 1935, 15 June-1 Sept.—Römerberg, commemorating the operatic festival performances for the summer of 1935 (Frankfurt a.M.).

☐ 1935, 22-23 June—Commemorating the 5th anniversary of Weapons Day/reunion of the German cavalry in Hamburg, and the opening phase of "Derby Week" which was part of Hamburg's "People's Festival."

☐ 1935, 23 June-3 July—Königsburg, commemorating the International East European Postal Exhibition. 5 Pf. (light green), and 6 Pf. (green). This version has the telephone number on lower left of card.

Ⓢ Cancellation with exhibition hall.

Ⓢ Cancellation with knight.

Ⓢ Königsberg (Pr)/Ostropa/Postwertz.-Ausstellung (Ordensritter).

Ⓢ Königsburg/Cranz-Rossitten Schiffspost/Ostropa 1935 & 5.

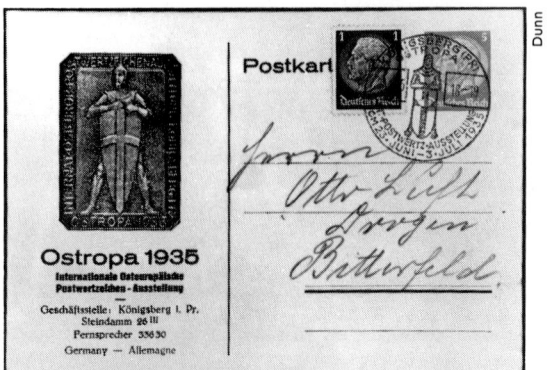

Dunn

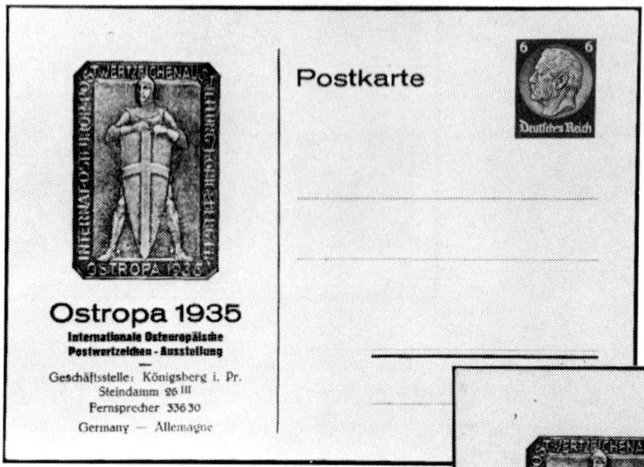

Dunn

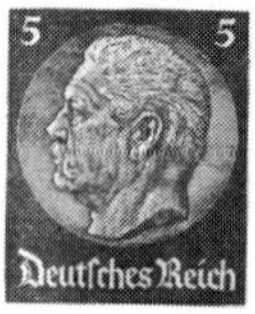

☐

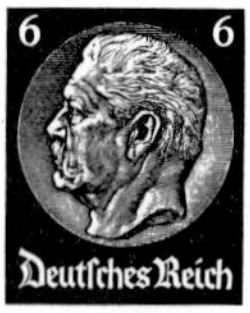

☐

☐ 1935, 23 June-3 July—Königsberg, as above but without the telephone number on lower left of card.

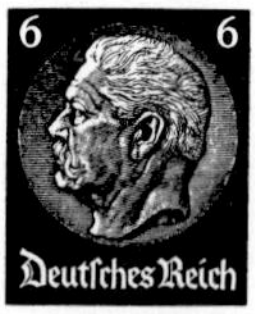

☐

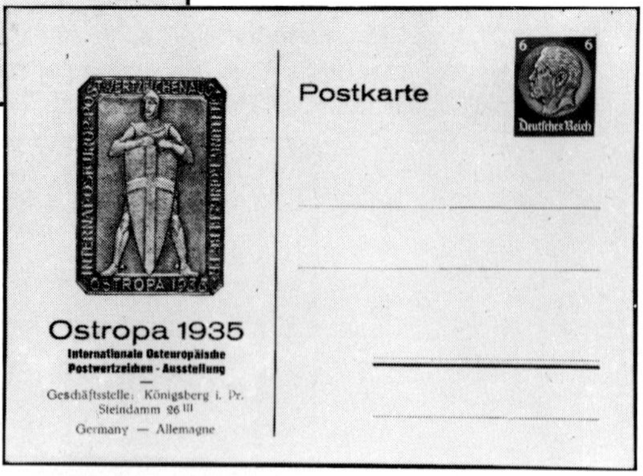

Dunn

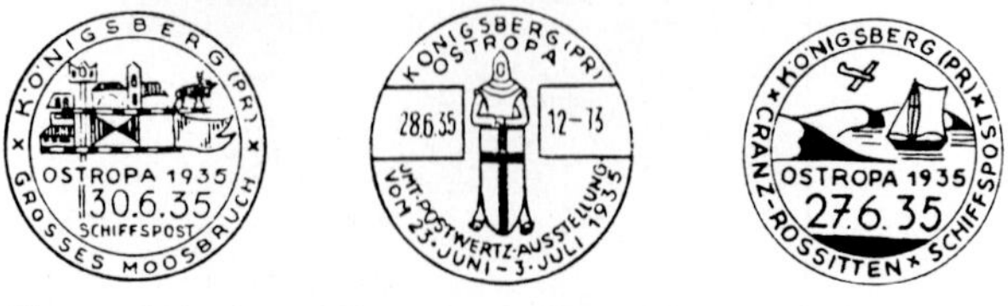

Three of the four different special cancellations for the International East European Postal Exhibition.

☐ 1935, 23 June-3 July—Königsberg, commemorating the International East European Postal Exhibition "Ostropa 1935." 15 Pf. (brown-violet).

☐ 1935, 28-30 June—Leipzig, commemorating the 2nd Saxon Singers Festival.

☐ 1935, 29 June-7 July—Zittau, commemorating the **postage-stamp** exhibition held during festival week. 3 Pf. (brown) and 6 Pf. (green).

Ⓢ Zittau/im grünen Ring/Briefmarkenausstellung.

☐ 1935, 30 June—Kanth, commemorating the riding tournament of military, police and SA riding detachments.

☐ 1935, July—Visit the Nordmark camp of Area (Gebiet) 6 for the Hitler Youth, which offers recreation and training for 20,000 boys.

☐ 1935, 16-19 Aug.—Mainz and Wiesbaden, 41st German Philatelic Day, 12th Mainz Club Day, Postage-Stamp Exhibition in Wiesbaden. 3 Pf. (brown), 5 Pf. (green) and 6 Pf. (dark green).

Ⓢ Mainz/41. Philatelistentag, 12. Bundestag.

Ⓢ Wiesbaden/Briefmarken-Ausstellung.

☐ 1935, 17 Aug.—Wiesbaden, part of a twelve card artist series depicting various parts of Germany. Designed by W. Lenz.

☐ Nr. 1
☐ Nr. 2
☐ Nr. 3
☐ Nr. 4
☐ Nr. 5
☐ Nr. 6
☐ Nr. 7
☐ Nr. 7
☐ Nr. 8
☐ Nr. 9
☐ Nr. 10
☐ Nr. 11
☐ Nr. 12

Nr. 4 Memel, Mole-Leuchtturm

☐ 1935, 18-25 Aug.—Commemorating the 1935 Reichenberg Fair.

Mesturini

Kaiser

☐ 1935, 18-25 Aug.—Saarbrucken, commemorating the 1st Southwest Gau Festival of the National League of Gymnastics.

☐ 1935, 24 Aug.-8 Sept.—Frankfurt/M., commemorating the Great Exhibition of the Rhine-Main Economy.

☐ 1935, 30 Aug.-1 Sept.—Berlin, commemorating the 2nd Postal Exhibition, "Beposta," held in the Berlin zoo building complex. 3 Pf. (brown), 5 Pf. (light green), 6 Pf. (green), 10 Pf. (brown) and 15 Pf. **(brown-violet)**.

Ⓢ Berlin W62/Beposta im Zoo, ect.

☐ 1935, 30 Aug.-1 Sept.—Berlin, commemorating the postal exhibition, "Beposta," held in the Berlin Zoo Building complex. 3 Pf. (brown), 5 Pf. (light green), 6 Pf. (green), 10 Pf. (brown and 15 Pf. (brown-violet).

Ⓢ Berlin W62/Beposta im Zoo. etc.

Ziegelhofer

All are printed in black except for the 3 Pf. versions listed below:

☐ With "Drucksache," black illustration   ☐ Blue illustration
☐ Red illustration   ☐ Brown illustration
☐ Black illustration   ☐ Green illustration

☐ 1935, Sept.-Oct.—Official postcard commemorating the 125th anniversary of the Munich "Oktoberfest" (1810-1935). Publ.: Kunstverlag Andelfinger, München.

☐ 1935, 7-11 Sept.—Munich, commemorating the postal exhibition, "Müpa," with this six-card set. 3 Pf. (brown), 5 Pf. (light green), 6 Pf. (green) and 10 Pf. Luftpost (red) next to 6 Pf. (green).

   ☐ 1. München, Bavaria mit Ruhmeshalle

   ☐ 2. München, Die Frauenkirche

   ☐ 3. München, Hofgarten und Armeemuseum

   ☐ 4. München, Mahnmal in der Feldherrnhalle

   ☐ 5. München, Schloss Nymphenburg

   ☐ 6. München, **Wittelsbacher Brunnen**

   Ⓢ Postwertzeichen-Ausstellung/MÜPA/München.

Nr. 1

264

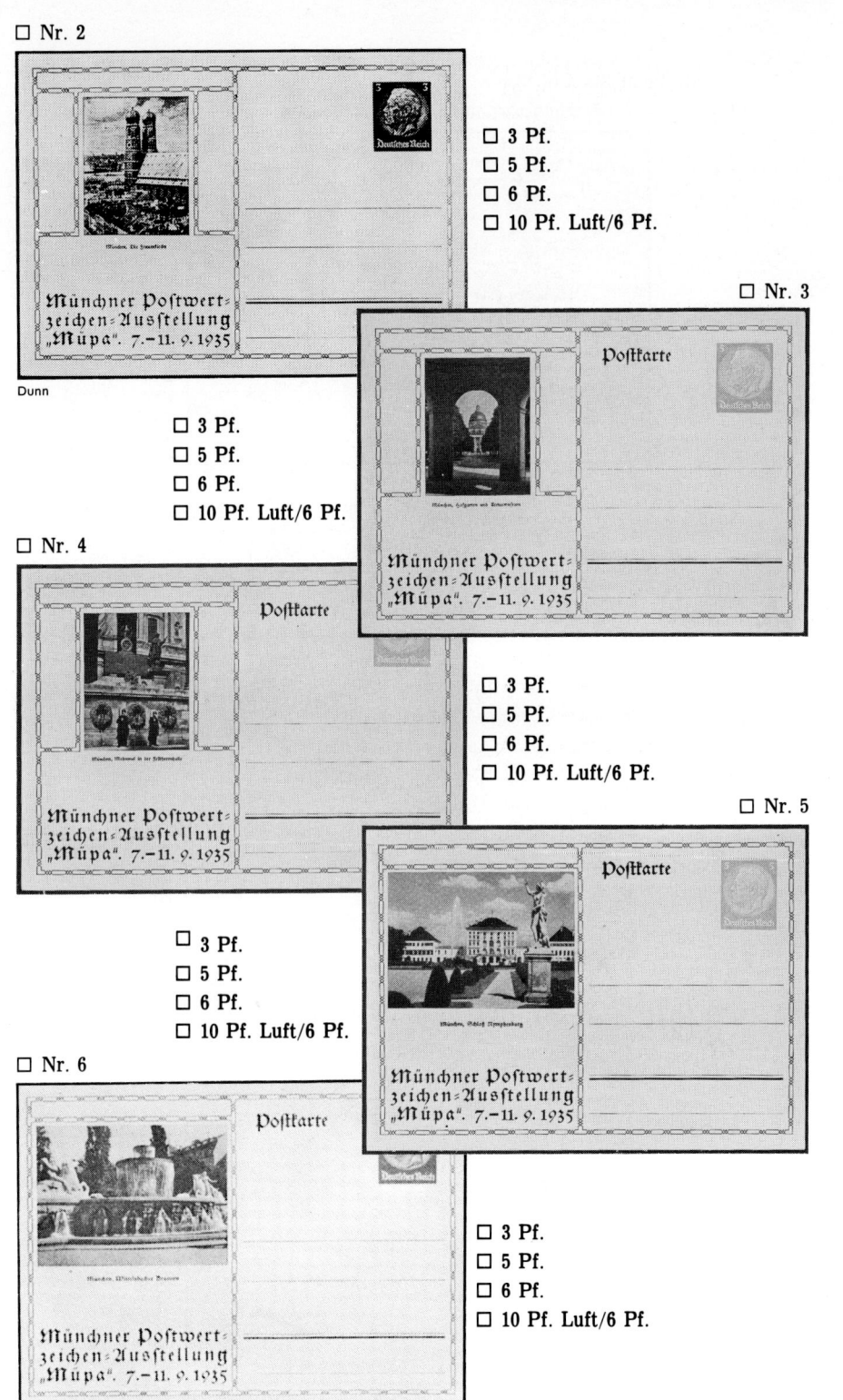

☐ Nr. 2

☐ 3 Pf.
☐ 5 Pf.
☐ 6 Pf.
☐ 10 Pf. Luft/6 Pf.

Dunn

☐ 3 Pf.
☐ 5 Pf.
☐ 6 Pf.
☐ 10 Pf. Luft/6 Pf.

☐ Nr. 3

☐ Nr. 4

☐ 3 Pf.
☐ 5 Pf.
☐ 6 Pf.
☐ 10 Pf. Luft/6 Pf.

☐ 3 Pf.
☐ 5 Pf.
☐ 6 Pf.
☐ 10 Pf. Luft/6 Pf.

☐ Nr. 5

☐ 3 Pf.
☐ 5 Pf.
☐ 6 Pf.
☐ 10 Pf. Luft/6 Pf.

☐ Nr. 6

☐ 3 Pf.
☐ 5 Pf.
☐ 6 Pf.
☐ 10 Pf. Luft/6 Pf.

□ 1935, 7-11 Sept.—As above but photo and border in light brown, reddish brown, or grey, and the addition of "Besucht die."

□ Postwertzeichen-Ausstellung/MÜPA/München.

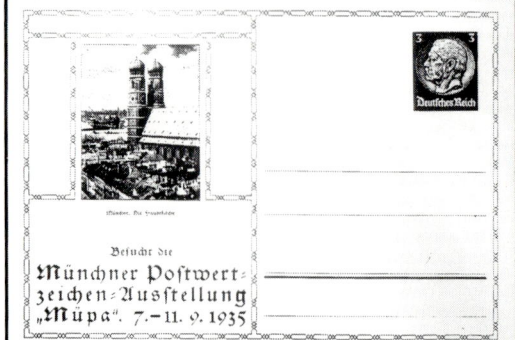

□ light brown
□ Reddish-brown
□ Grey
□ Grey, with triangular symbol for Metzner Verlag.

□ 1935, 7-11 Sept.—Munich, commemorating the postal exhibition, "Müpa." This "Learn to know Germany" card is overprinted with "Münchener Postwertzeichen-Ausstellung "Müpa" 7.-11.9.1935" in red. 6 Pf. (green).

□ 1935, 7-11 Sept.—As above but on a "Visit beautiful Silesia" card.

☐ 1935, 10-16 Sept.—Commemorating the march of the Political Leaders from Gau Saxony to the 1935 Reichsparteitage at Nuremberg.

☐ 1935—Nürnberg, a numbered pass for entry to the 1935 Reich Party Day Congress Hall.

267

□ 1935, 10-16 Sept.—Official 1935 Reichsparteitage postcard (Publ.: Verlag Franz Eher, München). Designed by Richard Klein.

□ 1935, 10-16 Sept.—Official 1935 Reichsparteitag postcard (Publ.: Verlag Franz Eher, München). Designed by Mjölnir.

The Führer speaks to his followers at the 1935 Party rally.

Ziegelhofer

□ 1935, 10-16 Sept.—Postally used during the 1935 Reichsparteitage. Rendering by Hermann Gärtner. Publ.: Hermann Gärtner, Nürnberg.

Crabb

□ 1935, 10-16 Sept.—Commemorating the 1935 Reichsparteitage. Publ.: Anton Hilbert, Kunstverlag, Nürnberg. Technically this card commemorates the city and not the rally.
Note: Part of a ten-card series.

□ 1935, 10-16 Sept.—Postally used during the 1935 Reichsparteitage. Publ.: Photo-Hoffmann, München. Nr. 45.

Note:

This card is identical to that produced by Hoffmann for the 1933 Reichsparteitage but without the "1923-1933" dates. It was also utilized in 1934 in this format, and some left-overs were used in 1935.

Nr. 50

☐ 1935, 10-16 Sept.—Commemorating the 1935 Reichsparteitage. Publ.: Photo-Hoffmann München. Nr. 49. As at left but with Hitler in front of the Frauenkirche.

☐ 1935, 10-16 Sept.—Commemorating the 1935 Reichsparteitage. Publ.: Photo-Hoffmann, München. Nr. 50. Hitler in front of a Nürnberg stadium eagle.

☐ 1935, 10-16 Sept.—Commemorating the 1935 Reichsparteitage. Publ.: Photo-Hoffmann, München, Nr. 446.

☐ 1935, 10-16 Sept.—Commemorating the 1935 Reichsparteitage. Publ.: Photo-Hoffmann, München. Designed by Hans Friedmann, Nr. 447.

☐ 1935, 10-16 Sept.—Commemorating the 1935 Reichsparteitage. Publ.: Photo-Hoffmann, München, Nr. 448.

The following publishers produced series of cards for the 1935 Reichsparteitage. Illustrated are samples of prominent series to acquaint you with the style and design of the various publishers.

☐ 1935, 10-16 Sept.—Commemorating the 1935 Reichsparteitage. Publ.: Photo-Hoffmann, München. "Opening of the Party Congress."

Eröffnung des Partei-Kongreſſes

Der Führer ſpricht zu den politiſchen Leitern

☐ 1935, 10-16 Sept.—Commemorating the 1935 Reichsparteitage. Publ.: Photo-Hoffmann, München. "The Führer speaks to the political leaders."

☐ 1935, 10-16 Sept.—Commemorating the 1935 Reichsparteitage. Publ.: Verlag H. Hunsinger, Nürnberg. "Germans of all Gaus meet each other within the walls of Nürnberg."

Deutſche aus allen Gauen
Treffen ſich in Nürnbergs Mauern

□ 1935, 10-16 Sept.—Commemorating the 1935 Reichparteitage. Publ.: Verlag Intra, Nürnberg.

□ 1935, 10-16 Sept.—Commemorating the 1935 Reichsparteitage. Publ.: Verlag Intra, Nürnberg. Nr. A1. "Roll-call of the political leaders."

□ 1935, 10-16 Sept.—Commemorating the 1935 Reichsparteitage. Publ.: Verlag Intra, Nürnberg. Nr. A5. "Roll-call of the political leaders."

273

☐ 1935, 10-16 Sept.—Commemorating the 1935 Reichsparteitage. Publ.: Verlag Intra, Nürnberg. Nr. A23. "Roll-call of the SA, SS and NSKK."

Capparelli

APPELL DER SA, SS UND NSKK

TOTENEHRUNG   Reichsparteitag 1935   A 28

☐ As above, but Nr. A28. "Honoring the dead."

☐ 1935, 10-16 Sept.—Commemorating the 1935 Reichsparteitage. Publ.: Verlag Intra, Nürnberg. Nr. 10. "Opening of the Party Congress."

Mesturini

ERÖFFNUNG DES PARTEIKONGRESSES

☐ 1935, 10-16 Sept.—Commemorating the 1935 Reichsparteitage. Publ.: Verlag Intra, Nürnberg. Nr. 12. "The Führer proceeds to the Party Congress."

DER FÜHRER BEGIBT SICH ZUM PARTEIKONGRESS   12

☐ 1935, 10-16 Sept.—Commemorating the 1935 Reichsparteitage. Publ.: Verlag Intra, Nürnberg. Nr. 15. "The master builder and tradesmen at the ground stone laying for the Congress hall."

☐ 1935, 10-16 Sept.—Commemorating the 1935 Reichsparteitage. Publ.: Verlag Intra, Nürnberg. Nr. 19. "The Führer at the ground stone laying."

☐ 1935, 10-16 Sept.—Commemorating the 1935 Reichsparteitage. Publ.: Verlag Paul Janke, Nürnberg.

Mesturini

275

☐ 1935, 10-16 Sept.—Commemorating the 1935 Reichsparteitage. Publ.: Verlag Paul Janke, Nürnberg. Nr. 1.

☐ 1935, 10-16 Sept.—Commemorating the 1935 Reichsparteitage. Publ.: Verlag Paul Janke, Nürnberg.

☐ 1935, 10-16 Sept.—Commemorating the 1935 Reichsparteitage. Publ.: Kunstverlag Liebermann & Co., Nürnberg-W. Nr. 2.

D. Geary

☐ 1935, 10-16 Sept.—Commemorating the 1935 Reichsparteitage. Publ.: Kunstverlag Georg Michel, Nürnberg-S. Nr. R27.

☐ 1935, 10-16 Sept.—Commemorating the 1935 Reichsparteitage. Publ.: Kunstverlag Georg Michel, Nürnberg-S. Nr. R28.

☐ 1935, 10-16 Sept.—Commemorating the 1935 Reichsparteitage. Publ.: Kunstverlag Georg Michel, Nürnberg-S. Nr. R29.

☐ 1935, 10-16 Sept.—Commemorating the 1935 Reichsparteitage. Publ.: Kunstverlag Georg Michel, Nürnberg-S. Nr. R31.

277

☐ 1935, 10-16 Sept.—Commemorating the 1935 Reichsparteitage . Publ.: Kunstverlag Georg Michel, Nürnberg-S. Nr. R32.

☐ 1935, 10-16 Sept.—Commemorating the 1935 Reichsparteitage. Publ.: Kunstverlag Georg Michel, Nürnberg-S. Nr. R33.

☐ 1935, 10-16 Sept.—Commemorating the 1935 Reichsparteitage. Publ.: Kunstverlag Georg Michel, Nürnberg-S. Nr. R34.

☐ 1935, 10-16 Sept.—Postally used during the 1935 Reichsparteitage. Publ. Entw. Pg. M. Molitor, München.

Ziegelhofer

REICHSKANZLER
ADOLF HITLER

☐ 1935, 10-16 Sept.—SS-motif card postally used during the 1935 Reichsparteitage. Publ. A. Nierhaus, Nürnberg.

Ziegelhofer

□ 1935, 10-16 Sept.—Commemorating the 1935 Reichsparteitage. Publ.: Bruno Panzer, Nürnberg. "Opening of the Party Congress by the Führer."

Eröffnung des Parteikongresses durch den Führer

□ 1935, 10-16 Sept.—Commemorating the 1935 Reichsparteitage. Publ.: Verlag Wilhelm Serz, Nürnberg. Serie 4.

ERINNERUNG AN NÜRNBERG

DIE STADT DER REICHSPARTEITAGE

□ 1935, 10-16 Sept.—Greeting card series of six to commemorate the 1935 Reichsparteitage. Publ.: Verlag Wilhelm Serz, Nürnberg. Serie I. Paintings by Kunz Weidlich.

Nürnberg - die Stadt der Reichsparteitage

□ Die Burg von Westen

280

□ Schöner Brunnen und Frauenkirche
am Adolf-Hitler-Platz

□ Fünfeckiger Turm (11. Jahrhundert) mit Kaiser-
stallung

□ Blick auf die Burg vom Hallertor aus

□ Albrecht-Dürer-Haus

□ Blick auf die Burg mit Sebalduskirche

☐ 1935, 10-16 Sept.—Postally used during the 1935 Reichsparteitage. This 1934 card was used in 1935 - note handwritten "5" over the "4." Publ.: F. Willmy, Nürnberg. "Arrival of the Führer in Nürnberg."

Panettiere

☐ 1935, 10-16 Sept.—Commemorating the 1935 Reichsparteitage. Publ.: E. Wirthmann, Nürnberg. Nr. 15. This was the last occasion the flags of the "Old Army" were paraded.

☐ 1935, 10-16 Sept.—Commemorating the 1935 Reichsparteitage. Publ.: E. Wirthmann, Nürnberg. Technically this card commemorates the city and not the rally.

☐ 1935, 10-16 Sept.—Commemorating the 1935 Reichsparteitage. Publ.: E. Wirthmann, Nürnberg.

☐ 1935, 10-16 Sept.—Commemorating the 1935 Reichsparteitage. Publ.: Zerreiss & Co., Nürnberg. Nr. 4.

"The Führer at a window of the Deutscher Hof during the Reichs-parteitage celebra-tions in Nürnberg."

☐ 1935, 10-16 Sept.—Commemorating the 1935 Reichsparteitage. Publ.: Zerreiss & Co., Nürnberg. Nr. 16.

"Roll-call of the Political Leaders on the Zeppelin Field."

Mesturini

☐ 1935, 10-16 Sept.—Commemorating the 1935 Reichsparteitage. Publ.: Zerreiss & Co., Nürnberg. Nr. 19.

Pechy

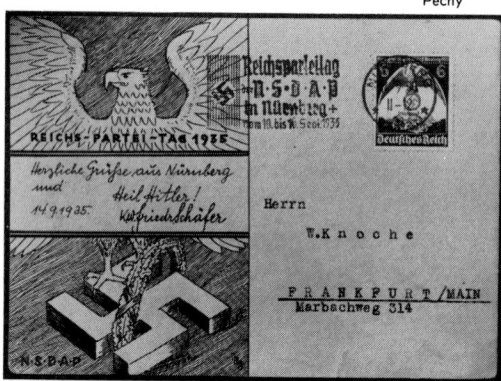

☐ 1935, 10-16 Sept.—Privately-produced card commemorating the 1935 Reichsparteitage.

☐ 1935, 28 Sept.—Nürnberg, commemorating the German Railways Centenary Exhibition. The painting by E. Schilling and Bruno Goldschmitt depict the first train (Nurnberg to Fürth) in 1935.

J. Rawlings

☐ 1935, 29 Sept.—Nürnberg, commemorating the Reichsbahn exhibition for 100 years of the German railway system. Publ.: Verlag Wilhelm Serz, Nürnberg.

☐ 1935, Oct.—Fund-raising card for the 1935/36 Winterhilfswerk programes. Produced by the Law Administration of Essen.

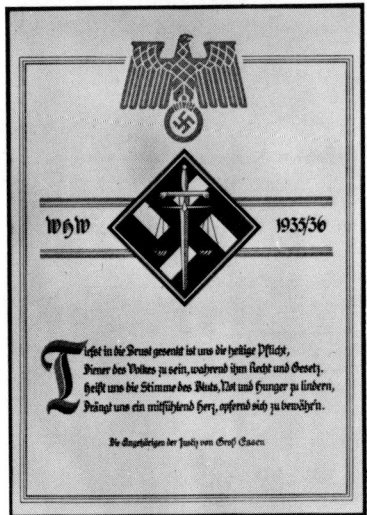

☐ 1935, Oct.—Munich, fund-raising card produced by that city's workers for the 1935/36 Winterhilfswerk programs. Publ.: Grassinger & Co., München.

☐ 1935, Oct.—Fund-raising card for the 1935/36 Winterhilfswerk programs. Publ.: Wüsten & Co., Frankfurt a.M.

☐ 1935, Oct.—Fund-raising card for the 1935/1936 WHW programs. Publ.: Wüsten & Co., Frankfurt a.M.

☐ 1935, 1 Oct.—Commemorating the Harvest Thanksgiving Festival at Bückeberg, with a surcharge for the Emergency Service. 6 & 4 Pf. (green).

Ⓢ "Bückeberg/Erntedanktag"

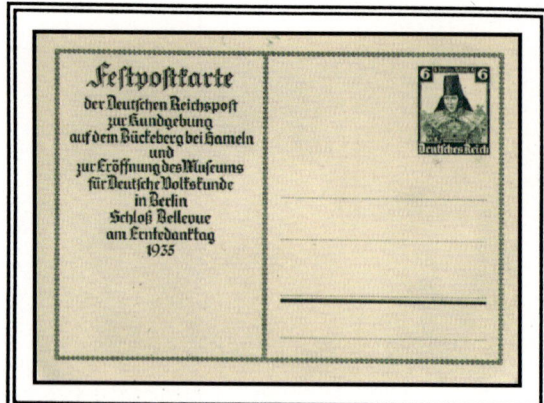

Valid until 30 June 1936.

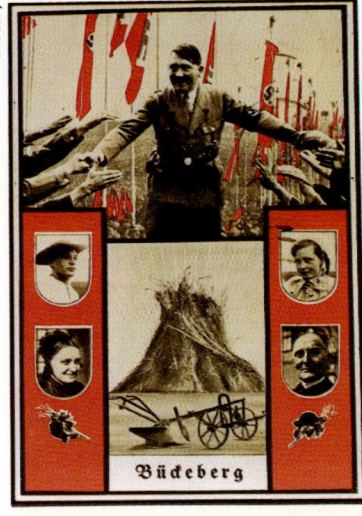

D Geary

Bückeberg

☐ 1935, 1 Oct.—Commemorating the Harvest Thanksgiving Festival at Bückeberg. Publ.: Photo Hoffmann, München. Nr. B.2.

Webb

☐ 1935, 1 Oct.—Bückeberg, commemorating the Führer's visit during the Harvest Thanksgiving Festival. Publ.: W. Tiedemann, Hannover-N.

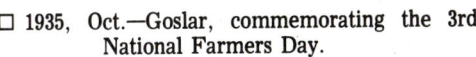

☐ 1935, 1 Oct.—Hameln, commemorating the Führer's visit during the Harvest Thanksgiving Festival.

☐ 1935, Oct.—Goslar, commemorating the 3rd National Farmers Day.

3.Reichsbauerntag Goslar 1935

☐ 1935, 1 Oct.—Special card for the German Emergency Service. 6 & 4 Pf. (green).

Valid until
30 June 1936.

☐ 1935, 12-20 Oct.—Hamburg, commemorating the Hanseatic Postal Exhibition. 3 Pf. (brown), 5 Pf. (light green), 6 Pf. (green), 10 Pf. (brown) and 15 Pf. (brown-violet). ⓈHamburg 1/Hansaposta/1935.

Note:
This series exists with two different length date lines. 43mm and 32mm. See examples at upper right.

☐ 43mm
☐ 32mm

☐ 43mm
☐ 32mm

☐ 43mm
☐ 32mm

☐ 43mm
☐ 32mm

☐ 43mm
☐ 32mm

288

43mm long date line. ▶

32mm long date line. ▶

☐ 1935, 19-27 Oct.—Leipzig-Eutritzsch, commemorating the 75th anniversary of the gymnastic and sports association.

☐ As above, but commemoration in Coburg.

☐ 1935, Nov.—Commemorating the One Pot Meal (with the money saved going towards social services). Publ.: Amt für Volks wohlfahrt, Gauamt Hamburg.

☐ 1935, 3 Nov.—Heinberg, commemorating a Hunting Association festivity (Hubertusfeier).

Mesturini

Nr. 1923/19

☐ 1935, 9 Nov.—Honoring the fallen of 9 November 1923 during the Munich Putsch. Publ.: Photo-Hoffmann, München.

Note:

The 1923/ series by Hoffmann is believed to have been issued in 1937 but the two illustrated cards from the series were postally used in 1935 indicating that at least part of the series was produced and used before 1937. In 1935 the memorial in Munich was officially opened, and the fallen heroes re-buried there. These cards apparently were published for that event.

Nr. 1923/24

☐ 1935, 9 Nov.—Honoring the fallen of 9 November 1923. The Feldherrnhalle in Munich is depicted. Publ.: Süddeutscher Kunstverlag M. Seidlein, München.

□ 1935, 9 Nov.—Honoring the fallen of 9 November 1923. The gold-leaf plaque with names of the fallen is separately affixed. Publ.: M. Grieger, Berlin.

Ziegelhofer

□ 1935, 25 Nov.—Publicity Card for the Olympic Winter Games at Garmisch-Partenkirchen. 6 & 4 Pf. (brown).

Ⓢ Garmisch-Partenkirchen/IV. Olympische Winterspiele.

Valid until 30 June 1937.

□ 1935, 25 Nov.—Publicity Card for the Olympic Winter Games at Garmisch-Partenkirchen. 15 & 10 Pf. (purple).

Ⓢ Garmisch-Partenkirchen/IV. Olympische Winterspiele.

Valid until 30 June 1937.

☐ 1935, 30 Nov.—Commemorating the 4th Hunters' Association Meeting and Antler Show. Publ.: Photo-Hoffmann, München.

☐ 1935, 30 Nov.-1 Dec.—Frankfurt, commemorating the Postage Stamp exhibit sponsored by the Frankfurt Collectors' and Traders' Club. 3 Pf. (brown), 5 Pf. (light green) and 6 Pf. (green).

☐ 1935, Dec.—Fund-raising card for the 1935/36 Winterhilfswerk programs.

☐ 1935, Dec.—"Oh German Danzig, now you are also awakening!"

Ziegelhofer

☐ 1935, 7 Dec.—Commemorating the 100th anniversary of the first German railroad connection between the cities of Nürnberg-Fürth. The train was called the "Ludwigsbahn." Publ.: Ludwig Riffelmacher, Fürth i. Bay.

D. Geary

☐ 1935—Coburg, commemorating the 75th anniversary of the German Gymnastic Association's founding.

293

Exact date of issuance not known on the following cards.

☐ 1935—Frankfurt a.M., commemorating National Handicraft Day.

☐ 1935—Kadenach, Saar, commemorating the reunion of German signals troops.

1936

☐ 1936, 4-7 Jan.—Breslau, commemorating the 5th Silesian Postal Exhibition. 3 Pf. (brown), 5 Pf. (light green) and 6 Pf. (dark green).

Ⓢ Breslau 1/Silesiaposta.

☐ 1936, 5 Jan.—Pankow, commemorating the postage stamp exhibition, "105 Jahre Stephan." 3 Pf. (brown). Red rubber stamp (upper left) on reverse of the Day of the Postage Stamp card (7 Jan. 1937).

Ⓢ Berlin Pankow/Postwert.-Ausstellung/105 Jahre Stephan.

☐ As Nr. 1, below.

☐ As Nr. 5, below.

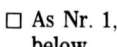
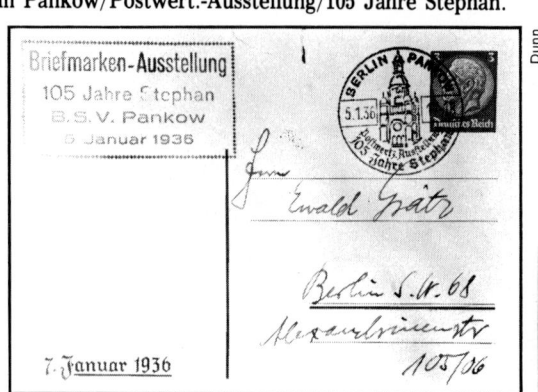

□ 1936, 7 Jan.—Day of the Postage Stamp, Founding Day of the National Philatelic Association. 3 Pf. (brown).

Ⓢ Berlin W62/1. Tag der Briefmarke/Gründungstag/des/Reichsverbandes der Philatelisten.

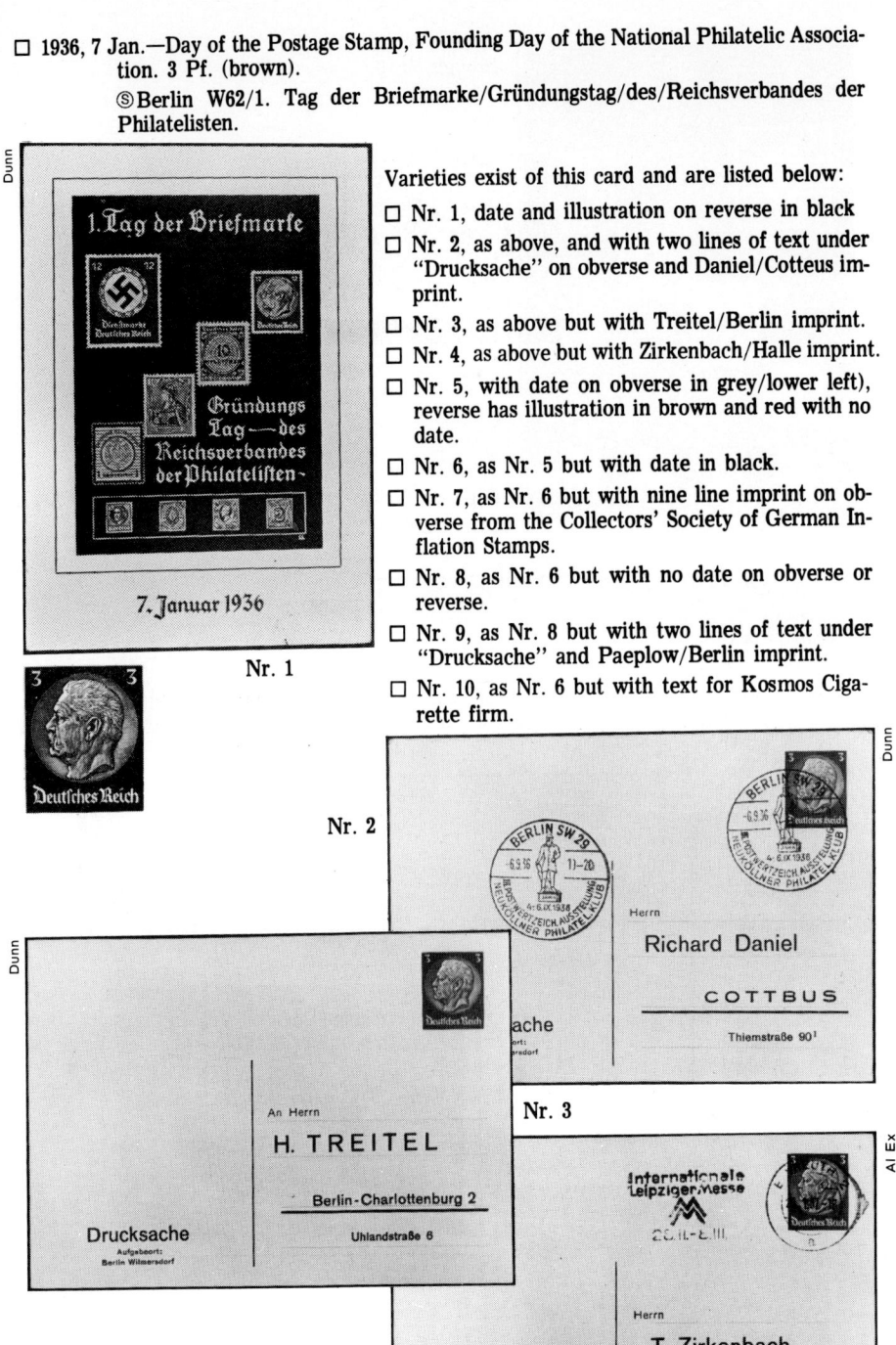

Varieties exist of this card and are listed below:

□ Nr. 1, date and illustration on reverse in black
□ Nr. 2, as above, and with two lines of text under "Drucksache" on obverse and Daniel/Cotteus imprint.
□ Nr. 3, as above but with Treitel/Berlin imprint.
□ Nr. 4, as above but with Zirkenbach/Halle imprint.
□ Nr. 5, with date on obverse in grey/lower left), reverse has illustration in brown and red with no date.
□ Nr. 6, as Nr. 5 but with date in black.
□ Nr. 7, as Nr. 6 but with nine line imprint on obverse from the Collectors' Society of German Inflation Stamps.
□ Nr. 8, as Nr. 6 but with no date on obverse or reverse.
□ Nr. 9, as Nr. 8 but with two lines of text under "Drucksache" and Paeplow/Berlin imprint.
□ Nr. 10, as Nr. 6 but with text for Kosmos Cigarette firm.

Nr. 1

Nr. 2

Nr. 3

Nr. 4

Obverse for Nr. 5
through Nr. 9.

Nr. 9

□ 1936, 7 Jan.-Sept.—Bernbeck, with "Recht schöne Grüsse/die zusammen mit dieser Kar-
te/10 Rpf kosten. Bitte abladen!" imprinted on the left reverse of Nr. 6 listed on
previous page.

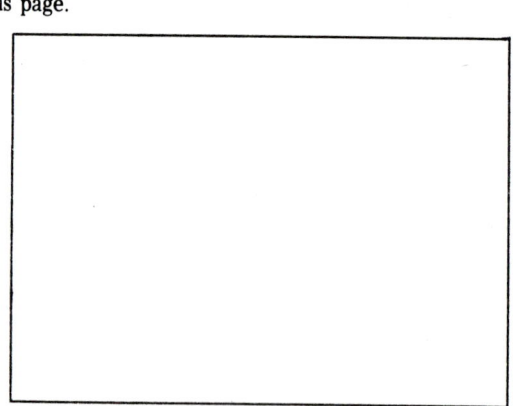

☐ 1936, 7 Jan.—Aschaffenburg, commemorating Day of the Postage Stamp. 3 Pf. (brown).
Ⓢ Aschaffenburg/Tag der Briefmarke.

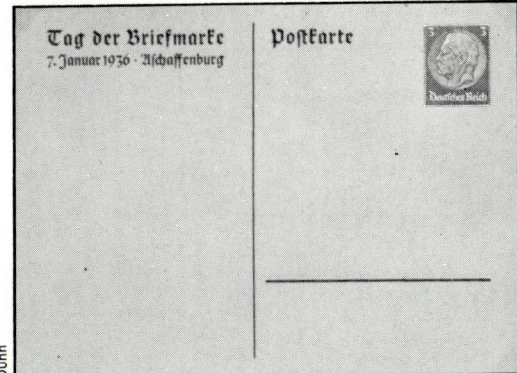

☐ Above is blank on reverse.
☐ Reverse has imprinted text in reference to the 1936 stamp exhibition.
☐ As above, with reverse showing coach before the city of Aschaffenburg (see below).

☐ 1936, 7 Jan.—Aschaffenburg, commemorating the Day of the Postage Stamp. This card has
an obverse as above and with illustration below on reverse. 6 Pf. (green).

☐ Blank on reverse, with "Tag der Briefmarke" text (see 3 Pf.).
☐ As above, with reverse showing coach before the city of Aschaffenburg.

☐ 1936, 11 Jan.—Leipzig, commemorating the 25th Anniversary (1911-1936) of the Leipzig Association of Postage-Stamp Traders. 3 Pf. (brown). Illustration was printed in:

    ☐ Blue

    ☐ Brown   Ⓢ Leipzig C1/25 Jahre/Verein Leipziger Briefmarken-Börse.

    ☐ Green

    ☐ Black

☐ As above but with 5 Pf. Luftpost (green) on green card.

☐ 1936, 25-26 Jan.—Munich, commemorating the 10th anniversary of the National Socialist Students' League.

☐ 1936, 30 Jan.—Commemorating the march of the Old Guard of the SA in Berlin.

☐ 1936, 30 Jan.—Commemorating the start of the 4th year of the National Socialist seisure of power (1933).

Ziegelhofer

☐ 1936, Feb.—"He beams so after his visit to the automobile and motorcycle exhibition because he . . . reads "Motor and Sport." Promotion card offering one free month of the magazine.

☐ 1936, 6 Feb.—Berlin-Lichtenberg, imprint of an invitation to join the stamp collectors' society on the 7 Jan. 1936 card (Day of the Postage Stamp), Nr. 6., 3 Pf. (brown).

☐ 1936, 6-16 Feb.—Commemorating the 4th Olympic Winter Games at Garmisch-Partenkirchen. This card was reproduced from a poster issued by the Reichsbahnzentrale für den Deutschen Reiseverkehr, Berlin. The text on reverse is in English. Designed by Ludwig Hohlwein.

☐

With text.

☐

□ 1936, 6-16 Feb.—Commemorating the 4th Olympic Winter Games at Garmisch-Partenkirchen, sponsored by the Austrian Olympic Foundation.

Mesturini

□ 1936, 6-16 Feb.—Commemorating the 4th Olympic Winter Games at Garmisch-Partenkirchen. Publ.: Hans Huber, Alpiner Verlag, Garmisch-Partenkirchen.

□ 1936, 6-16 Feb.—Picture postcard commemorating the 4th Olympic Winter Games at Garmisch-Partenkirchen. The construction of the winter stadium is shown. Publ.: Hans Huber, Garmisch-Partenkirchen. Nr. 340.

Mesturini

☐ 1936, 6-16 Feb.—Commemorating the 4th Olympic Winter Games at Garmisch-Partenkirchen. Publ.: Hans Huber, Alpiner Verlag, Garmisch-Partenkirchen. (Color.)

Garmisch-Partenkirchen mit Zugspitzgruppe (2964 m) im Zeichen der WINTER-OLYMPIADE 1936

☐ 1936, 6-16 Feb.—Picture postcard commemorating the 4th Olympic Winter Games at Garmisch-Partenkirchen. Illustrated is the winter stadium. Publ.: Verlag v.B. Johannes, Garmisch-Partenkirchen.

☐ 1936, 6-16 Feb.—Commemorating the 4th Olympic Winter Games at Garmisch-Partenkirchen. Publ.: Foto Verlag Eugen Wachter, Garmisch-Partenkirchen.

Olympiaort Garmisch-Partenkirchen

☐ 1936, 8-9 Feb.—Halberstadt, commemorating the 3rd National Farmers' Day.

☐ 1936, 15 Feb.-1 March—Berlin, commemorating the 1936 Berlin Auto Show. Designed by Axster-Heudtlass.

J. Rawlings

☐ 1936, 16 Feb.—Fund-raising postcard for German Sports (obviously for the upcoming Olympics). Card is numbered Nr. 11. Publ.: Reichssportverlag GmbH, Berlin-Charlottenburg.

Mesturini

To date, 30 different cards have been observed in this set.

☐ 1936, 9 March—Berlin, commemorating the annual Founder's Day, sponsored by the Berlin Postal Stationary Collectors' Club. 3 Pf. (brown).

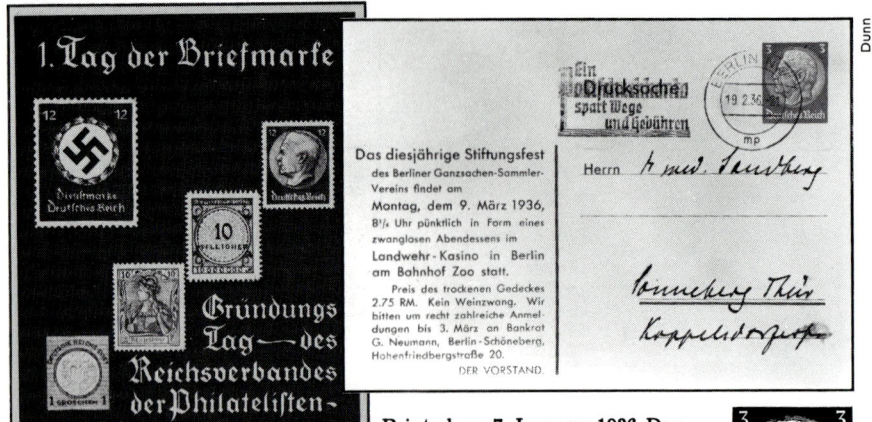

Printed on 7 January 1936 Day of the Postage Stamp card.

☐ 1936, 14-22 March—Berlin, commemorating the Great Water and Air Sport exhibition.

☐ 1936, 29 March—Honoring Adolf Hitler who gave Germany freedom and honor. Publ.: Traditionsgau München-Obb. der NSDAP. The date is of the 1936 Reichstag elections.

Jackson

☐ 1936, 29 March—Commemorating the 1936 Reichstag elections. "I gave my vote to the Führer!"

☐ 1936, 29 March—Italian-produced postcard from the German steamship "Genua" at a port call in Genua (Genova), Italy, which served as an absentee ballot for the 1936 Reichstag elections. "On the high seas we have fulfilled our duty."

Ziegelhofer

☐ 1936, 17-21 April—Berlin, commemorating merchants' day of the I.P.H.V. Text imprinted on a 7 Jan. 1936 card (Day of the Postage Stamp), Nr. 6. 3 Pf.

☐ 1936, 17-24 April—Frankfurt a. M., commemorating the 3rd National Agricultural Producers' Exhibition. The artist is Ludwig Hohlwein.

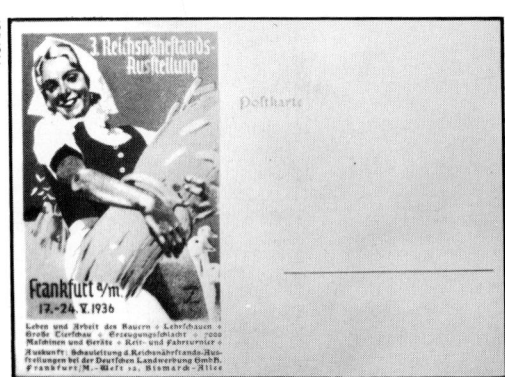

☐ 1936, 17-24 April—Frankfurt a.M., commemorating the 3rd National Agricultural Producers' exhibition.

☐ 1936, 20 April—Fund-raising card (Adolf Hitler birthday donation) for the Olympics, sponsored by government officials.

□ 1936, 24 April-11 Oct.—Dresden, commemorating the First National Exhibition of German Horticulture.

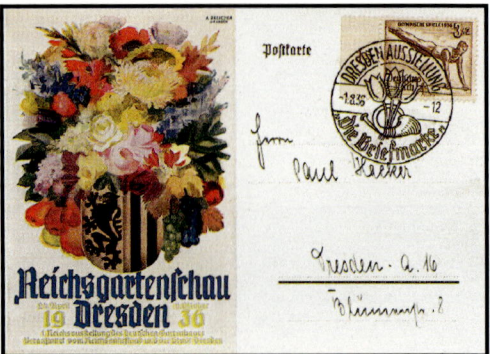

Webb

□ 1936, 24 April-11 Oct.—Dresden, commemorating the First National Exhibition of German Horticulture. Publ.: Verlag Pietzsch & Co., k.G., Dresden Nr. 104.

□ 1936, May—Official postcard commemorating Munich's Olympic Summer, May-October 1936, to include the annual thoroughbred race for "Das Braune Band von Deutschland" which was organized by Christian Weber.

☐ 1936, 1 May—Argentina, foreign Germans in Argentina commemorating the May Day meeting in the Luna Park. Note the Argentine flag is flanked by two German flags.

☐ 1936, 9-10 May—Leipzig, commemorating the Second Saxon, Wounded War Veterans' Day of the NSKOV (National Socialist War Casualty Assistance Organization).

☐ 1936, 16 May-14 June—Hamburg, commemorating the exhibition titled "The Working Nordmark."

311

☐ 1936, 16-19 May—Leipzig, official postcard commemorating the Day of German Lawyers and the 5th national convention of the Association of National Socialist German Lawyers.

Kaiser

Angolia

☐ 1936, 2 June—Commemorating National Craftsmen Day.

Ziegelhofer

☐ 1936, 6-7 June—Commemorating the Day of SA-Gruppe Nordsee, in Bremen.

☐ 1936, 6-7 June—Coburg, commemorating the Bavarian Ostmark Postage-stamp Exhibition. 3 Pf. (brown).

Ⓢ Coburg/Briefmarken-Ausstellung/Bayr. Ostmark.

☐ Also available with a special, red rubber stamping assigning a higher value of 6 Pf. ▶

☐ 1936, 6-7 June—Coburg, commemorating the Bavarian Ostmark Postage Stamp Exhibition. 6 Pf. (green).

Ⓢ Coburg,Briefmarken-Ausstellung/Bayr. Ostmark.

Webb

☐ 1936, 6-7 June—Coburg, commemorating the Bavarian Ostmark Postage Stamp Exhibition.

☐ 1936, 6-7 June—Lauenstein, commemorating the 42nd German Philatelic Day. 5 Pf. Luftpost (green).* The illustration and text on this card were printed in four colors.

    ☐ Blue   ☐ Green   ☐ Sepia   ☐ Reddish-brown

    Ⓢ Lauenstein/42. Deutscher Philatelisten tag (Gothic)

    Ⓢ Lauenstein/42. Deutscher Philatelisten tag (Grotesque)

    ☐ Also 1 Pf. (black) and 5 Pf. Luftpost (green) on a green printed card.

    ☐ Also 5 Pf. (green) and 5 Pf. Luftpost (green) on a blue card.

☐ Also 10 Pf. (brown) and 5 Pf. Luftpost (green) on a sepia printed card.

☐ Also 1 Pf. (black), 10 Pf. Luftpost (red) and 5 Pf. Luftpost (green) on a reddish-brown or blue printed card.

☐ Reddish-brown card
☐ Blue card

☐ 1936, 6-7 June—Lauenstein, as above but with "3. Philatelistische Ostlandtagung" imprint on upper left of card in all four different colors. 5 Pf. Luftpost (green).

    ☐ Blue   ☐ Green   ☐ Sepia   ☐ Reddish-brown

Ⓢ Königsberg/3. Philatelistische/Ostland-Tagung.

☐ 1936, 6-8 June—Cologne, commemorating the honor day for the League of Multi-Children Families.

☐ 1936, 12-14 June—Hanauer-Lamboy, commemorating the 300th anniversary of that city's founding.

☐ 1936, 12-14 June, Hildesheim, commemorating Gau Day.

☐ 1936, 14 June—Nürburg, commemorating the international races for sports cars, race cars and motorcycles.

☐ 1936, 15 June—Special Card for the Olympic Games in Berlin, 1-16 August. 6 & 4 Pf. (brown).

    Ⓢ "Berlin XI. Olympiade 1936"

Valid until
30 June 1937.

☐ 1936, 15 June—Special Card for the Olympic Games in Berlin, 1-16 August. 15 & 10 Pf. (purple).

    Ⓢ "Berlin XI. Olympiade 1936"

Valid until
30 June 1937.

☐ 1937, 19 June—"Defiance Forbidden!" Reference is to Party activity in Austria.

☐ 1936, 20-21 June—Freiburg/Breisgau, commemorating the day honoring the WWI front line soldier and wounded war veterans.

□ 1936, 20-22 June—Düsseldorf, a four card set commemorating the Rhine Postage Stamp Exhibit. 3 Pf. (brown), 5 Pf. (light green), 6 Pf. (green) and 10 Pf. Luftpost (red) next to 3 Pf. (brown).

Ⓢ Düsseldorf/Rheinische Briefmarken-/Ausstellung.

Freudiger Empfang der Ausstellungsgäste in Düsseldorf.

Die „Schirmherrin" der Spanienspezialisten trifft vor dem Ausstellungspalast ein

Der Ausstellungsstempel:
Die Freude des Markensammlers,
der Schrecken der Postbeamten.

Herzliche Luftpostgrüße von der Briefmarkenausstellung
Düsseldorf 1936

□ 1936, 20-25 June—Jena, commemorating the 700th anniversary of the city's founding.

□ 1936, 27 June—Heidelberg, commemorating the 550th anniversary of the university (1386-1936), Ruperto Carola. 5 Pf. (light green) and 6 Pf. (green).
Ⓢ Heidelberg/550 Jahre Universität.

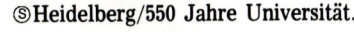

 □    □

□ 1936, 27-28 June—Commemorating the Gau meeting at Gelsenkirchen, Westfalen-Nord, 1936. This card is unique in that its central panel is of machine-woven silk and produced by Dr. R. Morisse & Co., Wuppertal.

Ziegelhofer

Note: Ludwig Knickmann was killed in the Ruhr-Abwehr battle on 21 June 1923.

□ 1936, 27-28 June—Official postcard commemorating the 1000th anniversary of the founding of Rochlitz (Sa.), the "City of Red Stones." 6 Pf. (green).

Rochlitz (Sachs)/Stadt des roten Porphyrs/Jahrtausendfeier.

□ 1936, 28 June-30 Sept.—Heidelberg, commemorating the Heidelberg historical exhibition. Note this postcard was printed on an old hand press from the Mainz Gutenberg Museum. 6 Pf. (green).

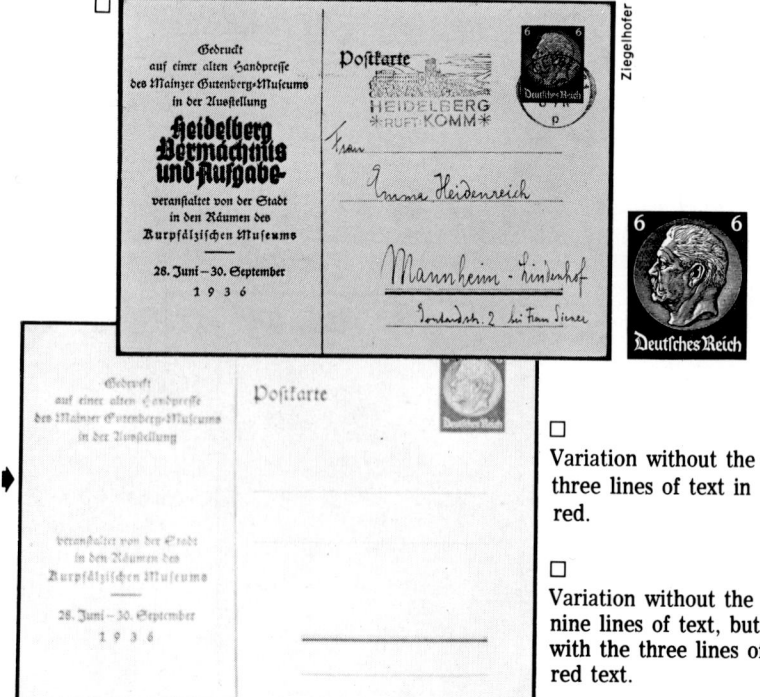

□ Variation without the three lines of text in red.

□ Variation without the nine lines of text, but with the three lines of red text.

☐ 1936, July—The Sudetenland, commemorating the Festival of all Germans, sponsored by the "Bund der Deutschen." Publ.: A. Schneider's Nachf. Mähr-Schönberg.

☐ 1936, 1-6 July—Commemorating the 150th anniversary of the German Veterans' Association in Kassel. Illustrated is the grenadier uniform and flag of Grenadier-Regiment Nr. 36.

Philip Baker

☐ 1936, 2 July-9 Aug.—Magdeburg, commemorating the summer encampment of the Hitler Youth in their tent city near Magdeburg.

☐ 1936, 3-5 July—Official postcard commemorating the 10th anniversary of the Parteitage in Weimar in 1926 (Publ.: NSDAP Gauleitung Thüringen).

☐ 1936, 3-5 July—Commemorating the 10-year anniversary of the Reichsparteitage at Weimar. Publ.: Rich. Schlothauer, Leipzig.

Ziegelhofer

322

□ 1936, 4-13 July—Warburg, commemorating the 900th anniversary of that city's founding.

□ 1936, 5 July—Stuttgart, commemorating the meeting of the 26th Reserve Division.

□ 1936, 11-12 July—Ulm/Do., commemorating the deployment of SA-Standarte 120 "Heinrich Förg."

☐ 1936, 17-19 July—Halberstadt, commemorating the German swimming championships.

☐ 1936, 20 July—Commemorating the start of the run which carried the Olympic torch 3075km from Greece to Berlin. Publ.: Werkstatt, Berlin.

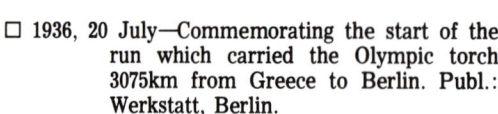

Mesturini

☐ 1936, 23-30 July—Hamburg, commemorating the World Congress for Leisure Time and Recreation. Publ.: Hans Andres, Hamburg.

☐ 1936, 23-30 July—Hamburg, commemorating the World Congress for Leisure Time and Recreation.

□ 1936, 25-27 July—Halberstadt, commemorating
the National Association Day of the
National Guild of Carpentry.

□ 1936, 25-26 July—Arnstadt, commemorating the
3rd district day.

□ 1936, 26 July—Nürburg, commemorating the auto
races in that city.   Publ.: Carl Werner,
Reichenbach i/V.

325

□ 1936, 29 July—Commemorating the arrival of the
Olympic Torch at Heldenplatz in Vienna
on 29 July 1936, at 8 p.m.

M.C. Voit

□ 1936, 29 July-16 August—The Olympic bell for
the Olympic games in Berlin.

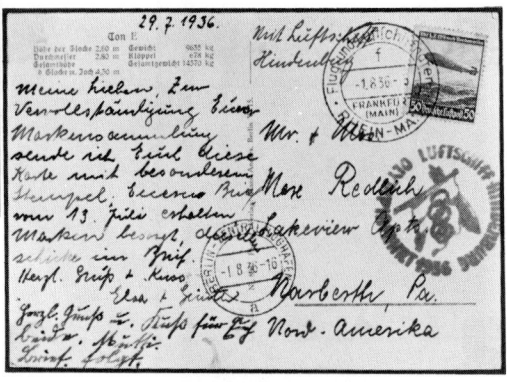

Note this card was carried on a
special airship flight, by the
Hindenburg, from Frankfurt to
Berlin on 1 August.

□ 1936, 1-2 August—Alsleben, commmemorating the
1000th anniversary of the town and the
district meeting of the NSDAP.

□ 1936, 1 Aug.—Publicity Card for the Olympic Sailing Competition at Kiel, 4-14 August. 6 & 4 Pf. (brown).

ⓢ "Kiel/XI. Olympiade Segeln 1936."

Valid until
30 June 1937.

□ 1936, 1 Aug.—Publicity Card for the Olympic Sailing Competition at Kiel, 4-14 August. 15 & 10 Pf. (purple).

ⓢ "Kiel/XI. Olympiade Segeln 1936."

Valid until
30 June 1937.

□ 1936, 1-16 Aug.—Ten-card fund-raising series for the 1936 Olympic Games in Berlin. Publ.: Reichssportverlag GmbH., Berlin.

D. Geary

Ziegelhofer

□ Nr. 1

□ Nr. 2

□ Nr. 3

□ Nr. 4

J. Rawlings

KIELER FÖRDE · KAMPFSTÄTTE FÜR SEGELN

☐ Nr. 5

BERLIN

FACKELSTAFFELLAUF OLYMPIA·BERLIN

☐ Nr. 6

Kaiser

REICHSSPORTFELD · DIETRICH ECKART · FREILICHTBÜHNE

☐ Nr. 7

Kaiser

GRÜNAU · KAMPFSTÄTTE FÜR RUDERN

☐ Nr. 8

329

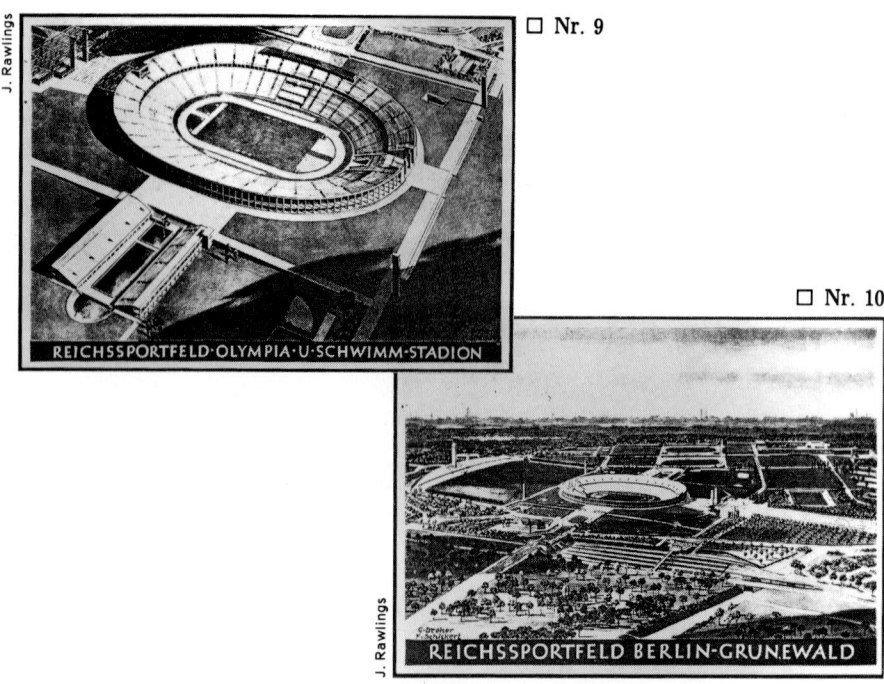

□ Nr. 9

REICHSSPORTFELD·OLYMPIA·U·SCHWIMM·STADION

J. Rawlings

□ Nr. 10

REICHSSPORTFELD BERLIN·GRUNEWALD

J. Rawlings

□ 1936, 1-16 August—Dresden, official postcard commemorating the Olympic Postal Exhibition, with German labor as its theme. 3 Pf. (brown) and no imprinted stamp.

  Ⓢ Dresden-Ausstellung/Reichsgartenschau.

  Ⓢ Dresden-Ausstellung/"Die Briefmarke."

Mesturini

□

□ No imprinted stamp.

☐ 1936, 1-16 Aug.—Dresden, commemorating the Olympic Postal Exhibition in Dresden, featuring the German family ("Deutsche Familie"). 3 Pf. (brown) and 5 Pf. (green). Also exists without imprinted stamp.

Ⓢ Dresden-Ausstellung/Reichsgartenschau.

Ⓢ Dresden-Ausstellung/"Die Briefmarke"

☐ No imprinted stamp.

☐ 1936/ 1-16 August—Dresden, official postcard commemorating the Olympic Postal Exhibition, with German music as its theme. 4 Pf. (grey-blue) and an imprinted stamp.

Ⓢ Dresden-Ausstellung/Reichsgartenschau.

Ⓢ Dresden-Ausstellung/"die Briefmarke."

☐ No imprinted stamp.

Ziegelhofer

☐ 1936, 1-16 August—Dresden, official postcard commemorating the Olympic Postal Exhibition with German aviation as its theme. 5 Pf. Luftpost (green) and no imprinted stamp.

Ⓢ Dresden-Ausstellung/Reichsgartenschau.

Ⓢ Dresden-Ausstellung/"Die Briefmarke."

☐ No imprinted stamp.

Mesturini

The following publishers produced cards commemorating the 1936 Olympics. Illustrated are samples to acquaint you with the style and design of various publishers.

☐ 1936, 1-16 Aug.—Picture postcard for the 1936 Olympic Games in Berlin. Publ.: Hans Andres, Berlin. Nr. 817.

☐ 1936, 1-16 Aug.—Picture postcard for the 1936 Olympic Games in Berlin. Publ.: Hansa-Luftbild GmbH, Berlin. Nr. 28969.

☐ 1936, 1-16 Aug.—Picture postcard for the 1936 Olympic Games. The olympic torch bearer is greeted by the Hitler Youth in the Lustgarten, Berlin. Publ.: Photo-Hoffmann, München. Nr. 03.

☐ 1936, 1-16 Aug.—Commemorating the 1936 Olympic Games in Berlin. The High School for Physical Fitness is shown. Publ.: Industrie-Fotografen Klinke & Co., Berlin. Nr. VI.

D. Geary

Mesturini

☐ 1936, 1-16 Aug.—Picture postcard for the 1936 Olympic Games. The Brandenburg Gate is illustrated. Publ.: Industrie-Fotografen Klinke & Co., Berlin.

D. Geary

☐ 1936, 1-16 Aug.—Commemorating the 1936 Olympic Games in Berlin. Official postcard showing the Olympic Stadium. Publ.: Industrie-Fotografen Klinke & Co., Berlin. Nr. 13.

Mesturini

☐ 1936, 1-16 Aug.—Official picture postcard for the 1936 Olympic Games. A view of the stadium from the east gate. Publ.: Reichssportverlag, Berlin.

Mesturini

☐ 1936, 1-16 Aug.—The national sports field is illustrated. Publ.: Reichssportverlag, Berlin. Nr. 9.

Mesturini

☐ 1936, 1-16 Aug.—The national sports field (stadium) is illustrated. Publ.: Reichssportverlag, Berlin.

Mesturini

☐ 1936, 1-16 Aug.—The national sports field with the Dietrich-Eckardt Arena is illustrated. Publ.: Reichssportverlag, Berlin.

Mesturini

☐ 1936, 1-16 Aug.—The swimming area is shown. Publ.: Reichssportverlag, Berlin.

Mesturini

☐ 1936, 1-16 Aug.—The Reich Sports Field is shown. Publ.: Reichssportverlag, Berlin.

□ 1936, 1-16 Aug.—Official picture post-
card for the 1936 Olympic
Games in Berlin. Publ.:
Reichssportveralg, Berlin
SW68.

□ 1936, 1-16 Aug.—Official picture postcard for the 1936 Olympic
Games. Publ.: Reichssportverlag, Berlin SW68). Nr. 104.

□ 1936, 1-16 Aug.—Picture postcard
for the 1936 Olympic Games
in Berlin. Publ.: Kunstanstalt
Stengel & Co., GmbH,
Dresden.

□ 1936, 1-16 Aug.—The olympic torch
is carried from the Lustgarten
to the olympic stadium. Publ.:
W.St.B. Nr. 735.

□ 1936, 1-16 Aug.—This card featuring
the airship"Hindenburg," was
carried by that airship from
Frankfurt to Berlin on 1
August.

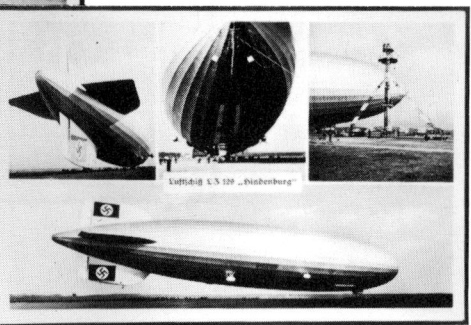

335

☐ 1936, 1-16 Aug.—Dresden, commemorating the National Garden Show and the Olympic Postal Exhibition.

Webb

☐ 1936, 1-16 Aug.—Commemorating the 1936 Olympic Games in Berlin. Identical to the official advertising poster of the Propaganda Committee for the Olympic Games, Berlin. Designed by F. Würbel.

Ziegelhofer

□ 1936, 1-16 Aug.—Publicity postcard for the 1936 Olympic Games, sponsored by the Austrian Olympic Foundation.

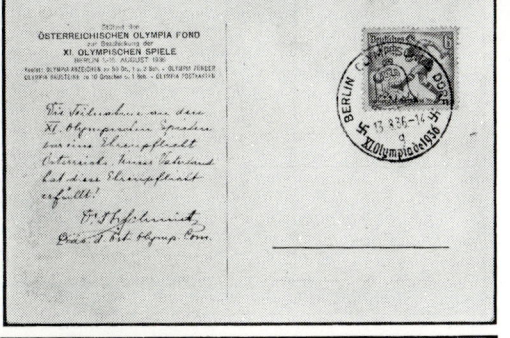

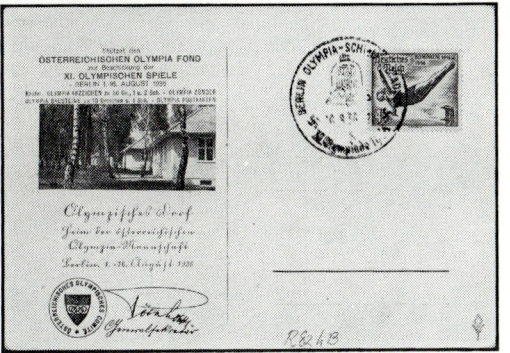

Note two different reverses on card.

□ 1936, 1-16 August—Artist relief card commemorating the 1936 Olympic Games in Berlin. Note the embossed foil medallion.

Angolia

☐ 1936, 1-16 August—Publicity card for the 1936 Olympic Games ("The Flags of participating Countries"). Publ.: Reichssportverlag, Berlin.

☐ 1936, 1-16 Aug.—Publicity card for the 1936 Olympic Games (showing the Olympic Village). The Olympic Village was built by the army near Döberitz/Berlin.

☐ 1936, 1-16 Aug.—Publicity postcard for the 1936 Olympic Games. Publ.: Der Reichsluftsportführer, Berlin.

☐ Also exists without Olympic rings.

☐ 1936, 1-16 Aug.—Commemorating the 1936 Olympic Games in Berlin. "I call the youth of the world." Publ.: Verlag Werkstatt Albu, Berlin.

D. Geary

☐ 1936, 1-16 Aug.—Publicity card for the 1936 Olympic Games featuring the torch-holder used in the relay race from Olympia to Berlin. Publ.: Hans Andres, Berlin.

Ziegelhofer

Mesturini

☐ 1936, 1-16 Aug.—The entrance to the olympic stadium is shown.

Webb

☐ 1936, 1-16 Aug.—Commemorating the 1936 Olympic Games in Berlin. National Sports Leader Hans v. Tschammer u. Osten is depicted.

☐ 1936, 14-21 Aug.—Postcard sent from the Hochland Camp by German Youth members while encamped there. The camp was located at Königsdorf near Bad Tölz. Used cards examined indicate that the same card was used for the 1937 and 1938 encampment as well. Designed by Harald Neles. Publ.: Vereinigte Kunstanstalten A.G. Kaufbeuren, Bayern.

Ziegelhofer

☐ 1936, 22-23 Aug.—Schmalkalden, commemorating NSDAP district day.

☐ 1936, 23-26 Aug.—Königsberg, commemorating the 24th German Eastern Fair. 6 Pf. (green).

Ⓢ Königsberg (PR)/DOK/Deutsche Ostmesse.

☐ 1936, 23-26 Aug.—Königsberg, as above but with "3. PHILATELISTISCHE OST-LANDTAGUNG" imprinted on upper left of card. 6 Pf. (green).

Ⓢ Königsberg/3. philatelistische/Ostland-Tagung.

☐ 1936, 23-26 Aug.—Königsberg, commemorating the 24th German Eastern Fair. 5 Pf. Luftpost (green).

Ⓢ Königsberg (PR)/DOK/Deutsche Ostmesse.

☐ 1936, 23-26 Aug.—Königsberg, as above but with "3. PHILATELISTISCHE OST-LANDTAGUNG" imprinted on upper left of card. 5 Pf. Luftpost (green).

Ⓢ Königsberg/3. philatelistische/Ostlandtagung.

☐ 1936, 29 Aug.-1 Sept.—Geithain, commemorating the 750th anniversary of that community's founding.

☐ 1936, 4-6 Sept.—Berlin Neuköln, commemorating the 3rd Postal Exhibition on the occasion of the 1936 Berlin Olympic Games. Sponsored by the Neuköln Philatelic Club. 5 Pf. Luftpost (green).
Ⓢ Berlin SW, 4.-6.9.1936.

□ 1936, 8-14 Sept.—Commemorating the "Adolf Hitler" march of the Hitler Youth to the 1936 Reichsparteitage. Publ.: Aufmarschstab der Hitler Jugend.

D. Geary

□ A variation of the above.

□ 1936, 8-14 Sept.—Commemorating the march of Gau Saxony participants to Nuremberg for the 1936 Reichsparteitage.

□ 1936, 8-14 Sept.—Official 1936 Reichsparteitage
   postcard. Publ.: Verlag Franz Eher,
   München. Designed by Richard Klein.

□ 1936, 8-14 Sept.—Official 1936 Reichsparteitage
   postcard. Publ.: Verlag Franz Eher,
   München. Designed by Richard Klein.

☐ 1936, 8-14 Sept.—Commemorating the 1936 Reichsparteitage. Publ.: Photo-Hoffmann, München.

D. Geary

☐ 36/1

Artwork by
Richard Klein

D. Gloster

☐ 36/2

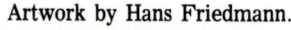

Artwork by Hans Friedmann.

☐ 36/3

Artwork by F.P. Glass.

D. Gloster

□ 36/4

Artwork by Hans Friedmann

□ 36/5

Artwork by Ludwig Hohlwein.

□ 36/6

Artwork by Hans Friedmann.

Artwork by Hans Friedmann

□ 36/7

D. Gloster

347

Artwork by Hans Friedmann

☐ 36/8

Artwork by Hans Friedmann

Reichsparteitag-Nürnberg

☐ 36/9

Reichsparteitag-Nürnberg

Hoffmann cards Nr. 36/10 to 36/52 are black/white photos of this event, of which a few samples are illustrated. The check-off list is provided for collectors' convenience.

☐ 36/10	☐ 36/19	☐ 36/28	☐ 36/37	☐ 36/46
☐ 36/11	☐ 36/20	☐ 36/29	☐ 36/38	☐ 36/47
☐ 36/12	☐ 36/21	☐ 36/30	☐ 36/39	☐ 36/48
☐ 36/13	☐ 36/22	☐ 36/31	☐ 36/40	☐ 36/49
☐ 36/14	☐ 36/23	☐ 36/32	☐ 36/41	☐ 36/50
☐ 36/15	☐ 36/24	☐ 36/33	☐ 36/42	☐ 36/51
☐ 36/16	☐ 36/25	☐ 36/34	☐ 36/43	☐ 36/52
☐ 36/17	☐ 36/26	☐ 36/35	☐ 36/44	
☐ 36/18	☐ 36/27	☐ 36/36	☐ 36/45	

Der Führer begrüßt die sächsische Abordnung auf dem Zeppelinfeld

36/33

36/34

Mesturini

36/41

Samples of other publishers' cards commemorating the 1936 Reichsparteitage.

☐ 1936, 8-14 Sept.—Commemorating the 1936 Reichsparteitage in Nürnberg. Publ.: Verlag Intra, Nürnberg.

G. Notarpole

☐ 2

Kaiser

☐ 3

349

□ 43

"Opening ceremony in the city hall."

Eröffnungsfeier im Rathaus. Reichsparteitag 1936.

□ 63

"Roll-call of the RAD at the 1936 Party Day. The March-by."

Crabb

Appell des Reichsarbeitsdienstes Parteitag 1936. Vorbeimarsch.

"Party officials' roll-call on the Zeppelin Field."

Anhlungsappell auf der Zeppelinwiese. Reichsparteitag 1936.

□ 88

"Party officials' roll-call on the Zeppelin Field."

□ 89

350

Catella

"Party officials' roll-call on the Zeppelin Field."

"Roll-call of the SA, SS and NSKK on the Luitpold Arena.

G. Notarpole

☐ 105

"March-by on the Adolf Hitler Platz.

☐ 115

☐ 1936, 8-14 Sept.—Commemorating the 1936 Reichsparteitage. Publ.: Verlag Th. König, Berlin. Nr. 1027.

☐ 1936, 8-14 Sept.—Commemorating the 1936 Reichsparteitage. Publ.: Liebermann & Co., Nürnberg. "Luitpold Arena."

☐ 1936, 8-14 Sept.—Commemorating the 1936 Reichsparteitage. Publ.: Kunstverlag Georg Michel, Nürnberg-S.

☐ 1936, 8-14 Sept.—Commemorating the 1936 Reichsparteitage (publisher unknown).

□ 1936, 8-14 Sept.—Commemorating the 1936 Reichsparteitage. Publ.: Verlag von Ludwig Riffelmacher, Fürth i Bay.

□ 1936, 8-14 Sept.—Commemorating the 1936 Reichs-parteitage. Publ.: Verlag Wilhelm Serz, Nürnberg. Nr. 5 of the series.

□ 1936, 8-14 Sept.—Commemorating the 1936 Reichsparteitage. Publ.: Verlag Paul F. Weber, Leipzig. Nr. 454.

☐ 1936, 8-14 Sept.—Commemorating the 1936 Reichsparteitage. Publ. E. Wirthmann, Nürnberg. This card was produced for the 1935 Party rally, but with a silver over-print to cover the 1935 date.

☐ 1936, 8-14 Sept.—Commemorating the 1936 Reichsparteitage. Publ.: Graphische Kunstanstalt Zerreiss & Co., Nürnberg.

☐ Nr. 12

"The RAD gathers."

☐ Nr. 43

"The Führer on the balcony of the German Hotel (Deutscher Hof)."

354

John D. Griffin

☐ 1936, 8-14 September—Commemorating the 1936 Reichsparteitage (privately published in limited quantities).

Ziegelhofer

Ziegelhofer

☐ 1936, 8-14 Sept.—Commemorating the 1936 Reichsparteitage.

☐ 1936, 8-14 Sept.—Sold and used at the 1936 Reichsparteitage. Originally produced as an artist relief card. Note embossed foil medallion.

☐ 1936, 21 Sept.—W.H.W. card commemorating the opening of 1000 km of the Autobahn (started 23 Sept. 1933 and completed on 23 September 1936). 6 & 4 Pf. (brown).

Valid until
30 June 1937.

355

Ziegelhofer

Durch Luftsport zur fliegenden Nation.

Mahnke

☐ 1936, Oct.—"Becoming a flying nation through aviation sports." This is a propaganda slogan to make Germany aviation-minded.

☐ 1936, Oct.—Marathon runner Pottschulte starts his run in Wittenberg with the finish line in Berlin 100km away. This run was to raise money for the 1936/37 Winterhilfswerk programes.

Lutherstadt Wittenberg

Kaiser

Zu Gunsten des W.H.W.

☐ 1936, 1 Oct.—Hameln, commemorating the Harvest Thanksgiving Festival.

Webb

Hameln/ Erntedanktag

Rattenfängerspiele

□ 1936, 3-4 Oct.—Jena, commemorating the 1st Thüringen Postage Stamp Exhibition. 3 Pf. (brown) and 6 Pf. (green). The market square and memorial are illustrated. Ⓢ Jena/Thürposta 1.

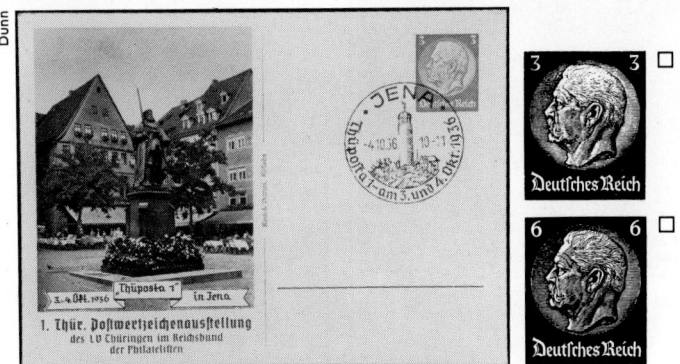

□ 1936, 3-4 Oct.—Jena, commemorating the 1st Thüringen Postage Stamp Exhibition. 3 Pf. (brown) and 6 Pf. (green). The city gateway is illustrated. Ⓢ Jena/Thüposta 1.

□ 1936, 10-12 Oct.—Eisenach, commemorating the 3rd National Meeting of German Christians.

□ 1936, 11-12 Oct.—Erfurt, commemorating the 1st great people's festival in the flower city of Erfurt.

□ 1936, 16-18 Oct.—Münster (Westf.), commemorating the Third Postal Exhibition.

Webb

□ 1936, 16-18 Oct.—Münster (Westf.), commemorating their 3rd Postage Stamp Exhibition. 5 Pf. (light green) and 5 Pf. Luftpost (green).

Münster (Westf.) 2/3. Briefmarken-Ausstellung.

Ziegelhofer

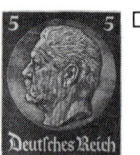

J.B. Terry

□ 1936, 17-18 Oct.—Zwickau, commemorating the 15th anniversary of the formation of the first political branch of the Party outside of Bavaria (1921).

□ 1936, 21 Oct.—Commemorating the laying of the foundation stone for the House of German Justice in Munich. 6 Pf. (dark green).
  Ⓢ München/Grundsteinlegung des "Hauses des Deutschen Rechts 24.10.36."

□ 1936, 24-25 Oct.—Königswald, commemorating the 17th German Association and Philatelic Day.

□ 1936, Nov.—Fund-raising card for the Winterhilfswerk 1936/37, commemorating the week of land communication in the traditional Gau of Bavaria. Publ.: Deutsche Kunst- und Verlagsdruckerei & Co., München.

□ 1936, Nov.—Fund-raising card for the Winterhilfswerk 1936/37, commemorating the week of transportation service in the traditional Gau of Bavaria. Publ.: Grassinger & Co., München. Designed by P. Neu.

□ 1936, Nov.—Fund-raising card for the Winterhilfswerk 1936/37, commemorating the week of aviation service in the traditional gau of Bavaria. Publ.: Grassinger & Co., München. Designed by P. Neu.

□ 1936, Nov.—Deutsche Lufthansa promotional series.

"Information and tickets available in all travel agencies."

"Fast to the destination."

"Europe to South America in two days - air mail post sent twice a week."

Mesturini

"In three days to South America with airships of the German Zeppelin Shipping Company.

Mesturini

"Also in winter."

Mesturini

362

□ 1936, 1 Nov.—1st Berlin Airmail Collectors Club Show. 3 Pf. (brown) and 15 Pf. Luftpost (blue) next to 1 Pf. (black).

Ⓢ Berlin-Schöneberg/1. Berliner/Luftpost-Werbeschau.

□ As above, but with additional vertical line, and one broken and one bold solid address line. 3 Pf. (brown).

Catella

□ 1936, 9 Nov.—Honoring the fallen of 9 November 1923. The Feldherrnhalle in Munich is depicted (Publ.: Grusskarten-Verlag Deutsch, Schwalbach).

363

□ 1936, 14-15 Nov.—Fund-raising card commemorating the street collections of the Greater Essen postal service for the 1936/37 Winterhilfswerk programs.

□ 1936, 14-15 Nov.—Fund-raising card commemorating the street collections of the Essen law administrators for the 1936/1937 Winterhilfswerk programs.

□ 1936, 22-29 Nov.—Goslar, commemorating the 4th National Farmers' Day. Publ.: Reichsnährstand, Vorbereitungsstelle für Kundgebungen.

Ziegelhofer

☐ 1936, 5 Dec.—In memory of contributions made to the 1936/37 Winterhilfswerk program on 5 December 1936.

Ziegelhofer

☐ 1936, Dec.—Berlin, commemorating the 1936 Berlin Christmas Market in the Lustgarten.

Used also during the 1937 Christmas season.

☐ 1936, Dec.—Berlin, commemorating the 1936 Berlin Christmas Market.
  Ⓢ Berlin C2/Berliner Weihnachtsmarkt 1937

Used also during the 1937 Christmas season.

□ 1936, Dec.—German Christmas greetings.
"The Führer thinks of you!"

D. Geary

□ 1936, Dec.—Christmas greetings for 1936.

Exact date of issuance not known on the following card.

□ 1936—Saxony, honoring the workers of the
German Labor Front in that state.